PHalarope
Books

PHalarope books are designed specifically for the amateur naturalist. These volumes represent excellence in natural history publishing. Most books in the PHalarope series are based on a nature course or program at the college or adult education level or sponsored by a museum or nature center. Each PHalarope book reflects the author's teaching ability as well as writing ability. Among the books:

The Amateur Naturalist's Handbook
Vinson Brown

Biography of a Planet: Geology, Astronomy, and the Evolution of Life on Earth
Chet Raymo

A Complete Manual of Amateur Astronomy: Tools and Techniques for Astronomical Observations
P. Clay Sherrod with Thomas L. Keod

Owls: An Introduction for the Amateur Naturalist
Gordon Dee Alcorn

Thoreau's Method: A Handbook for Nature Study
David Pepi

365 Starry Nights: An Introduction to Astronomy for Every Night of the Year
Chet Raymo

The Wildlife Observer's Guidebook
Charles E. Roth, Massachusetts Audubon Society

A Field Guide to the Familiar: Learning to Observe the Natural World
Gale Lawrence

D0107606

THE SKY OBSERVER'S GUIDEBOOK

CHARLES E. ROTH

PHalarope Books

PRENTICE HALL PRESS

New York   London   Toronto   Sydney   Tokyo

Dedicated to
Miriam Dickey
warm friend,
talented colleague,
devoted naturalist,
and
"sky coach" to amateurs of all ages

Copyright © 1986 by Charles E. Roth

Published by Prentice Hall Press
A Division of Simon & Schuster, Inc.
Simon & Schuster Building
Rockefeller Center
1230 Avenue of the Americas
New York, New York 10020

PRENTICE HALL PRESS is a trademark
of Simon & Schuster, Inc.

Printed in the United States of America

Library of Congress Cataloging-in-Publication Data

Roth, Charles Edmund

The sky observer's guidebook.

Includes bibliographies and index.
1. Sky. I. Title.
QC879.R85   1986   551.5   85-19248

ISBN 0-13-812785-9

10 9 8 7 6 5 4 3 2

CONTENTS

Quotes on pages 10-12 are from a paper by Dr. Leonard Duhl, delivered at the For Spacious Skies Conference and used by permission of Dr. Duhl and Sage Publications. The paper will appear in the *Journal of Humanistic Psychology*.

Page 12 contains a quote from *The Intellectual Adventure of Ancient Man,* by Henri Frankfurt et al., reprinted with the permission of the Chicago University Press.

Quotes by Henry David Thoreau on pages 30, 34, 43, and 92 were selected from a collection compiled from his journals by the Thoreau Lyceum for Spacious Skies.

The quotes on pages 35, 206, and 208 are used by permission of *Arizona Highways.*

The quote on pages 60-61 from "A Windstorm in the Forests," by John Muir, appeared in *The Mountains of California* (The Century Co., 1898) and is reprinted by permission of E. P. Dutton, Inc.

Pages 67-68 contain quotes from George Miksch Sutton's essay "In A Dust Storm," published in *Discovery,* an anthology edited by John K. Terres and published by J. B. Lippincott in 1961. Segments of it are reprinted by permission of Dr. Dorothy S. Fuller.

The cartoon sequence on page 126 by Walt Kelly is from his book *Impollutable Pogo,* published by Simon & Schuster in 1970. The sequence is used with the kind permission of Mrs. Walt Kelly.

Page 126 contains a quote by J. E. Lovelock from *Gaia: A New Look At Life On Earth* (Oxford University Press, 1979), reprinted with the permission of the author.

The quotes on pages 128-129 are from Anna Botsford Comstock's *Handbook of Nature Study* (Comstock Publishing Associates, 1939) and are reprinted with the permission of Cornell University Press.

Pages 138-139 contain quotes from *The Wandering Albatross,* by William Jameson and Robert Cushman Murphy, and are used with permission of William Morrow and Co. and John Farquharson, Ltd.

The quotes on page 140 from *Borne On The Wind,* by Stephen Dalton (Reader's Digest Press, 1975), are reprinted with the permission of the author.

Quotes on pages 146 and 186-187 are reprinted by permission of Nancy Wood, from *Hollering Sun,* published by Simon & Schuster in 1972.

Page 177 contains a quote from *Topophilia* by Yi-Fu Tuan, copyright 1974, reprinted by permission of Prentice-Hall, Inc.

The poem "To The Thawing Wind," by Robert Frost, found on page 188, is from *The Poetry Of Robert Frost,* edited by Edward Connery Lathem. Copyright 1936 by Robert Frost. Copyright 1964 by Lesley Frost Ballantine. Copyright 1969 by Holt, Rinehart and Winston. Reprinted by permission of Holt, Rinehart and Winston, Publishers, the Estate of Robert Frost, and Jonathan Cape, Ltd., London.

Quotes by Yehudi Menuhin on pages 189 and 191 are from *The Music of Man,* by Yehudi Menuhin and Curtis W. Davis, published in 1979, and are reprinted with permission by the publisher, Methuen, Inc.

The quote on pages 194-195 by E. H. Gombrich is from his book *The Story of Art,* (Phaidon Publishers Inc., 1958).

The photograph on page 206, *Cloud, Sierra Nevada, California, 1936,* by Ansel Adams, is reproduced by courtesy of the Ansel Adams Publishing Rights Trust.

The paintings *The Buffalo Trail* (p. 203), *Moonlight Sonata* (p. 200), *The Harp of the Winds* (p. 202), *Storm Over Lake Otsego* (p. 203), *River Scene* (p. 196), *A Rough Sea* (p. 196), *The Slave Ship* (p. 198), *Top View Of Turkey Buzzard* (p. 137), and *Weymouth Bay* (p. 198) are reproduced with the permission of the Museum of Fine Arts, Boston, Massachusetts.

FOREWORD

How is it possible that we can live under a vast canopy so everchanging that its one face seldom wears the same expression—and not truly *see* it? How is it possible that we can fly through spectacular cloudscapes yet prefer to pull down the little shade at our plane window so the cabin will be darker for the in-flight movie?

In 1981, For Spacious Skies engaged Dr. Ervin Zube, the eminent professor of environmental design, to do a survey of sky awareness among Americans. The study showed that only 50 percent of the public is sufficiently aware of the sky to be able to identify accurately its appearance from clues such as very clear, a few scattered clouds, many clouds, hazy, overcast.

In his paper delivered at the For Spacious Skies Conference at Grand Canyon, Arizona, psychiatrist Dr. Leonard Duhl cited sensory detachment from the natural environment, typified by not seeing the sky, as a causal factor in personal and social ill-health.

I myself became alive to the presence of the sky through a sudden awakening on a Massachusetts hillside. Moved to share with others this new awareness, I founded For Spacious Skies, a non-profit organization, in 1981. The first step in this movement was the conference at Grand Canyon. Preparation for that unprecedented gathering brought me in contact with Chuck Roth, who not only served on our steering committee but delivered the conference's most significant paper—"The Education of Sky Beings." In that paper he reminded us that we dwell at the bottom of the sky and that it's time we learned about our habitat. Additionally, he outlined a broad scale educational approach using the sky as cornerstone for all learning.

As our friendship developed, I complained to Chuck that despite its profound relationship to our collective existence there is no truly comprehensive book of the sky. Meteorology, astronomy, aviation, birds—the endless topics on the sky-related list—all have their literature. It is as if there were books on arms, legs, noses, organs—but no book on the body.

A book was needed that would explain how we can live out our lives under such a magnificent dome, its glory freely available to all but the physically blind, and yet reduce the sight of it to something less than visual "background music"—seldom registering on our consciousness unless it

vii

threatens to wash out a picnic, weekend sailing trip, or holiday double-header. Indeed, even the word *cloud* is synonomous with unpleasantness.

A book was needed that not only exhorts us to behold the beauty and wonder of this overarching, awesome, all-embracing container of our existence but also spells out every aspect of its influences on life. Chuck responded by writing that very book!

JACK BORDEN
Founder, For Spacious Skies

PREFACE

This book was conceived simply to raise people's consciousness of the sky, an oft-overlooked, undervalued, but major component of our environment. Within these pages you can explore the physical nature of the day and night skies; the biology of the sky; and the impact of the sky on our culture past, present, and future. There are sky-observing activities suggested at the end of most chapters along with suggestions for further reading. The further readings can provide greater detail on many interesting points that I can only hint at in a book of this broad scope.

Although titled a "guidebook," it is not a typical guide to locating and identifying sky phenomena; rather, it is a book to guide readers to see the sky in a broader sense than just a place for weather and astronomy observations. The purpose of the book is to look at the sky not only in terms of scientific phenomena, but in terms of the meaning of the sky to our lives. I trust it will help the reader discover the sky as a major part of our home and living environs; a part of our world to contemplate with wonder, pleasure, and affection. Hopefully, it will also spark a desire to protect the processes of the sky, for they are essential to our lives. We cannot afford to continue to pollute the sky excessively with gases, particulates, and radioactive materials.

Although this book is informative, it is basically designed to be a steppingstone for your own continued observation and enjoyment of the sky. If it does not lead you to spend more time looking out of building and car windows and/or walking unfettered, head up, beneath spacious skies, it will have failed in its purpose. It may even spark you to some artistic or scientific endeavors related to the sky and its phenomena.

Additionally, sky observing is actually quite healthful, fostering a head-up position while walking that expedites delivery of oxygen to the lungs, which makes you feel more lively. The head-up position is also the position of someone who feels good about him- or herself and has a positive attitude toward life and living. Sky watching heads you right, with your head in the clouds but your feet on the ground.

Compiling a book of this nature engenders a feeling of indebtedness to many people although they are far too numerous and spread over too

ix

long a time to fully acknowledge individually. No slight is intended by not tendering individual recognition here, nor is there any desire on my part to take unwarranted credit; we all stand upon the shoulders of those who went before us, with the assistance of our contemporaries.

However, some people have contributed to this book in ways that must be specially recognized. Verne Rockcastle stimulated my first writing about the sky more than twenty years ago by urging me, then a graduate student, to make a presentation to the American Nature Study Society about observing the atmosphere. Miriam Dickey, a valued co-worker, has shared her enthusiasm for the night sky over many years in many workshops; and Jack Borden, founder of For Spacious Skies and indefatigable promoter of sky watching, rekindled my thinking about the sky in general education and nudged me into finally preparing this book. My knowledge and feeling for the sky were also greatly enhanced over the years by the writings and illustrations of the late Eric Sloane and the opportunities to roam the sky with my pilot father-in-law, Doug King.

The staffs of the Reuben Hoar and Massachusetts Audubon Society libraries have been most helpful in my research, particularly Betty Smith, Sue Moody, and Louise Maglione. Mary Rogers patiently read the evolving manuscript and bolstered morale along the way.

Ultimately, it is to his family that the author owes his greatest gratitude. My daughter, Amy, was part of the basic inspiration for this book because she has on many occasions dropped whatever she was doing, from sports to eating, to dash out, camera in hand, to record the sunset. She has been more than patient and I hope understanding of her father's mental absences while writing just across the hall. My wife has shared the same neglect while being helpful in many ways, not the least of which was the gift of the word processor that has made the work flow so much more easily.

To these folks and all the multitude of authors, scientists, painters, musicians, ancient and modern, who have presented their insights on the sky and permitted me to reiterate them here, I express my sincerest thanks. I hope that this book will inspire you to greater appreciation of the sky as their writings and works of art have inspired me.

If there is nothing new on earth, still there is something new in the heavens. We have always a resource in the skies. They are constantly turning a new page to view. The wind sets the type in this blue ground, and the inquiring mind may always read a new truth.

Henry David Thoreau
JOURNAL, November 17, 1837

CHAPTER 1

MIND, EYE, AND SKY

At eventide, clouds often seem drawn toward the setting sun as if by an unseen magnet, to be set aglow with shades of orange and red light and etched against the darkening sky. The spectacle delights our eyes and sets our minds to contemplation of the mysteries of our universe. Our spirits tend to be lifted, our minds cleared.

Yet at other times there is a strong tendency for most of us to overlook events that are happening in the sky. We seem to be so preoccupied with the mundane happenings in our daily lives that we become blind to the rest of our surroundings, particularly the sky. With noses to the grindstone, our eyes are to the ground, and we lose sight of the sky. What a great misfortune that is, for the sky is, in essence, a vast panoramic screen upon which we can view a host of beautiful and mysterious events. Such events are changing constantly, some almost minute by minute. Some are here briefly, then gone forever, while others recur periodically.

Throughout this book we will examine many of these sky events, along with the myriad ways the sky affects both our lives and the lives of other living things. The sky governs our lives in ways we seldom think about; it even helps shape our moods. It is to our advantage to be more consciously and regularly aware of it. Truly a global commons, the sky belongs to all of us without regard to race, creed, or social status. Arching over city, suburb, farm, and wilderness, it is a reality no living soul is untouched by, regardless of how ignorant he or she may be of that fact.

1

WHERE IS THE SKY?

The sky is up, of course. Doesn't everyone know that? Well, yes and no. Conventional wisdom conceives of the sky as being above us, but just where does the sky begin? And just how high is the sky? Although these are the kinds of questions children often ask, they are not silly questions. Nor are the answers as simple and straightforward as one might think. Once-simple answers have been particularly complicated by findings of our space-age explorations of other parts of the solar system and the universe in general.

The word *sky,* which is of Middle English origin, was coined by earthbound people whose concept of their universe placed earth at its center and the sky as a domed surface across which clouds drifted and stars moved. To them, the sky was that layer overhead where the clouds and stars were. Corresponding words in other European languages, such as the French *ciel,* or the Spanish and Italian *cielo,* similarly connote "ceiling"; the impression of a room's ceiling was probably created in large part by the clouds in the sky.

Conventionally, we think of the sky as a blue dome overhead, even though we know that it becomes gray when overcast with clouds and that it is essentially black at night. At least, that is how the sky appears when we contemplate it from earth. But what did our astronauts see in the sky when they stood on the moon? What do the space-probe television cameras reveal about the sky of Mars or Venus once they have landed? Do the moon and the planets have skies? Indeed, just what is sky? Is it just up from wherever you happen to be in the universe?

WHAT IS THE SKY?

Dictionary definitions of sky are of little help in answering those last two questions. In fact, it is almost impossible to find a clear definition of sky that provides any information that would help with the answers to some of the questions we have raised here. Indeed, as we seek answers we discover the idea of sky is as much a product of the human mind as it is of an objective reality perceived through our eyes and other senses. In this book the sky is defined as coterminus with a planet's atmosphere; beyond that is space. Thus, the astronauts saw nothing in the sky when on the moon because the moon has no atmosphere and thus no sky. However, the space probes' cameras sent back photos of the skies of the respective planets. The height of a sky depends upon the gravitational pull of its planet and thus will vary from planet to planet. Also, according to our definition, there are no stars in the sky; they are beyond the sky and are viewed *through* the sky. We will specifically answer the question of how high earth's sky is in the following chapter.

By extrapolation from our definition, the sky begins not up but down. The atmosphere is all around us and even under our feet as it infiltrates the

2

upper layers of the soil. As we go about the business of living, we bear the sky upon our shoulders and are continually, though unconsciously, pushing our way through the sky. We are actually bottom-dwelling organisms of the ocean of air that is the sky, or, as author Guy Murchie put it, "We are the crabs of the airy depths."

Not only is *sky* a term whose origins were earthbound, it was also a placebound term. Sky was described as an arch that ran from horizon to horizon in a circle; in essence, like a bowl inverted over us. Science has revealed that to be a perceptual illusion of our minds. Our vision is bounded by the horizon, and such celestial objects as the sun and moon appear to rise from that horizon ever higher in the sky until overhead and eventually to descend to disappear below the opposite horizon line. Thus, people in different geographic locations do not see the same view when they contemplate the sky. We then say there are different skies. However, different skies are in reality only perceptual segments of the one sky of earth. We more properly refer to "skies" when we consider the atmospheres of the different planets.

THE SHAPE OF THE SKY

If an inverted bowl shape for the sky is only a perceptual illusion, what shape is the sky? Earth's sky is like a layer of transparent plastic wrap around the planet. Relative to our size it seems vast, reaching out from the surface several hundred miles. Relative to the diameter of the planet, however, it is very thin. It has been variously described as comparable to the thickness of your condensed breath on a marble or as merely a decal on the surface of the earth. This thin transparent layer, tethered to the planet by gravity, is not of uniform thickness, being almost twice as thick at the earth's equator as at its poles. Additionally, gravitational forces from the moon and pressure from solar winds regularly distort its symmetry.

Only a few centuries ago, before the rise of modern science, the sky

FIGURE 1.1. Three perceptions of the sky: (a) an idealized celestial dome; (b) the perceptual celestial dome which is wider than high; (c) the sky (exaggerated scale) as earth's atmosphere to the limit of the magnetopause.

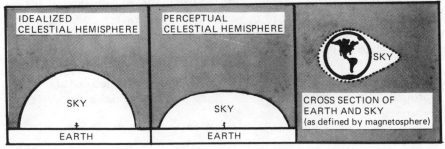

3

was conceived of primarily as a background for various celestial objects and events and as a home for various deities. Sky was a fuzzy concept that begged clear definition. Today, science has taken a closer look at what is "up," and we are able to have a sharper conception of the nature of the sky. That is not to say that all the mystery that has traditionally been associated with the sky has been removed or that there is universal concensus on the nature and structure of the sky; only that we have increased our knowledge and understanding since those earlier days.

SKY AWARENESS

Another change that has occurred over those centuries has been to our general awareness of the sky; it has lessened dramatically! Recent studies indicate that most people today spend 95 percent of their time indoors, so it probably is not surprising that they are less aware of the various cyclical events that occur in nature, including the continuously changing events in the sky. In earlier times, however, most people were at least part-time farmers or spent time outside traveling by foot or animal. These people saw the sky, observed it carefully, and could interpret what they observed there, at least in terms of what it foretold for their comfort and safety. Far more of them were also aware of the stunning beauty of sunrise, sunset, starry nights, and rainbows. Most did not ask for detailed explanations of what they saw; they simply enjoyed or feared it and took its changes as various signs of the pleasure or wrath of their deity or dieties.

The majority of us today have lost such direct awareness of the sky, not because it is unavailable to us, but because we tend to ignore its presence for any of a number of reasons beyond our general tendency to spend so much time indoors. After all, even building-bound people can look out the window to view the sky if they want the contact. Perhaps one of the most pervasive reasons people do not see the sky or regularly turn to it for beauty, spiritual uplift, or general recreation is our modern alienation from nature. We have become so accustomed to the creations of our culture and to living in urban areas that we never gain a real appreciation of the raw materials that make all this possible and the natural systems and cycles that provide these raw materials. We have lost sight of the fact that we breathe the sky and that it plays a major role in delivering our water. Most of us don't realize at all that it shields us continually from the more harmful radiations of the sun. Instead, we thoughtlessly use it as an aerial dump for the gaseous byproducts of our industry and transportation, and we have caused some alteration of the shielding mechanism of the upper sky through the prolonged use of certain propellant and refrigerating gases, along with some industrial gaseous wastes.

TURNING ON TO THE SKY

There are, of course, a number of other possible reasons for our turning off our awareness of the sky. In some places, tall buildings or foliage form a near horizon in our major line of sight, forcing us to deliberately raise our point of view if we are to see the sky. Another major reason is our mental capacity not to respond to incoming sensual messages that we have learned are not of immediate importance. This capacity is known as *habituation*. Because the sky is constantly providing sensory messages to us, and because our biological adaptation to the pressure of the sky and the gases it provides and disposes of is so well tuned, our minds can generally ignore sky messages safely. There are so many other messages arriving that must be processed that to process regularly and consciously all the background sky messages might cause overload. Unfortunately, such habituation causes us to miss much of the beauty of the sky. Once we are aware of this natural tendency to habituate to certain incoming information and have determined that we no longer want to miss the pleasures of the sky, we can override much of the habituation. In essence, we can reprogram our minds not to tune out all sky messages. People in professions that demand sky awareness do this all the time, and it is clearly within the capacities of the rest of us as well if we will it to be.

Related to the concept of habituation is the countertrend of *positive reinforcement*. It is really the tool one uses to reprogram an area diminished through habituation. By seeking meaning or enjoyment from sky events and doing it over and over, we positively reinforce the mind's response to those kinds of stimuli or sky messages. It has been suggested that we tend not to notice the sky because very few dangers come from there, and that we notice the weather when we do look at the sky because it is one of the few potential dangers the sky does present to us. Therefore, we must use the principles of positive mental reinforcement if we want to respond regularly to the sky as a source of beauty, recreation, and spiritual and creative inspiration.

FIGURE 1.2. The ground/figure concepts.

| GROUND | FIGURES ON GROUND | MIXED GROUNDS AND FIGURES |

5

Our longstanding cultural perception has been that of the sky as a background against which a "figure" is sought. Figures may be such things as birds, planes, kites, balloons, comets, meteors, and clouds. The rest of the sky is the background. (Actually, clouds can also be background, particularly when they cover a major portion of the sky.) When our minds perceive messages in the sky, the figure is most important and the background secondary. The mind seldom focuses on details of background. We have to train our minds through positive reinforcement to deal with the whole sky as a figure, responding to its varying colors and the patterns created by clouds, stars, and other celestial objects and events.

In reality, we do look at the sky more frequently than we are consciously aware. Our minds process the incoming messages quickly, reading the broad pattern and dropping the information from our short-term memories unless it deviates significantly from what we have come to perceive as normal and friendly. Only the unexpected or unusual do we retain, respond to, and store in longer-term memory. At that, we tend to retain only the broad pattern, not the minor details. Details require concentration if they are to be absorbed and retained in our memories, at least our conscious memories.

Much of our conception of the sky is symbolic. It is not only the place where we see the stars and clouds but is the place of gods and angels—heaven, the happy hunting ground, Valhalla. Each of these represents in its own way the greatest mysteries and unrestricted power. Even from a purely humanistic view, the sky as the source of incredibly powerful storms, vast space, and awesome spectacles of light represents a symbol of uncontrollable powers that dwarf the powers of humans to alter the environment and affect living things. Many people, committed to the idea of humanity as all-powerful and capable of total control over nature, want no reminders of the real limitations of human powers. The sky provides a constant reminder of such limitations, so we feel it is best to habituate to its presence and not let perception of the sky and its phenomena enter our consciousness on any regular basis.

In his studies of how people respond to each other, E.T. Hall described each person as surrounded by a series of concentric spatial distances. The smallest and nearest is intimate distance—the space in which touch is possible. Next comes personal distance, which is the space in which we can interact with another individual who is beyond touch; this is usually limited to eye contact with only one other person. Beyond that is social distance, the area in which you can relate comfortably to several people at once. The next distance is that in which a speaker is addressing a large group; there is normally a considerable space between speaker and the first row of listeners. To Hall's list should be added spiritual space, which is that distance or space which makes us perceive ourselves as small and less significant. Cathedral architects are intuitively aware of the power of such

6

FIGURE 1.3. Spaces shape our sense of importance.

space and design accordingly. The sky is the ultimate spiritual space and tends to place a person in perspective. Such a perspective is unacceptable to many; they need to feel more important, more secure, which they can do by spending more time in structures designed for a more human perspective, one in which people seem larger and more important in relation to the rest of their surroundings. Involving, as it would, altering the philosophy and world view of such people, changing their viewpoints is a task greater than we can suggest realistic approaches for here. But their attitude does represent one more reason some people tend to ignore the sky.

Of course, people in some regions fail to remain tuned in to the sky because of its tendency to exhibit apparent sameness over long stretches of time. They habituate to it because it does not send significant new messages frequently enough. This is because the sky varies geographically in its weather activity, producing, in some areas, long stretches of clear blue skies or heavy overcast, while in other places the changes are much more frequent, with the sky seldom remaining static for more than a few days at a time. The sky is always in dynamic interaction with the other major realms with which it is in constant contact—land, water, and space. It is these varied interactions that cause changes in the clear, fluid nature of the sky; that generate the weather changes and their patterns of movement. Dedicated sky watchers note that, even in areas with long stretches of apparent sameness, the sky is regularly changing, but in subtle ways that require close, detailed observation. Geographic variation in the skies is one of the factors that adds a certain zest to travel. Some places are as notable for the quality of their sky, and the lighting and backdrop it provides to the area, as for their landscape and architecture. Actually, there are few landscapes that are not improved by a good skyscape.

7

REVERSE THE TREND

Although there are a number of reasons and rationales for why various people today are less aware of the sky than their ancestors were, none of them is valid enough for you not to reacquaint yourself with the sky and encourage others to do so as well. In addition, there are some clear indications that sky awareness and sky watching can lead to improved mental and physical health. For example, just lifting your head to view the sky while walking opens the breathing passages for more efficient oxygen intake and all that that implies for feeling better about yourself physically and mentally. Furthermore, sky watching requires no special equipment (although some may enhance or extend your experiences) and can be done virtually anywhere. A case in point is that of an apartment-bound senior citizen whose walls are crowded with an extensive series of paintings of the sky which she made of the sky view from the single window in that city apartment. There are also numbers of prisoners who tell of maintaining their contact with reality through regular sky watching from their jail cells. Few of us are that constrained in our opportunities for sky watching, but we all need to take fuller advantage of those more abundant opportunities we do have.

SKY WATCHING

Sky artist and author Eric Sloane invested much of his career in helping people better understand the sky and the weather it engenders and transports. He writes:

> While you and I enjoy weather wisdom in an amateur manner, we get to look at the sky; we argue about and slosh around in hail and snow and rain and wind. We experience the weather to its fullest, and living with the weather is more rewarding than analyzing it.
>
> Fish probably are not generally aware of the stuff they swim in any more than we are generally aware of the invisible stuff that we live in. But becoming aware of air is a strange and wonderful experience that certainly adds to the joy of living. . . . Once I became introduced to the sky and to that lower part of the sky which I live in, my life became very much richer.

Sloane's interest in the sky has not been confined to weather interest alone. He goes on to say: "I constantly find its spiritual qualities outweighing its weather influences. I believe that the sky was created for pure beholding: that one of man's greatest joys can be simply looking at the sky."

Indeed, sky watching can have a variety of positive impacts on a person's life—practical, aesthetic, and spiritual. In fact, most of these three aspects are interrelated and contribute to an overall feeling of well-being and good health. Time taken from the hurly-burly pace of modern living to lose one's self in observation and contemplation of the sky tends to give

8

FIGURE 1.4. Sky—a source of power and mystery.

both mind and spirit gentle massage and uplift. The release of tensions is communicated throughout the body; muscles relax a bit, blood pressure tends to decline, some of the mental garbage that generates stress is discarded, and in general one feels more refreshed and vigorous. Sky viewing tends to lift us out of our everyday constraints of time and space, expanding our horizons and perspectives. Regular sky watching can be a positive alternative to tranquilizers and many other drugs—and the price is right.

Day or night, the sky can produce great beauty. Despite the rantings of some scoffers, beauty is an essential ingredient of our lives if we are to maintain a sense of health and well-being. The Navajo people have been deeply aware of this for centuries and have reflected it in such ceremonies as the "Yiebechei Chant":

> *Beauty below me, I walk*
> *in beauty, I walk*
> *To the direction of the rising sun,*
> *in beauty, I walk*
> *To the direction traveling with the sun,*
> *in beauty, I walk*
> *To the direction of the setting sun,*
> *in beauty, I walk*
> *To the direction of the Dippers,*
> *in beauty, I walk*
> *All around me my land is beauty,*
> *in beauty, I walk.*

The sky is an intimate part of the "land" for these people and beauty an essential part of their lives. We can and should make it the same for us. Beauty is in essence a reflection of harmony between our outer and inner environments, and it is such harmony that in large measure is responsible for a state of good health.

During one of his lectures, Leonard Duhl, Professor of Public Health and City and Regional Planning at the University of California—Berkeley, was presenting some personal experiences with the sky and pointing out that, although they didn't fit the requirements of hard science, he

> would like to argue nevertheless that such experiences, synthesizing as they do the internal and external environments, inner space and outer space, carry meaning, knowledge, and health. During these timeless moments, there is no barrier between inner and outer space; in fact, time and space melt away and reveal themselves as the mental constructs they really are. With this harmony comes awe, and an overwhelming sense of well-being, one that nurtures and heals. The sense of interconnection and relationship that such events carry can be overpowering. Their peace and playfulness evoke visions of the womb and remind us of our wistful imaginings that this was how human life was long ago, timeless, spacious, without boundaries or separation and without the need to control.[1]

[1]Journal of Humanistic Psychology (Leonard Duhl, in press).

10

Later in the lecture he discussed our tendency to desire to "know" the details of how and why and what and to push aside pure experience. He commented: "And so, although we look at the stars and the moon and 'ooh' and 'ah,' we do not permit ourselves to appreciate the feeling they evoke in us until we can comprehend, cognize, analyze, and name the celestial bodies and their connection to us and the world. The spontaneity of complete response to the sky has been denied us by our history, our traditions, and our conventions about what real knowledge is." It is my hope that this book will help you use a fuller range of your mental powers, to use both that aspect of your brain that deals with analytic, perceptive, controlled thinking and that which is responsible for processing responsive, intuitive, dream-like, nonlinear, diffuse knowledge.

In whole, healthy persons there is no real division between feelings and cognition. What we know rationally colors and enriches our feelings; how and what we feel can alter our knowledge. Sky watchers can have a fulfilling experience on a purely emotional level, but that can be further enriched by knowledge of what is happening and what it may portend. Sky watching provides food for mind and soul.

As has been suggested earlier, the effects of the sky on the mind may have much broader ramifications for the body as a whole and its general health. They sky can also be a place for various forms of more active physical recreation than passive recreation, activities that engage both mind and body, such as kite flying, hang gliding, sky diving, ballooning, and sailplane piloting. Although primarily done on water, sailing vessels of all sorts—boats, windsurfers, iceboats, and land schooners—depend on the sky's winds for their propulsion. Nor should we overlook various forms of birding, such as hawk watching, that, although land-based, keep our eyes to the sky.

Contemplation of the sky through the centuries has stimulated much creative thinking that has brought to human culture understanding of mathematical properties and navigational techniques, growing understanding of the universe and the place of our planet in it. It has stimulated poets and writers past and present, along with many painters. Cultural perceptions of the sky have literally shaped many ancient cities. Music, which is such an important part of so many of our lives, has been inspired by the sky and is primarily transported from its source to our waiting ears by the sky. All of these benefits will be explored more fully in later chapters.

SKY FEARS

Until now I have focused largely on the positive influence of the sky on our lives, but the sky can impart fears as well. The unbridled power of a towering thunderstorm, hurricane, tornado, sandstorm, or other violent storm can

11

cause damage and destruction that imprint themselves indelibly on the mind. Incessant winds can set our nerves on edge, making attempts at stress reduction, through sky watching or any other means, farcical. All are sky phenomena. For some people such phenomena engender fear; for others, religious reverence for the power of the God or gods that control such power. It has been so throughout most of human history. Henry Frankfurt and others, writing in *The Intellectual Adventure of Ancient Man,* point out that

> The sky can, at moments when man is in a singularly receptive mood, reveal itself in an almost terrifying experience. The vast sky encircling one on all sides may be felt as a presence at once overwhelming and awesome, forcing one to his knees merely by its sheer being. And this feeling which sky inspires is definite and can be named: it is that inspired by majesty. There comes a keen realization of one's own insignificance, of unbridgeable remoteness. The Mesopotamians express this well when they say, "Godhead awesome as the faraway heavens, as the broad sea." But though a feeling of distance, this feeling is not one of absolute separation; it has a strong element of sympathy and of the most unqualified acceptance.

Thus, as you embark upon further adventures with the sky through this book, expect to engage your eyes and other senses, your mind, and indeed your whole body. Expect not only to learn but to feel. Remember that many modern astronomers and physicists believe that what is seen depends upon who is looking because the observer cannot truly be separated from the observed. You bring to your observations a filter composed of your life experiences to date, and subsequent observations may alter the filter through which you observe and perceive sky objects and events. You are embarking on an adventure.

As you enlarge your sky-observing activities and learning, it is hoped that you will decrease your alienation from the natural world; become more concerned about becoming attuned to its cycles and systems; and even engage in social activity to prevent their further disruption. You may come to appreciate more fully Leonard Duhl's candor when he commented,

> I realize that [the sky] is a symbol of universal vastness, openess, and nearly unimaginable meaning, and at the same time that it cannot be separated from myself, from my own health and the health of all who live. We carry the universe, both vast space and intricate form within us, although we live—I have lived—for the most part alienated from any knowledge of this intimate link between our body-minds and the sky.

FURTHER READING

FRANCK, FREDERICK. *The Zen of Seeing.* New York: Alfred A Knopf, Inc., 1973.

GREGORY, R. L. *Eye and Brain. The Psychology of Seeing.* New York: McGraw-Hill, 1970.

PARMENTER, ROSS. *The Awakened Eye.* New York: Wesleyan University Press, 1968.

12

FIGURE 1.5. Sky—sometimes a remote, overwhelming, awesome presence.

13

PART I
THE PHYSICAL NATURE OF SKY AND SPACE

CHAPTER 2

SKY ANATOMY AND PHYSIOLOGY

The sky is earth's outer skin, an ocean of air with a distinctive layered structure and internal movements that, although very real, are largely invisible to the naked eye. However, in order to understand and appreciate most of the phenomena that occur in the sky it is most helpful to have some knowledge of sky anatomy and physiology. Those readers who wish to get right to the heart of exploring sky objects and phenomena may wish to skip over this chapter for the moment but should return later to broaden their understanding of what occurs where in the sky and why.

The sky envelope is even less of a perfect sphere than the earth itself. It bulges outward at the equator and is much less thick at the poles. This distortion affects all of the component layers of the sky as well, so that the actual height of a given layer above the earth's surface varies with latitude; it is greatest at the equator, least at the poles. (Figure 2.1 presents a rough approximation of the shape of the atmosphere and the planet as they might appear in cross section.)

The gaseous envelope around the earth that makes up what we generally think of as our sky can be conceived of as being structured something like an onion; that is, as a sequence of concentric layers. There are two primary subdivisions, the *homosphere* and the *heterosphere,* both composed of several other layers, each with its own characteristic chemical and physical properties.

The layer closest to the planetary surface, the homosphere, contains the physical bulk of the material of the atmosphere. Within the homosphere, nitrogen and oxygen, the dominant gases, along with the rarer gases argon, xenon, krypton, carbon dioxide, neon, methane, nitrous oxide, and helium, are thoroughly and evenly mixed together and behave as if they were a single gas. In the heterosphere, on the other hand, the gases tend to sort out

16

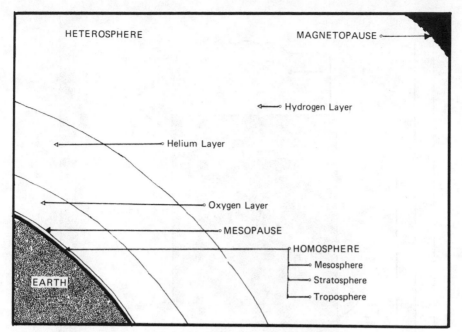

FIGURE 2.1. Cross section of the sky indicating the major zones or layers.

into layers according to their weight, with the heavier ones, like nitrogen and oxygen, at the lower altitudes and the lightest, such as hydrogen, at the highest altitudes and in interstellar space. The dividing line between the homosphere and the heterosphere occurs at about 55 miles (90 km) of altitude.

The innermost layer of the heterosphere is composed primarily of molecular nitrogen—two atoms of nitrogen bonded together. It extends from 55 miles to about 125 miles (90 to 200 km) of altitude. Boundaries between the layers of the heterosphere are not sharply defined but rather are zones of mixing. Above the nitrogen layer is one of atomic oxygen. That is, instead of the normal two-atom oxygen molecule, the oxygen of this layer exists primarily as single atoms. The atomic oxygen layer extends from roughly 125 miles to 700 miles (200 to 1100 km). Next is a helium layer ranging from 700 miles to 2200 miles (1100 to 3500 km), followed by the outermost layer of hydrogen. This hydrogen layer extends out to the limits of the earth's magnetic field, an odd-shaped boundary affected by the solar wind of electrically charged particles. More about this later.

STRUCTURE OF THE HOMOSPHERE

The homosphere consists of three quite distinct layers that are distinguished by their temperature behavior. Boundaries between them are fairly sharp. The layers are known as the *troposphere, the stratosphere,* and the *meso-*

17

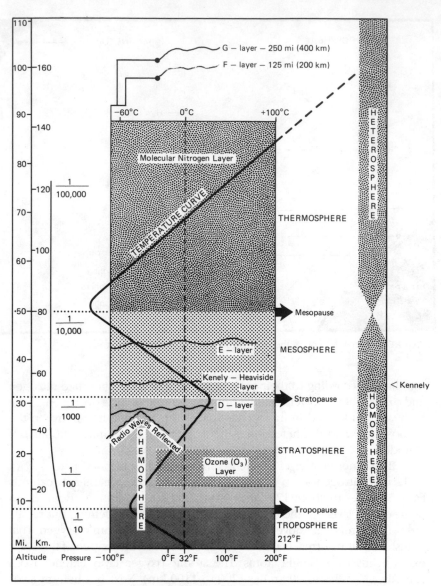

FIGURE 2.2. Anatomy of the Sky. This diagram indicates the various zones of the sky described by scientists and indicates what generally happens in terms of temperature, pressure, and molecular layerization within the various zones.

sphere; the boundaries are called, respectively the *tropopause,* the *stratopause,* and the *mesopause.* The mesopause is actually the boundary between the homosphere and the heterosphere.

The Troposphere

The troposphere is the bottom layer of the sky, the one with which we are all most familiar. Here the concentration of gas molecules is most dense, the pressure most heavy, and the turbulence the greatest. It is the zone of clouds, storms, thunder and lightning, rainbows, gale winds, and sandstorms. It contributes most to the beauty of sunsets and sunrises.

Within the troposphere, as it increases in altitude from the earth's surface, temperature declines steadily. The rate of temperature decline is called the *lapse rate,* and in the troposphere the lapse rate is quite steep. Although you cannot see the boundaries of temperature change, you can surely gain a feel for the temperature characteristics of the troposphere by climbing mountains or taking hot-air balloon rides. As you ascend you will find that the temperature decreases at a rate of about 1° F for every 300 feet (or 0.5° C for every 100 m). Eventually, you would reach a point where the lapse rate declines and the temperature remains quite constant. This point is the tropopause; the actual height of the tropopause above the planet's surface varies widely with latitude and season but is usually somewhere around 5 miles (8 km) near the poles and 10 miles (16 km) near the equator. Temperature at the tropopause is about −112° F(−80° C) over the equator and −50° F (−46° C) above the poles. Over the temperate regions, tropopause occurs at about 7 miles (11 km) altitude, at a temperature of −65° F (−54° C). The apparent anomaly of the tropopause being colder over the equator than over the poles is explained by the greater altitude of the tropopause at the equator than at the poles.

Because the troposphere rests upon the surface of the earth and receives heat conducted, radiated, and reflected from the surface, it is the site of a great many vertical air currents. These cause turbulence, which generates winds, clouds, and precipitation. Thus, all of our ordinary weather develops in this layer.

The Stratosphere

Just above the tropopause the temperature begins to rise slowly but steadily until at the stratopause it reaches about 32° F(0° C). This occurs at an altitude of roughly 30 miles (50 km). This temperature rise is due to the action of very shortwave, ultraviolet light on the molecules of oxygen gas at that level. Each of the oxygen molecules is composed of two atoms of oxygen bonded together with energy. The force of the ultraviolet rays breaks the bond, releasing two atoms of oxygen. This monatomic oxygen then combines, by processes not clearly understood, with a normal two-atom oxygen molecule to form the three-atom oxygen molecule known as *ozone.* It is the heat released through the ozone formation process that generates the increase in temperature in this region of the sky.

Although concentrated ozone is toxic at the surface of the planet, at this altitude it is a protector of living things. If the incoming ultraviolet rays reached the ground at their full strength, their destructive, penetrating powers would cause very serious damage to living tissues. However, the process of ozone formation robs them of much of their power. Thus, the upper stratosphere serves as a vital shield for life at the bottom of the sky. What is most amazing is that such a rare substance can have such an

19

important shielding function; for if all the ozone were brought down to sea-level density, it would form a layer only about $^1/_{10}$ inch (2.5 mm) thick! Of course, at its altitude of greatest concentration, 16 miles (25 km), it is much more widely distributed. Its presence there is largely due to an abundance of shortwave radiation, which splits the oxygen molecules, and to a great enough density of other diatomic oxygen molecules with which the freed oxygen atoms can collide and bond.

The stratopause occurs at an altitude of 32 miles (50 km), and at that point the temperature has risen to not much less than that at sea level. However, because ozone is not evenly distributed around the earth and its concentration varies both over time and in space, the temperatures that its formation creates vary also, creating strong seasonal winds within the stratosphere layer. Very little water penetrates the stratosphere; that which does is usually in the form of water vapor, so clouds are a rare occurrence in this layer.

The Mesophere

The mesosphere extends upward from the stratopause to about 50 miles (80 km) from earth. In this zone temperature again decreases with altitude to a reading of about $-203°$ F ($-95°$ C) at the mesopause, the coldest point in the atmosphere. The lapse rate in the mesosphere, however, is only about half that in the troposphere. There is a small amount of vertical mixing in this zone, with erratic horizontal winds that may reach extremely high speeds. Although there is some ozone in the lower reaches of the mesosphere, most of that substance is generated in the stratosphere below. The mesophere is, in reality, a transition zone between two energy-absorbing layers: the ozone layer of the stratosphere below and the ionized layers of the ionosphere above.

There is almost no solid or liquid state matter in the mesosphere; thus, we should expect that there are no clouds to be seen here. But there is one rare but notable exception—*noctilucent* clouds. These are very high-level clouds that form in the upper part of the zone and can be seen only at twilight, although they may actually be present at other times. Noctilucent clouds are best seen when the sun is 5° to 8° below the horizon. As might be expected, these rare clouds are most often observed in high latitudes where there are the longest periods of twilight.

STRUCTURE OF THE HETEROSPHERE

From the point of view of its temperature behavior, the heterosphere can be thought of as a single layer, the *thermosphere*. Here the atoms of gas absorb vast amounts of energy that cause them to have individual temperatures of

20

around twenty-one hundred degrees Fahrenheit or more. However, this does not create the torrid zone that would seem to be implied because the individual atoms are too far apart to have many of the collisions that would transmit such heat. The subzones of the heterosphere are distinguished by the behavioral phenomena of the gases at those altitudes.

The Ionosphere

Above the mesopause air molecules are few and far between, so far between in fact that sound cannot be transmitted here and silence reigns supreme. However, the key feature of this layer is that most of the air is electrically charged. Electrically charged particles are known as *ions* (from the Greek word for "wanderer"), and from such ions this region of the upper sky gets its name.

The ionosphere becomes ionized because it is subject to extensive electromagnetic bombardment from a broad range of the energy radiation spectrum—visible light, ultraviolet radiation, infrared radiation, cosmic rays, and radio waves among them. Of particular import are the ultraviolet rays that knock electrons from molecules or split the molecules into single atoms, and the cosmic rays that smash into atomic nuclei with incredible force, scattering highly energetic debris.

Within the ionosphere particles are not uniformly distributed but tend to concentrate in distinct zones of electrically charged air. These more concentrated zones of charged particles are not constant in thickness but expand during exposure to sunlight and shrink in the darkness. Electric currents are generated in these zones by the same basic process by which we generate electricity here on the ground when moving a wire through a magnetic field. In the ionosphere ionized particles replace the wire, and the magnet is the magnetic field of earth itself. Movement is created by the atmospheric tides. As the gravitational pull of the moon exerts its force, the atmosphere exhibits tidal movements just as the oceans do. Furthermore, the flow of electric current itself generates other magnetic fields. The electromagnetic processes of the ionosphere are exceedingly complex.

The electromagnetic activity of the various zones of concentration in the ionosphere have a distinct impact on the transmission of radio and television signals and also give rise to the phenomenon of auroras, about which we will have more to say in Chapter 4. These zones are also subject to electromagnetic storms, triggered in large measure by solar storms, that are very disruptive to radio and television communications and often generate spectacular auroras.

Temperature soars as altitude increases within the ionosphere. It starts at a few hundred degrees Fahrenheit and reaches somewhere over two thousand degrees in the uppermost regions; that is, at a height of about 350 miles. Density of the air in this zone is highly rarefied, with the particles

21

of nitrogen and oxygen primarily in atomic rather than molecular form and highly energized by solar radiation.

The Exosphere

Transition between the ionosphere and the exosphere is not sharply delineated but generally occurs somewhere between 350 and 500 miles altitude. Here, gas particles are still charged but are separated by vast distances. They are too widely scattered to form the ionized layers characteristic of the ionosphere. However, the exosphere has two enormously thick, electromagnetically charged belts. One band begins at about 2500 miles from earth and is hundreds of miles thick; the other starts at around 10,000 miles and is thousands of miles thick. These two bands, known as the Van Allen radiation belts, are made up of swarms of electrons and protons that have been expelled from the sun as solar wind and have been recruited and trapped by the earth's magnetic field.

The exosphere extends outward from the planet for about 18,000 miles, but its boundaries are not sharp. The top of the sky is determined by the pull of earth's gravity on the various particles. The action of the sun's energy on the gases is great, and particles may heat to over 3000° F. Some particles get enough energy to accelerate to speeds over 25,000 miles per hour, which allows them to escape the gravitational pull of the planet and into space beyond. The loss of these particles is roughly balanced by the number of incoming particles trapped by our gravity.

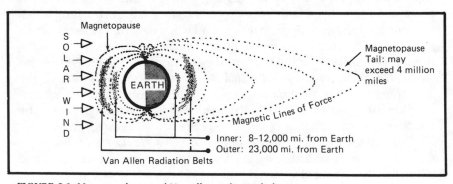

FIGURE 2.3. Magnetosphere and Van Allen radiation belts.

Relative Emptiness

Beyond the exosphere are the vast reaches of cosmic space. Such space is far from empty, housing a host of objects such as planets, comets, stars, and plasmas. However, these objects are relatively so distant from one another that we can only conceive of the space between them as empty.

We need to understand that about 95 percent of the substance of our atmosphere is concentrated in the first 12 miles above the earth, while only 5 percent fills the remaining 17,988 miles. Loebsack emphasizes this in a slightly different way; he remarks that "for every ten million million air molecules at sea level there are only one thousand at six hundred miles and only one molecule at nine hundred miles."

It is the lower reaches of the sky that house the majority of the sky phenomena which have intrigued us over the centuries, and which alter our perceptions of the celestial objects that compose the rest of the universe but actually lie beyond the sky. Our sky is our window on the universe, and it proves to be less transparent than we might believe or wish it were. Like many panes of glass it has impurities whose optical properties alter our perception of reality.

We can observe sky phenomena in most of the different layers of the sky, but the majority lay within the troposphere. Thus, much of our explorations will deal with this region of the sky. It is useful, however, to be familiar with the general anatomy of the sky in order to understand something of the nature and location of all of these objects and phenomena.

THE SKY IN MOTION

The substance of the sky is fluid and thus in constant motion. Even when the sky is apparently calm, air molecules are zipping about, caroming off each other like microscopic billiard balls. The sky obeys the laws that govern fluids, and thus pressure applied at one point is distributed equally in all directions. The very weight of the sky, created by the pull of gravity toward the center of earth, creates a basic pressure. Gravity also helps concentrate most of the air molecules at the bottom of the sky, which means that those in the troposphere have a far greater likelihood of hitting others in their movement than those in the ionosphere or exosphere. Where molecule density is greatest, distribution of pressure forces will be greatest.

If we look at an arbitrary "package of air" in the lower sky, we find that pressure exerted on it encounters differential resistances from different directions. Upward pressure is countered by the sheer weight of the air column above; downward pressure is resisted by the greater density of the earth. Least resistance comes from packets of air to the side; thus, this is the direction of most air movement, parallel to the earth. Such movement causes breezes and winds.

Wind itself is invisible; we know it by its effects. It dries our skin, chills our extremities, rustles the leaves, raises waves, flutters flags, raises dust and debris, turns windmills, and transports the clouds. At its worst it levels buildings, increases tidal flooding, and generally causes sheer mayhem. We judge the wind as good or bad depending upon its effect on our lives, but the wind is neutral. It is simply the circulation mechanism of the sky.

23

FIGURE 2.4. The wind is seen by its actions. Ira Spring photo.

To make the point that pressure differentials generate winds, I deliberately oversimplified, implying that the weight of the air column was the cause of the pressure. Actually, it is only one source of pressure. The other major source is the energy imparted to the air molecules themselves from a variety of sources. As they take on more energy, they move more rapidly, hit others with more force, and generally cause an expansion of the packet of air they are in, thus generating an increase in pressure. As the reverse occurs and they lose energy, they move with less force and exert less pressure.

Air molecules get their energy from the radiant energy of the sun or earth and transmit or lose it by conduction (transmission by contact from particle to particle), radiation (transmission as energy waves), or the processes of convection (mass movement of energized particles). Above the troposphere there is relatively little wind action, but within the troposphere there is a great deal, and its patterns are complex. They are shaped by the impact of local earth topography and by the celestial motions of the planet itself. When moving air encounters a mountain, it tends to flow up and over. In effect, the air is lifted, and when you lift air it expands and cools. By contrast, as air sinks it becomes compressed and heats up. Mountains are not

24

the only causes of air lifts. As another air mass of greater density is encountered, it may have an impact similar to the mountain. Such cycles of rising and falling air help create reasonably discrete masses of air that interact with each other and with the earth and seas beneath them, generating varying degrees of turbulence and changing weather patterns.

In any fluid such as the sky, objects, such as air masses, rise or fall depending upon whether upward pressure from their energies or the downward pull of gravity wins the vertical tug of war of the moment. The vertical force resulting from such a tug of war is called *buoyancy*. The buoyancy of a particular air mass depends upon how the air above it is vertically stratified with respect to temperature. If the temperature lapse rate of the air above is less than $1°$ C per 100 meters, the air is considered stable, and it will resist an upward push from an air mass below it. However, if the temperature lapse rate of the upper air is greater than $1°$ C, it will favor the upward push of the air mass below. At a lapse rate of exactly $1°$ C, the upper air is neutral, neither favoring nor resisting the upward push of the lower air mass. Thus, stable air aloft discourages vertical motion of air masses, while unstable air aloft is very amenable to such mixing motion. All of this is of great import to the nature of clouds and winds.

All fluids, like the sky, possess the property of *viscosity;* that is, a dissipative force that opposes motion. The viscosity of the sky acts much as the shock absorber of a car to squelch motion. If driving forces are not added, air motion comes to a standstill. In most of the troposphere this seldom happens except in a few narrow bands: one over the equator, the *doldrums* region; and the other between the trade winds and the prevailing westerlies, known as the *horse latitudes*. Pressure forces are the most fundamental of the driving forces, and they get the wind blowing and thus the air moving.

Despite our discussion of air parcels we must always realize that the air is continuous and that a flow of air into one region must always be accompanied by a flow out of that region. The net affect of all this is that the atmosphere, the sky, functions as a massive heat engine, converting energy from one form to another and circulating it around our planet.

GLOBAL PATTERNS

The "air parcels" we have mentioned are created by rising and sinking air which establishes more or less circular convection currents. Since warm rising air is of a different density than cooler sinking air, the differing densities create boundaries that are almost as effective as more solid walls. Such bounded units of air, with relatively similar temperature and moisture regimes, differentiate themselves from each other and move about with the winds, changing temperature, moisture, and pressure characteristics as they move over the earth's surface.

There are several forces at work creating these air parcels and shaping the direction of their movement. Within the first few miles of the sky, the planet's topography creates a variety of barriers that the air must flow over or around, depending upon temperature conditions. These barriers and temperature conditions alter more clearcut air-movement patterns that can be seen or determined higher in the sky. Such local disruptions of the bigger patterns make for the interesting diversity of skies in different regions, and we will discuss them in greater detail under specific sky phenomena. At this point, however, let us focus on the broader patterns of movement in the sky around the planet.

In a very broad sense the air of the planet rises at the equator and settles at the poles, but in reality a great deal happens in between. As the hot equatorial air rises, it expands and cools, and the cooler air sinks, with the spin of the earth giving it a twist. This results in a circulation of equatorial hot air rising and spinning poleward and easterly and, as it cools, settling down around the two 30°-latitude tropics of Capricorn and Cancer. It then flows back toward the equator. At the planet's surface this backflow creates the broad belt of winds blowing from the northeast called the trade winds. At the equator itself the wind direction is primarily upward, so relative calm prevails at the surface, creating a quiet region known as the doldrums. In the regions where the cooling tropical air actually descends, there tend to be seasonal periods of little or no surface winds. This creates areas known as horse latitudes. These are so called because in the days of the sailing ships it was not unusual to become becalmed there for long periods, sometimes

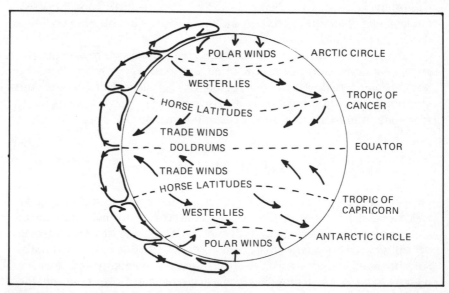

FIGURE 2.5. General global wind-circulation patterns.

26

necessitating throwing the livestock overboard when food and water shortages emerged, or to reduce the ship's load and thus gain some tiny advantage of movement in the painfully light breezes that might occur.

North of the tropics the descending cool air is turned northward and westward near the surface in its prevailing motion until it meets denser, cooler polar air. It is then deflected upward and aloft to flow southward toward the tropics. A comparable pattern occurs in the southern hemisphere. This major circulation creates the prevailing westerlies of the earth's temperate regions.

Even further poleward are the polar wind systems. Dense, frigid air descends at either pole and flows southward and westward. Along this route it becomes relatively warmer and rises as it butts into the prevailing westerlies. It then rises and, aloft, flows northward to sink again at the poles.

This circulation pattern is, of course, a great oversimplification of reality. Although temporary temperature and pressure boundaries to air masses do exist, the atmosphere nonetheless remains a continuous fluid whose particles are constantly mixing and being distributed around the planet. However, the simplification gives us a basic model of the grand circulation that we can grasp for the moment. Figure 2.5 helps visualize this scheme of things.

A variety of factors complicate this fundamental flow pattern. In addition to energy from direct solar radiation, air takes on energy from the sea and land over which it travels. The amount varies with various ocean currents and land topography. Moisture evaporating into the air often cools it, and precipitation tends to warm it. Reasons for this fact will be explored later; for now it is introduced only as a complicating factor that can affect the operation of the global heat engine which is the sky.

In the upper part of the troposphere, between the polar air masses and the prevailing westerlies, flow strong currents called *jet streams*. Jet streams change their course from time to time, creating great arching curves that tend to pull the adjacent air masses into comparable flow patterns. Temporal changes in the paths of jet streams have strong effects on the weather patterns of a region at any given point in time.

Between the influence of jet streams and the variety of near-ground circulation alterations, the global patterns seldom operate as might be predicted from basic theory. In spite of almost a century of careful observation and record keeping—highly sophisticated recording equipment operating at different levels of the atmosphere, weather satellites constantly monitoring cloud movement, computer modeling and data manipulation, and many practical incentives for precise prediction of weather events—we remain a long way from accurate, consistent results. There are just so many interactions of so many interrelated variables over vast expanses of territory that mystery continues to reign, even though we have made considerable progress in the reliability of short-range weather predictions.

27

HEAT BUDGETS

As a heat engine, the sky and its movements are affected by an overall heat budget. For all practical purposes, 100 percent of the energy of the sky comes directly or indirectly from the sun. As that energy comes through the sky, 10 percent of it is scattered and reflected back to space by the molecules of air. Ozone layers absorb another 2 percent of the energy, and water vapor absorbs another 8 percent. Thus, on a clear day, 80 percent passes through the sky and strikes the land and seas. The situation is quite different on a cloudy day. Then the clouds reflect 30 to 60 percent back toward space, while another 5 to 20 percent is absorbed by the clouds. Depending upon the density of the cloud layer, only from as much as 45 percent to as little as none may strike the planetary surface.

FIGURE 2.6. Some general components of Earth's heat budget.

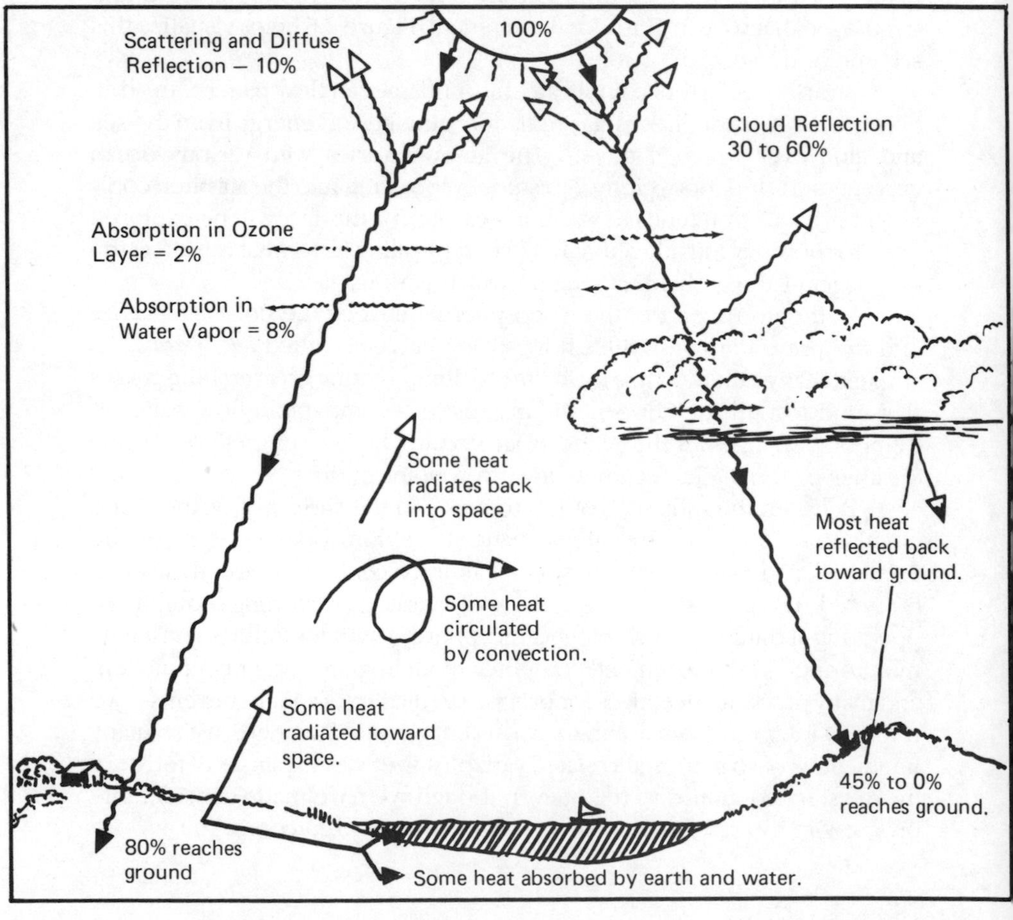

Scattering and Diffuse Reflection — 10%

100%

Cloud Reflection 30 to 60%

Absorption in Ozone Layer = 2%

Absorption in Water Vapor = 8%

Some heat radiates back into space

Most heat reflected back toward ground.

Some heat circulated by convection.

Some heat radiated toward space.

45% to 0% reaches ground.

80% reaches ground

Some heat absorbed by earth and water.

28

Much of what energy reaches the surface heats the land and water or is utilized in the photosynthetic processes. As the air passes over the land and water, it takes on some energy by conduction, radiation, and convection in some places and gives up some energy by the same processes in other places. Amounts vary from day to day, season to season, and location to location, but on average about as much heat is lost as is gained. This heat gain and loss is the ultimate driving force behind the various motions of the sky. It is the motions of sky and sea that are the great heat transfer mechanisms of the planet. Sky and sea are intimately interrelated, and water is constantly being exchanged between them. The various changes of state of water in the atmosphere are also important factors in the overall heat budget. Sea and sky together comprise a grand planetary system that permits the existence and functioning of many of the environmental phenomena of earth.

FURTHER READING

BLUMENSTOCK, DAVID I. *The Ocean of Air*. New Brunswick, NJ: Rutgers University Press, 1959.

GOODY, RICHARD M., and JAMES C.G. WALKER. *Atmospheres*. Foundations of Earth Science Series. Englewood Cliffs, NJ: Prentice-Hall, Inc., 1972.

LOEBSACK, THEODORE. *Our Atmosphere*. Translated by E.L. and D. Rewald. New York: Pantheon Books, Inc., 1959.

MILLER, ALBERT, and JACK C. THOMPSON. *Elements of Meteorology*. Columbus, Ohio: Charles E. Merrill Publishing Co., 1970.

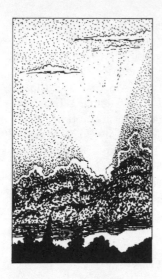

CHAPTER 3

SKY PHENOMENA

Although blue is the color that immediately comes to mind when the sky is mentioned, and is the common response, in a psychologist's free-association word test, to the word *sky,* in actuality the sky is not blue; it is transparent and colorless. The apparently clear blue skies that we perceive are essentially daytime phenomena; night skies are black or deep blue-black. Classic blue skies are seen only when the atmosphere is dry, because the addition of moisture droplets to the air creates surfaces that reflect white light and that act like white paint to dilute the deep blue color to paler hues. Other particles in the air reflect or refract other wavelengths of visible light to add other colors such as yellows and reds, which in turn mix with each other and the blue to form a broad spectrum of subtle colors in the sky. Indeed, to think of the sky only in terms of blue or gray is to have a very limited perception of the range of color which the sky can appear to be. Nor is the sky usually uniform in color. As the earth turns, causing the sun to appear to move across the sky, the different quadrants of the sky may well have quite different hues, with the clearest blue at the zenith.

Henry David Thoreau truly appreciated the variety of colors and changing light to be found in the sky. His *Journal* entry of April 25, 1852 illuminates his observations:

> What different tints of blue in the same sky! It requires to be parted by white clouds that the delicacy and depth of each part may appear. Beyond a narrow wisp or feather of mist, how different the sky! Sometimes it is full of light, especially toward the horizon. The sky is never seen to be of so deep and delicate a blue as when it is seen between downy clouds."

30

THE ELECTROMAGNETIC SPECTRUM

The light that we perceive as color is actually a very narrow portion of a broad band of electromagnetic energy waves. Length of these waves is measured from crest to crest or trough to trough. At one end of the spectrum we have the long radio waves with a wavelength of 100,000 meters; on the other, the gamma rays with wavelengths of less than 0.0001 micron. The wavelengths that our eyes can respond to, that we call visible light, include a range from about 0.400 micron (violet light) to 0.710 micron (red light). Within that narrow range our eyes are able to discriminate among very tiny differences that create some of the beauties of the sky, and indeed of all nature. The chart below indicates the wavelength range of the various colors we can perceive:

violets	0.400 micron to 0.423 micron
blues	0.424 micron to 0.490 micron
greens	0.491 micron to 0.574 micron
yellows	0.575 micron to 0.584 micron
oranges	0.585 micron to 0.646 micron
reds	0.647 micron to 0.710 micron

Such a chart may seem a bit technical, but its information may help us to understand why the sky appears basically blue. The apparent color of the sky is a function of the scattering of light by particles of the atmosphere. Blue is the color we see because of the size of the particles that do the scattering.

WHY DOES THE SKY APPEAR BLUE?

Studies indicate that the primary light-scattering particles in the air are the molecules. Such studies also reveal a law of nature, designated Rayleigh's Law after its discoverer. Technically, this law says that the light energy scattered per unit volume of air containing particles smaller than 0.1 micron is inversely proportional to the 4th power of the wavelength of the illuminating radiation. Simply put, this means that the shorter wavelengths of the spectrum will be scattered more intensely than the longer ones. Wavelengths of radiation from the sun travel in a straight line, but if they strike particles of certain sizes and densities they may be deflected from that path. Since molecules function essentially as spheres, they will tend to deflect the wavelengths in many directions, in essence scattering them. Thus these wavelengths, instead of appearing to come from one direction, appear to come from all directions at once.

You will note from the chart above that the violet and blue wavelengths are the shorter ones, thus the ones most scattered by the air molecules. The result is that we perceive the sky as basically blue. But the

31

FIGURE 3.1. Haze over the mountains. C.E. Roth photo.

higher one rises into the sky, the darker it appears, primarily because there are fewer and fewer air molecules to scatter the incoming light. If you climb or drive up a high mountain, you may be able to observe this change in the apparent color of the sky above you. Those few people who travel to the moon or in the space shuttle soon reach the outer limits of the atmosphere and enter interstellar space, where blackness reigns, for there is little or no matter to scatter or reflect the light.

OTHER COLORS

Scattering of the short blue waves thus gives the basic apparent color to the essentially transparent atmosphere, but that accounts for only a small part of the color phenomena of the sky. Reflection and refraction are the two other processes that play major roles in creating the sky's visual beauty. In large measure they operate through the presence of water in the air in the form of clouds. Other small particles in the air, such as dust and salt, also play a role as well, particularly in scattering and reflecting certain wavelengths of radiation.

The greatest amount of dust and haze is in the lowest part of the atmosphere, and that is the part we see nearest the horizon. These larger

FIGURE 3.2. Crepuscular rays behind a cloud. C.E. Roth photo.

particles are less selective than air molecules in the wavelengths they scatter, so that they scatter longer wavelengths as well as shorter ones. The end result is that the blue is diluted with the white of the other light, and thus the horizon area is usually a lighter blue than what is seen directly overhead. However, in some places where extensive mountain forests exist, during parts of the year the forests release large amounts of volatile organic molecules of a size that scatters the blue and violet light and thus creates the distinctively colored haze that creates the phenomena of blue and purple hills.

Twilight, or crepuscular, rays are a light-scattering phenomenon that attract our attention. These are the apparently fan-shaped rays that may reach up from behind a cloud at sunset or down through the misty forest at sunrise. They often create a very dramatic, even spiritual effect. They are simply light being scattered by fine particles suspended in the atmosphere, such as dust and light mist. They are never to be seen in extremely clean air and thus are largely absent from such regions as the open North Atlantic, the Central Pacific, and polar regions. The appearance of converging rays is actually an optical illusion; all the rays are parallel. Artists use this illusion when they represent parallel railroad tracks receding into the distance as coming closer and closer together until they converge at the horizon. If you have taken a flashlight out at night and shone it skyward and observed the milky beam, you have observed the same scattering effect as creates crepuscular rays. The same flashlight will produce no observable beam on a crystal-clear and dry night.

33

FIGURE 3.3. The solar disc at sunset. C.E. Roth photo.

SUNRISE, SUNSET

There are few people who have not marveled, at some time in their lives, at the glorious hues of red, orange, and yellow that predominate at sunrise and sunset, flooding the sky itself with color and/or reflecting off the clouds. These colors make their appearance only when the sun appears relatively close to the horizon. At such time the sun's rays travel through the maximum thickness of atmosphere, and the segment that contains the most particles of moisture and dust. This results in the greatest amount of scattering of the short blue and violet wavelengths and the passage through to your eyes of the longer red, yellow, and orange radiation waves. Optical phenomena, related to light's interaction with the various particles in the air, plus differing temperatures and thus air densities near the ground, create a complex of factors that we appreciate as the beauty of the sunset in all its gradually changing glory. The same is true for sunrise, although in our culture more people tend to see the sunset than the sunrise. What is most wonderful is that such beauty is available almost daily, as Thoreau noted in his *Journal* for January 7, 1852. "Every day a new picture is painted and framed, held up for half an hour, in such lights as the Great Artist chooses, and then withdrawn and the curtain falls. And then the sun goes down, and long the after glow gives light."

34

And after all this explanation is said and done, I still feel that the editors of *Arizona Highways* were right on target when they wrote in a 1976 feature: "While scientific explanation of the hows and whys of these silent heralds of day and night are interesting, all that is put aside when we experience the quiet majesty of a day's borning or the twinkling-on of the evening's stars. For us, that enchanted interval of color and quiet is a time of peace, a time of marvel and wonder, a time of, well—of magic."

FROTHY MIRRORS

Clouds are the great reflectors in the sky. Composed of vast clusters of water or ice droplets, each coalesced around a minute speck of dust, clouds absorb relatively little radiant energy but reflect and transmit a great deal. The thicker and denser the cloud bank, the more light it reflects and the less it transmits. This accounts for the observation that a thin cloud cover still

FIGURE 3.4. Silvered edges of cumulus cloud. C.E. Roth photo.

35

GRAY

WHITE

FIGURE 3.5. Cloud color depends upon relative positions of observer, clouds, and sun.

gives us reasonable light and that a towering thundercloud will reflect silvery edges and flashing white turrets but underneath will be virtually black. A large part of the magic of clouds is that they not only reflect the white light coming directly from the sun but also the scattered and reflected light of sunrise and sunset. Thus the delightful forms of clouds can be tinted across the rainbow in both strong tones and delicate pastels. They may also reflect back earth tones in some parts of the world, such as the pinkish tones reflecting from some desert sands.

The apparent colors of clouds depend upon a variety of factors but particularly on the relative position of the observer, the cloud, and the sun. As each of these things changes, the light we observe from the cloud changes (see Figure 3.5). Also, as the individual cloud ages over several hours, it tends to form larger drops and fewer of these drops per square centimeter. Under these conditions the cloud becomes a more efficient absorber of radiant energy, and thus appears darker. We may see several fluffy, fair-weather cumulus clouds near each other, with some radiantly white and others a murky gray due to this relative difference in age (actually only a matter of hours).

HALOS AND CORONAS

Other types of color are added to the sky by clouds through the *halo* phenomenon. This occurs when a thin veil of cirriform clouds lies between the viewer and the sun or moon. Cirriform clouds, about which we will have more to say a bit later in the chapter, are composed of ice crystals. Often

36

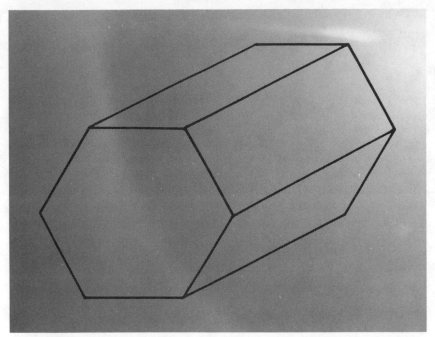

FIGURE 3.6. Insert illustrates columnar crystals that produce a halo effect like that in the photo. C.E. Roth photo.

these crystals are in the shape of six-sided prisms, this pattern forming when the temperature at that elevation is below about 5° F (-15° C).

Such crystals are column-shaped, the equivalent of two 60° triangles glued base to base with their points lopped off (see Figure 3.6). Optical laws for light passing through such a prism indicate that the minimum angle of deviation from a straight line for light passing through is 22°. The violet end of the spectrum will deviate slightly more than the red end. Consequently, light from the sun or moon shining through such a cloud will create a ring of colored light, caused by the diffraction of the light in the ice crystals. The inner edge of this ring will appear red, followed by bands of yellow, green, white, and blue toward the outside of the ring. From a straight line between the viewer and the sun or moon, the inner edge of the halo will diverge a fraction less than 22°, which, for rough measurement purposes, is the distance between your outspread thumb and little finger when held at arm's length.

A larger, 46° halo is occasionally seen. It can occur optically when the prism angle of the ice crystals is 90°, and is a greater rarity as a phenomenon than the smaller halo. Keep in mind that these ice crystals are tumbling randomly about in the cloud and only those light rays that strike a crystal at just the right angle will be diffracted. There are many variations on ice-crystal shape and movement patterns in the sky that may produce unusual

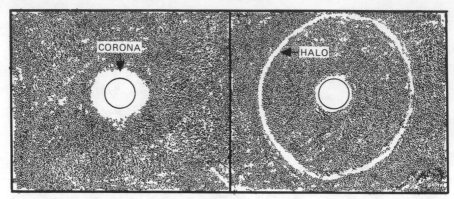

FIGURE 3.7. Comparison of *corona* with *halo*.

occurrences such as circumscribed halos, which tend to be oval in shape and may surround a 22° halo when the sun is higher than 29° above the horizon. You might even spot a curved bar, or Parry arc, across the upper circumscribed halos. Also to be occasionally observed are two bright, often brilliantly colored patches, sometimes with long white tails, known as *mock suns, sun dogs,* or *parhelia.* These will be seen on the edge of the halo, or by themselves, on a level with the actual sun. They tend to be located on the halo at low elevations of the sun but recede from it as the sun rises. Sometimes it is possible to spot small arcs curving downward from the mock suns to the halo; these are known as *Lowitz arcs.* Pillars of light may also be seen occasionally stretching above and below the sun itself, much like the column of light we sometimes see on water reflections when the sun is low in the sky.

These are the most commonly observed halo phenomena, but there are other, rarer forms that have been described in the literature, and the avid sky watcher will be ever alert for spotting them for himself. Asymmetrical arcs, even elliptical halos and an inexplicable square halo have been legitimately recorded. Somewhat more frequently, offset, interlocking halos and arcs are seen. Mock moons are observable, and there are records of lunar halos with horizontal cones of light extending from the moon to the mock moons; there are even records of lunar halos with a cross running through the moon, dividing the halo into four quadrants. These only begin to suggest some of the rare and unusual halo phenomena that have been recorded, some of which are difficult, if not impossible, to explain by standard optical principles. Every attempt should be made to try and record photographically such anomalous effects.

Coronas are essentially halo formations that occur very close to the edge of the moon or sun, although sun coronas are seldom seen due to the sun's brightness. However, coronas are not usually generated by light coming through ice crystals but rather by light passing through small

38

FIGURE 3.8. Sundogs, or *parhelia*, along a halo.

spherical water droplets and being refracted. The more uniform in size these droplets are, the purer will be the colors in the corona. Normally, the border of the corona nearest the moon will be bluish and will merge outward into a yellowish white; the outer edge, at roughly a distance of one or more moon diameters, will be brownish. This corona may in turn be followed by 1 to 3 multihued bands; each band will have the following sequence of colors from the inside out: blue, green or yellowish, then red.

The size of the diameter of the corona is determined by the size of the water droplets in the cloud. The smaller the droplets, the greater the corona diameter. Young clouds have the most uniform droplets and thus produce the best corona effects; older clouds tend to have more variation in droplet size, resulting in poorer color brightness and overlap in the ring diameter.

RAINBOWS

Rainbows are among the most beautiful of sky phenomena and have intrigued humankind from the earliest times; they continue to fascinate and to find a place not only in the sky but in song, myth, and symbol as well. Few people today have not daydreamed at some time about the mythical pot of gold at the end of the rainbow, hummed a few bars of "Somewhere, Over the Rainbow," or seen translucent rainbow decals on the windows of cars and homes. Some are aware that in the biblical Book of Genesis, God spoke to Noah after the Flood, saying: "This is the sign of the covenant which I make between me and you and every living creature that is with you, for all future generations: I set my bow in the cloud, and it shall be a sign of the covenant between me and you and every living creature of all flesh. When the bow is in the clouds, I will look upon it and remember the everlasting covenant between God and every living creature of all flesh that is upon the earth." What a truly glorious symbol!

It is a particularly appropriate symbol because its formation comes from both the rain and the sun. It occurs when light tries to pass through a

39

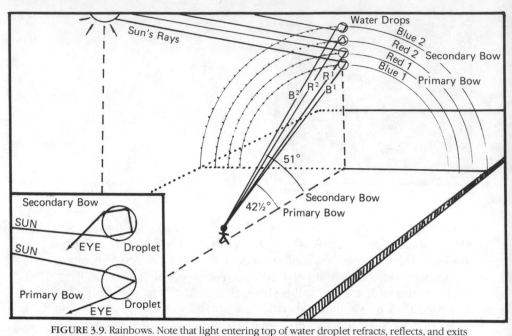

FIGURE 3.9. Rainbows. Note that light entering top of water droplet refracts, reflects, and exits to form the primary rainbow the ground observer sees; while light entering the bottom of a droplet refracts and reflects twice before exiting toward the viewer. This reverses the color band of the secondary bow.

raindrop; thus, to see a rainbow the sun must be behind you and fairly low in the sky. With the sun overhead earthbound people see no rainbows, although those up in the sky may see not only a rainbow, but a full circle of color.

Suspended water droplets are nearly spherical, although falling ones may be flattened beneath due to air resistance. As light rays strike the drop, most go through and are bent slightly and focused as if through a lens. But those striking the upper and lower sections of the sphere penetrate and are deflected at such an angle that when they reach the far side they are reflected back inside the drop rather than exiting directly. They will exit the drop headed back toward the observer. Light striking the top sector of a drop will be exiting from the bottom sector and contribute to the primary rainbow; light striking the lower sector may be twice reflected inside and exit the top side, and will contribute to the weaker secondary bow. (See Figure 3.9.) The key to the color sequence of the rainbow lies in the fact that the different wavelengths of the beam of white light will be deviated from their path at slightly different angles, thus separating each one to be perceived separately by our eyes. In the primary rainbow, you see the innermost circle as violet and the outermost as red, with the colors between arranged as in our chart of visible light wavelengths on page 31. In the secondary bow the arrangement of colors will be reversed, since the light ray got turned around inside the water drop.

40

If you are a hunter of rainbows, you will want to do most of your hunting in the afternoon or evening, for more showers are likely to occur then than in the morning. For the most complete rainbow arcs, look to the setting or rising sun. The higher the sun, the less full an arch you are likely to see. The top of the arch will be cut off, and you will experience only one or both legs of the potential full arch. Although there is pleasure enough in viewing a standard rainbow, there is an extra sense of adventure in looking for unusual rainbow events. Red rainbows are one such; they can occur at sunset when blue and violet waves are scattered out and primarily orange and red waves pass through the atmosphere to strike the raindrops and create the bow. At any time be alert to extra arcs near the primary rainbow. These supernumary bows may be above the main arch or may intersect that arch, and some supernumary bows may be white rather than the spectral colors.

Another rare rainbow event is a lunar bow. Because moonlight is so much weaker than sunlight, lunar bows are seldom seen and are usually a pale whitish arch without the rainbow colors. Occasionally, the spectrum colors are seen, more often with the reds weak or missing. Occasionally also, double lunar rainbows may be seen, some even with intersecting arches. Fogbows are an interesting variant that form when the sun or moon shines on minute droplets of water suspended in air; because fog droplets are so small, the wavelengths have little room to spread out. Thus, the light leaving the droplets still essentially appears white, making fogbows white.

DISTORTIONS AND FLASHES

When the sun is low in the sky, its rays must pass a greater distance through atmosphere than when it is overhead. Of course, the atmosphere nearer the surface also contains more suspended particles and layers of air of different densities. Either or both of these factors may create situations that can distort apparent images from the transmitted light, creating unusual effects, some of rare beauty. These are not everyday occurrences, but to see one or more of them adds spice to the joy of sky watching.

Light flashes are among the more interesting of these effects, and their actual cause stimulates controversy. Some of the flashes are clearly real and can be photographed, while others may occur only in the mind, essentially as an afterimage on the retina of your eye. (If you stare at a bright light for a while and then close your eyes, you will still see an image of the light, usually in a complementary color.) The most famous of the light-flash phenomena is the green flash which can occasionally be seen just as the last of the sun disappears below the horizon. Normally, for this to be seen the atmosphere must be extremely clear; thus, green flashes are most likely to be seen at sea. Green flash is generally explained as the scattering and

41

dispersion of the green wavelengths. Actually, blue and violet flashes usually occur at the same time, but these shorter waves are more readily absorbed by the atmosphere, and only the green gets seen. On occasion, however, both the blue and violet flashes are perceived, sometimes in succession.

On the other hand, a green flash effect can be created by using an artificial horizon such as a concrete wall, and raising or lowering your head to make the sun appear or disappear below the wall. The sun, at such twilight times as make this illusion possible, is often glowing red, and since you have been staring at it when it disappears, your retina retains the image in the complementary color—green. This, then, is only an apparent green flash.

When the sun is setting and appears to descend below a succession of cloud layers that form artifical horizons, you may spot a red flash as the sun reappears below each layer. A similar red flash may be seen just as the sun's orb breaks the horizon at sunrise. It may be preceded by a green flash. Actually, such flash phenomena are not confined to the sun but may occur at the rising or setting of any sufficiently bright celestial object, such as the moon or Venus, when atmospheric conditions are right.

Light passing through air of different densities changes its velocity and direction slightly; physicists say that it is diffracted. As light from the sun, moon, or other celestial objects passes through several layers of different density, such as may be created by temperature inversions, it will be variously refracted. The result may be the appearance of multiple images of the object; or the image may be grossly distorted so that the object appears rectangular or drawn out in odd ways as if seen in the fun-house mirrors of an amusement park. Such images can be enough to make you question your sobriety.

Similarly, *mirages* are sky phenomena that are the result of refraction through layers of differing density. The most familiar mirage effect is that seen over roadways on hot summer days. Radiation and reflection from the road surface heat a thin layer of air just above it which is trapped by cooler denser air that overlies it. Low-angle light striking this layer is refracted upward, making the layer function like a mirror reflecting the sky and some low-lying objects. Since the image is dependent upon the angle at which the light is hitting, as you move closer and change the angle the image disappears, only to be seen still ahead of you. Essentially, the same thing may happen on a grander scale over deserts, grasslands, and calm water surfaces. If the warmed air layers are not level but bulge upward unevenly, they may create lens-like layers that magnify the images and invert them as does a mirror. Particularly over water, conditions arise that may produce a double mirage, one image over the other with the lower one inverted. It is this type that may create the effect of castles in the air. Such mirages are most often observed in the Straits of Messina between Italy and Sicily, over the Toyama Bay on the western coast of Japan, and over the Great Lakes of North America.

Layers of air of differing densities may also refract and reflect the

INFERIOR MIRAGE

Cold air layer

Warm air layer

SUPERIOR MIRAGE

Warm air layer

Cold air layer

FIGURE 3.10. Mirages: inferior and superior.

colors of sunset upward onto the bases of clouds, further enhancing the beauty of a sunset. We also know that bubbles of air of a density different from the main air mass are trapped in the air mass and travel along with it. These bubbles defract light passing through them and distort the images slightly. It is such bubbles that contribute to the twinkling effect of stars at night.

THE REALM OF CLOUDS

To those early English peoples who coined the word *sky,* it was primarily the realm of clouds. Clouds have long captured the imagination because of their diverse shapes and forms and their movement. The young and the young at heart down through the ages have enjoyed lying back on the ground and watching the fair-weather clouds drift by while letting their minds discover the forms of animals, ships, castles, and the like in the shifting and dissolving shapes. To Thoreau, "a sky without clouds is a meadow without flowers, a sea without sails."

Writing in his *Journal* on June 24, 1852, Thoreau seems to sum up the captivation of clouds:

> The drifting white downy clouds are to the landsman what sails on the sea are to him that dwells by the shore—objects of a large, diffusive interest. When the laborer lies on the grass or in the shade for rest, they do not too much tax or weary his attention. They are unobtrusive. I have not heard that white clouds, like white houses, made any one's eyes ache. They are the flitting sails in that ocean whose bounds no man has visited. They are like all great themes, always at hand to be considered, or they float over us unregarded. Far away they float in the serene sky, the most inoffensive of objects, or, near and low, they smite us with their lightnings and deafen us with their thunder. . . . What could a man learn by watching the clouds? The objects which go over our heads unobserved are vast and indefinite. Even those clouds which have the most distinct and interesting outlines are commonly below the zenith, somewhat low in the heavens, and seen on one side. They are among the most glorious of objects in nature.

FIGURE 3.11. Clouds spur imagination and wonder. C.E. Roth photo.

CLOUD CLASSIFICATION

Although each cloud is as unique as a fingerprint, it does not take a long period of cloud watching to recognize that there are several distinct types of clouds and that these tend to form at particular levels in the sky. We can usually distinguish extensive flat layers of cloud; round, fluffy clouds; and high, thin, wispy ones. And we note that some kinds are found more commonly in the lower reaches of the sky, some in the higher reaches, and others in the middle area between them. Scientists, seeking a sense of order in the sky and trying to understand how and why clouds form and the kind of weather that each implies, have developed a classification of the clouds that builds in detail on the simple observations we have noted above and on the classification scheme first suggested by Luke Howard in 1803.

The International Cloud Classification recognizes the three height categories noted and establishes a range of altitude for each. These altitudes vary somewhat with latitude, but for the middle latitudes the heights are essentially as follows: *low-level* clouds, from the surface to 6500 feet; *middle-level* clouds, ranging from 6500 feet to 23,000 feet; and *high-level* clouds, from 16,500 feet to 45,000 feet. Another group of "towering" clouds is also recognized; the bases of these may be only a few hundred feet above the earth's surface, but the cloud builds upward and may reach more than 80,000 feet. Thunderstorm clouds are examples of towering clouds.

A basic division of cloud types is based on how they are formed. There are those formed by rising air currents; they are called *cumulus* clouds, from a Latin word meaning "to accumulate or pile up." Other types of clouds are formed when water vapor in the air condenses into a cloud without benefit of upward motion. These are *stratus* clouds. These two main cloud divisions are further divided into ten subcategories, or *genera,* depending primarily on their height and whether or not they generate precipitation. (The highest clouds are designated category nine, and thus has evolved the phrase, when someone is undergoing some sort of high, of being "on cloud nine.")

The Nimbus Category

The Latin term *nimbus* indicates rain, and so by combining the term with the division name we have the two genera for rain clouds—*cumulonimbus* and *nimbostratus.* Nimbostratus clouds are generally middle-level clouds that are dark gray colored and trail gray rain skirts, or *virga,* beneath them. Nimbostratus clouds are made of suspended water droplets, sometimes supercooled, and of falling raindrops and/or snow. They are tall clouds, usually rising several thousand feet into the atmosphere, and are older clouds that generally form from the thickening of altostratus clouds, a cloud genus we will describe shortly. Generated by the steady ascent of air over a broad area, they are usually associated with frontal weather systems.

Cumulonimbus clouds are thunderstorm clouds, the most awesome and spectacular of the ten genera. Their bases are at low-cloud level, but they build higher and higher, through processes we will detail in Chapter 4, until they literally bump into the stratosphere above. When they reach this point the tops of the clouds flatten out against the warmer air of the stratosphere to form a flattened, anvil-shaped top to the formation. These clouds develop from strong convective currents and may have very powerful internal updrafts and downdrafts. Cumulonimbus clouds are composed of water in all its phases—gas, liquid, and solid. They may occur as isolated clouds or in groups along a squall line. We will have much more to say about

45

FIGURE 3.12. Rain skirts, or *virga,* hanging from cumulonimbus clouds. C.E. Roth photo.

these clouds when we explore storms. Like nimbostratus, cumulonimbus are older clouds, and their bases appear very dark and threatening.

The High Clouds

There are three genera of the third, high-level type of clouds, all located very high up and all distinguished in name by a form of the Latin word *cirrus.* You might assume this word referred to height, but actually it means curly. The three genera are *cirrus, cirrostratus,* and *cirrocumulus.* Cirrus have the most distinct form of the basic division, for they are thin wispy forms that tend to have a curl. They resemble locks of hair, or horse tails, or down feathers. Composed entirely of ice crystals, usually of columnar form, cirrus clouds form at or above 25,000 feet, where freezing temperatures prevail. They generally form in air that is ascending slowly and steadily over a broad area and are often the first type of cloud to appear in advance of an approaching cyclonic disturbance.

When you see high patches of small thin clouds arranged in a pattern, often like fish scales, you are probably viewing cirrocumulus clouds. The pattern of scaly light and dark that they create is often called a "mackerel sky." Cirrocumulus clouds are formed of either highly supercooled water droplets, or columnar and prismatic ice crystals, or both. These clouds generally form somewhere between 20,000 and 25,000 feet.

46

FIGURE 3.13. Cirrus clouds. C.E. Roth photo.

47

FIGURE 3.14. Cirrostratus clouds. C.E. Roth photo.

FIGURE 3.15. Cirrocumulus clouds. C.E. Roth photo.

48

Forming at the same height, but made entirely of ice crystals, are the cirrostratus clouds. They create the appearance of thin sheets or a milky veil and often cover all of the visible sky. It is these clouds that are generally responsible for the halo effects discussed earlier. If you want to observe halos, you should be alert to the appearance of cirrostratus in the sky.

Middle-Level Clouds

The middle-level cloud genera are characterized by the prefix *alto* to the two division names; thus, *altocumulus* and *altostratus*. In this case the prefix does derive from the Latin word for high. Altostratus clouds often cover the whole visible sky and in reality may cover several thousand square miles. Very uniform in appearance, they are usually gray or gray-blue sheets hundreds to thousands of feet thick. As you might expect from their altitude and thickness, their composition is quite complex, usually layered, with ice crystals at the top, ice and/or snow crystals in the middle, and supercooled or ordinary water droplets in the lower regions. It is not always easy to distinguish altostratus from cirrostratus because it is difficult to determine their actual altitude accurately from the ground. Altostratus, however, are thicker, so they do not create halo effects, and they tend to move across the sky more rapidly.

Altocumulus clouds are puffy white or gray clouds that occur in

FIGURE 3.16. Altostratus clouds. C.E. Roth photo.

49

FIGURE 3.17. Altocumulus clouds. C.E. Roth photo.

patches or layers, often with a waved pattern. These form when the slow lifting of an unstable air layer leads to convective motion. They too are often difficult for a ground observer to distinguish with certainty from their cirrocumulus cousins. However, they are thick enough to create shadows, which cirrocumulus cannot do, and they do not create halo effects. They are composed of small, liquid water droplets and often occur in advance of a cold front.

Low-Level Clouds

Our remaining genera are low clouds: *stratus, cumulus,* and *stratocumulus.* Stratus are usually the lowest of clouds and are composed of relatively widely dispersed water drops. Fog is essentially a stratus cloud resting on the ground, but it is not technically designated a stratus cloud until its base has lifted somewhat off the ground. It is not surprising, then, that stratus clouds often form from lifting fog. However, stratus clouds can form from as low as a hundred feet off the ground to as high as several thousand feet. There is virtually no vertical movement within a stratus cloud, so there never is serious precipitation from this genus, only an occasional fine drizzle. The base of true stratus clouds is normally very uniform.

Stratocumulus clouds are something of a hybrid that may develop

50

FIGURE 3.18. Stratocumulus clouds. C.E. Roth photo.   FIGURE 3.19. Fleet of cumulus clouds. C.E. Roth photo.

from the rising of a stratus cloud or the transformation of a stratus or nimbostratus. They are whitish or grayish clouds but, unlike stratus, have a rounded appearance and uneven bases. You might think of them as lumpy stratus clouds. They frequently form in clear air, and while they do not produce rain, they often transform into nimbostratus clouds. Primarily composed of small water droplets, they may be accompanied by larger droplets, snowflakes, and soft hail.

In many ways cumulus clouds are the most interesting genus. They are the products of rising, vertical currents of air, and once born they take on something of a life of their own, with internal development that may permit them to grow and assume constantly changing shapes. These are the billowing white clouds that we generally associate with fair weather. As heated air rises, it eventually reaches cooler elevations where the moisture condenses to form the cloud. Winds aloft will tend to push the cloud horizontally, and a new cloud will form above the rising air column. Thus, fleets of cumulus clouds are set adrift across the sky. However, there is still vertical motion within each cloud, so it can continue to grow larger and larger, and the size of the water droplets in it will also enlarge. This also changes the reflectivity of the cloud, and its color will slowly change as it ages and grows. Cumulus clouds often exhibit a great deal of vertical growth and normally reach a greater height than do stratus or stratocumulus. Sometimes the cumulus clouds begin to mass together as they grow, developing into powerful cumulonimbus.

51

FIGURE 3.20. Expanding cumulus cloud. C.E. Roth photo.

Special Cloud Types

Although the clouds described constitute the major cloud types, there are some further subgroups and some special, localized cloud formations that are of interest. For example, within the cumulus genus one may speak of cumulus *humulis* clouds, which are essentially the young, fair-weather cumulus with poorly developed vertical circulation. There are cumulus *congestus* clouds, which are essentially imminent rainshower clouds crowded together in heaps, with moderate development of vertical circulation between cumulus and cumulonimbus clouds. They are heavy with

FIGURE 3.21. Lenticular cloud. Ira Spring photo.

moisture in all its forms but are not yet precipitating. Similarly, there are several other adjectives added to generic cloud names to further describe their appearance. *Fractus* is used to indicate broken, jagged fragments of either stratus or cumulus clouds. These usually appear as the clouds are disintegrating. As cirrocumulus and altocumulus show strong vertical circulation, they often lose the tops that look like a head of cauliflower and develop towers and turrets like castles; thus they are granted the adjective *castellanus. Uncinus* means "hook-shaped" in Latin and is a descriptor applied to cirrus clouds that bear that shape and look much like giant commas in the sky.

Often, over a high mountain peak, you may observe a *lenticular,* or standing wave, cloud. Such a cloud appears to remain stationary while the air continues to blow through it. The rising air cools and forms the cloud at its crest, but as the air descends it warms, and the droplets revaporize. Such a lenticular cloud only appears stationary; actually, it is continuously forming and dissipating at the one location. In places where lenticular clouds form you may also find, at lower levels on the lee side of the mountain, what appear to be ragged cumulus clouds or fractocumulus. Pilots consider these "rotor clouds" particularly dangerous because they represent highly turbulent air below the mountain summits.

You may also occasionally spot lenticular-shaped clouds away from mountains. These form when upper winds take on a wave motion and the crests of the waves form clouds. This form is given the adjective *lenticularis* and is applied mostly to cirrostratus, altocumulus, and stratocumulus cloud genera. Sometimes you see only one arched cloud when only a particularly high wave displacement forms a cloud, but usually you see a series of such clouds formed in this manner.

The cloud most of us are most likely to experience intimately is *fog.* As previously stated, it is essentially a stratus cloud resting on the ground. Normally, fog is a suspension of fine water droplets, but under some conditions tiny ice crystals prevail, and we have ice fog. *Mist* is related to fog and usually precedes or follows a fog, but the droplets are even finer, and the air doesn't feel wet as it does in fully developed fog. Most fog and mist form with the cooling of moist air. They can form, however, from the rapid addition of moisture to a cooler air flow, such as when cool air comes across a much warmer body of water.

Some special clouds are fairly limited in their geographic range, but you might be alert for them if you travel. For example, the morning glory of tropical Australia is a very long (often over a hundred miles), rolling-pin-shaped cloud only 300 to 600 feet thick that appears on the eastern skyline around sunrise. It approaches rapidly, like an advancing sea wave, producing squally winds but seldom any precipitation. The morning glory comes in low, often not more than 200 feet off the ground and traveling at from 30 to 70 miles per hour. Double morning glories are not uncommon, and as many as seven in a row have been recorded. There is little agreement on how they are formed or why. They usually appear in calm or cloudless conditions. In places like Florida and Hawaii you may see a superficially

54

FIGURE 3.22. Fog nestled in a mountain valley. C.E. Roth photo.

similar type roll of clouds that stretches downward from the burning of sugar cane fields. These are more than just smoke; the fine particles form condensation nuclei that generate true cloud structure. These clouds may persist for quite a distance. In tropical oceans you can often see long streamer clouds downwind of mountainous tropical islands. These are caused by moist air being deflected aloft by the island to form the cloud, while the bulk of the air flows around and past the island without such cooling and cloud development.

A particularly odd and seldom-seen set of streamers is formed from thin high cirrus clouds. These bands have a distinctive, true north-south orientation and apparently follow the lines of geomagnetism. This type of formation was first formally noted by the explorer Alexander von Humbolt. The bands are always quite thin and tenuous.

The seeker of odd clouds should keep alert for rotating ring clouds, much like giant smoke rings. These form from small whirling vortices that rise from the ground until they reach a point where their moisture condenses into a cloud. The center of such a whirling air bubble is a downdraft, so no cloud forms over it; thus the donut-shaped cloud. Look also for clear round holes punched through a solid deck of stratus clouds. When scientists seed a cloud with silver iodide crystals to stimulate rain, they often get the same hole-in-the-cloud phenomenon. It may be that such natural holes develop from some sort of natural cloud-seeding mechanism which remains unknown at present.

Large meteors often leave clouds in their wake. The upper winds disturb these streaky clouds and distort them in wild and crazy shapes.

55

Check the star guides for meteor shower activity (see Chapter 5), and then check the appropriate quadrant of the sky for meteor-formed clouds.

A rare cloud form, seen mostly in high-latitude countries, is the noctilucent cloud. These clouds form in the upper stratosphere at heights of around 50 miles, where there is practically no water vapor. The question of the composition of these clouds remains unanswered. When they can be seen at all, noctilucent clouds are apparent after sunset or before sunrise in a generally wavy pattern. They are a sight primarily for the hardy northern traveler.

Today we cannot ignore man-made clouds; not simply low clouds forming over factory stacks, or those from the burning of cane fields, but also high clouds, the contrails of high-flying aircraft. Initially linear trails, as contrails age they may spread out even to the point of creating broad sheets of cirrostratus cloud. At other times they break up and develop hanging streamers from which precipitation may fall. Upper winds often shear the contrails and contort them. Some people enjoy observing the behavior of contrails, while others think of them as an unwarranted intrusion of the purity of the sky.

The form of clouds is a great aesthetic treasure. They are objects to be observed and enjoyed whether or not you can name the appropriate classification. Within many of the cloud genera there seems to be endless variation on the theme, with shapes enriched by the brilliant colors of sunset or sunrise or highlighted by the contrast with blue sky or the brilliant reflections of raw sunlight. They create an ongoing feast for the eyes. People have also learned to associate certain cloud types with weather patterns, which is most useful, particularly in providing advanced warning of potentially dangerous storms. But in developing the pragmatism of weather forecasting we must never abandon the sheer joy of seeing the sky, the clouds, and other sky phenomena for their own sake and our aesthetic pleasure.

SKY-OBSERVER ACTIVITIES

• It is fun to make a simple color spectrum chart with a wooden frame and old paint-color chips from the paint store, and spend time afield seeing how many different hues you can match with the sky on different days.

To make such a chart simply arrange all the color chips around the edge of the frame, with the hues of each major color arranged in a sequence of increasing intensity. Although a wooden frame is most sturdy, you can achieve the same effect by cutting a frame from cardboard and gluing the color chips around the edges of the frame. To use the device simply view through the frame and match the sky color as closely as possible with one of the color chips.

Even overcast days should not be passed over for sky viewing, since

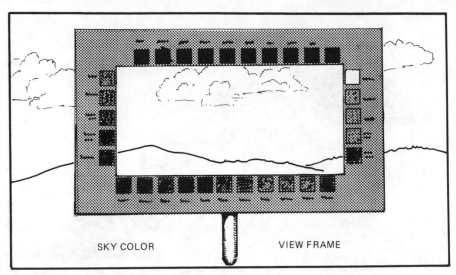

SKY COLOR | VIEW FRAME

FIGURE 3.23. Color frame for sky observing.

there are a great variety of blue-gray hues to be seen at such times. As you become more sensitive to the subtle variations of colors that exist, you will discover just how diverse in color the sky actually is over the course of even a few days but particularly over the course of a year.

• Establish a sky log where you regularly record objects you see in the sky and the variety of hues. Be sure to note as many conditions of the sky as you can relative to the objects you record; that is, such items as time, temperature, air pressure, humidity, and clarity of the air.

• Develop a collection of sky photographs to augment your sky log. Taking photos of the sky is not particularly difficult, but there are some pointers to keep in mind:

+ Filters are a must for good sky pictures. With black and white film a medium-yellow filter (No. 8-K2) or a deep-yellow filter (No. 16-G) will darken the shades of gray which the blue of the sky registers as and thus make any clouds appear whiter and crisper. You can heighten this effect, making the sky almost black, by utilizing a red filter such as No. 25-A. A polarizing filter should be used with color film to deepen the blue color of a sky and help even filmy clouds stand out.

+ If you have a camera with interchangeable lenses, use your wide-angle lenses (i.e., 24mm, 35mm) for broad skyscapes and sunsets and sunrises. Telephoto lenses, such as a zoom 80−200mm, will let you focus on specific clouds, halo effects, and the like so that they fill the frame. If you have access to a "fisheye" lens you may want to take some sequences showing a 360° skyscape, particularly with a front approaching or thunderstorms forming.

57

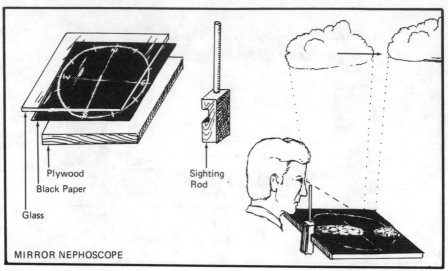

Plywood
Black Paper
Glass
Sighting Rod

MIRROR NEPHOSCOPE

FIGURE 3.24. Mirror nephoscope.

• You might enjoy plotting the direction clouds are moving with a homemade cloud tracker or mirror nephoscope. You will need a sheet of glass, a piece of plywood, and a sheet of black paper all 1 foot square. With white ink or marking pencil, on the black paper draw a circle 10 inches in diameter. Then mark the circle with each 10 degrees of azimuth, or mark the 16 major points of the compass rose. Connect all the opposite points through the center of the circle with a line. Mount the black paper and its drawing on the plywood, and cover it with the glass. Bind the sandwich together around the edges with cloth tape. You will also need to create a sighting rod by making a notch in a small block of wood so that the block will slip over the sandwich snugly. Bore a hole in the top of the block into which you insert and glue a ¼ inch dowel about 5 inches long.

When all is finished, take your mirror nephoscope outside and set it on some level support, like a tripod, set at about waist height. Orient it with a compass but with all points reading precisely the reverse of the compass; that is, south on the scope should be where north is on the compass. Choose a cloud mirrored on the scope to follow. Walk around the mirror until your cloud appears in the center and seems to be moving directly along one of the compass lines. Slip the sighting rod on the edge at this point. Sight over its top and follow the cloud to the edge of the mirror. The compass marking on the mirror at that point tells you the direction *from which the cloud was moving*. You can roughly calculate the speed the cloud is moving as well if you have a fairly accurate reckoning of its height above you.

• Following are a series of folk rhymes about the weather. From your observations of the sky, determine their reliability for predicting changes in sky and weather.

58

Evening red and morning gray
Send the traveler on his way.
Evening gray and morning red
Send the traveler wet to bed.

Sounds traveling far and wide
A stormy day will betide.

When wooly fleeces spread the heavenly way,
No rain, be sure, will mar the summer day.

When the clouds appear like rocks and towers
The earth's refreshed by frequent showers.

When hill or mountain has a cap
Within six hours we'll have a drap.

Mackerel sky, mackerel sky—
Not long wet, not long dry.

Rain before seven, clear before eleven.

Rainbow to windward [west], foul falls the day.
Rainbow to leeward [east], damp runs away.

FURTHER READING

CORIS, WILLIAM R. *Handbook of Unusual Natural Phenomena.* Garden City, NY: Anchor Press/Doubleday, 1983.

GREENLER, ROBERT. *Rainbows, Halos and Glories.* New York: Cambridge University Press, 1980.

HOBBS, PETER V., and A. DEEPAK. *Clouds: Their Formation. Optical Properties and Effects.* New York: Academic Press, Inc., 1981.

LYNCH, DAVID and SCIENTIFIC AMERICAN EDITORIAL STAFF. *Atmospheric Phenomena: Readings from Scientific American.* San Francisco: W.H. Freeman & Co., 1980.

MINNAERT, M. *The Nature of Light and Colour in the Open Air.* New York: Dover Publications, 1954.

O'CONNELL, D.J.K. *The Green Flash and Other Low Sun Phenomena.* New York: Interscience Publishers, Inc., 1958.

PERRIE, D.W. *Cloud Physics.* Toronto University of Toronto Press, 1980.

RUBIN, LOUIS D., SR., and JIM DUNCAN. *The Weather Wizard's Cloud Book.* Chapel Hill: Algonquin Books of Chapel Hill, 1984.

SCORER, R.S. *Clouds of the World.* Harrisburg, PA: Stackpole Books, 1972.

SHAFER, VINCENT J., and JOHN A. DAY. *A Field Guide to the Atmosphere.* Boston: Houghton Mifflin Co., 1981.

Periodicals

"Beauty on the Horizon—A Portfolio of Sunsets and Sunrises." *Arizona Highways,* September 1976.

SHELLIE, DON. "The Dramatic Skies of Arizona." *Arizona Highways,* June 1979.

59

CHAPTER 4

SKY DYNAMICS

In Chapter 2 we explored some of the major global air-circulation patterns. Here we look more closely at somewhat more localized winds, many of which are related to storms of one form or another. Although you cannot see the winds, you can certainly feel them, and they are clearly sky phenomena to be aware of, an invisible force to be reckoned with. In hot, humid climates and seasons some of these winds bring welcome temporary relief from discomfort even though they may be followed by stormy weather. There are also some warm dry winds that appear in colder climes and seasons to bring a relief of sorts to seemingly unending cold and snow.

WINDS AND STORMS

To be fully appreciated, winds have to be experienced. Few people have experienced winds with a greater sense of exuberance than the great naturalist and wilderness advocate, John Muir. On one occasion he headed out in a December gale in the high Sierras and climbed a giant Douglas fir to ride the wind from a perch high in this elastic species where he was "safe, and free to take the wind into my pulses and enjoy the excited forest from my superb outlook." Excerpts from his writing concerning this experience give rare insight into the potency of winds:

> Most people like to look at mountain rivers, and bear them in mind; but few care to look at the winds, though far more beautiful and sublime, and though they become at times about as visible as flowing water. When the north winds in winter are making upward sweeps over the curving summits of the High Sierra, the fact is sometimes published with flying snow-banners a mile long.

60

Those portions of the winds thus embodied can scarce be wholly invisible, even to the darkest imagination. And when we look around over an agitated forest, we may see something of the wind that stirs it, by its effect on the trees. Yonder it descends in a rush of water-like ripples, and sweeps over the bending Pines from hill to hill. Nearer, we see detached plumes and leaves, now speeding by on level currents, now whirling in eddies, or, escaping over the edges of the whirls, soaring aloft on grand, upswelling domes of air, or tossing on flame-like crests. Smooth, deep currents, cascades, falls, and swirling eddies, sing around every tree and leaf, and over all the varied topography of the region with telling changes of form, like mountain rivers conforming to the features of other channels. . . . The sounds of the storm . . . the profound bass of the naked branches and boles booming like waterfalls, the quick, tense vibrations of the pine needles, now rising to a shrill, whistling hiss, now falling to a silky murmur, the rustling of laurel groves in the dells, and the keen metalic click of leaf on leaf—all this was heard in easy analysis when the attention was calmly bent. . . . Winds are advertisement of all they touch, however little we may be able to read them, telling their wanderings even by their scents alone. Mariners detect the flowery perfumes of land winds far at sea, and sea-winds carry the fragrance of dulse and tangle far inland, where it is quickly recognized, though mingled with the scents of a thousand land-flowers.

WIND GENESIS

In examining the nature of winds we need to think in terms of two different directions of movement—horizontal and vertical—and two patterns of flow—linear and whirling. Air flows from areas of high pressure to areas of low pressure to create wind. With no other forces at work the wind would blow in a straight line along the gradient from high to low pressure. But there are other forces.

Let us consider the spinning of the earth on its axis. It creates the effect of a giant merry-go-round with us aboard. If you ride a carnival merry-go-round and attempt to throw a ball at a target on or off the carousel, the ball will always appear to curve to the right of your target. But to an observer off the carousel the ball will appear to have traveled in a straight line. This is because you moved relative to the traveling ball. The same effect occurs on our planetary carousel. The wind direction appears to be deflected slightly to the right in the northern hemisphere and to the left in the southern one. This is often referred to as the *Coriolis force,* although in fact it is not a true force but an effect. Whether you call it a force or an effect, it always acts at right angles to the pressure gradient that generates the wind. Because the effect is small, it has relatively little impact on local winds but becomes important in terms of larger air masses traveling long distances, particularly for the cyclonic patterns we will discuss a bit later.

A true force that affects wind direction and power is friction from the interlocking of surface irregularities and the adhesion of molecules of two surfaces in contact with one another. The effect of friction is to slow down or eliminate forward motion. In an air mass in motion there may be internal

61

friction of the gas molecules from vertical and horizontal eddies, and where the mass is in contact with the earth's surface there will be even stronger friction. Frictional forces act in a direction opposite to that of the prevailing wind. They are much less of a factor at higher altitudes than near the ground.

The other major force to influence the wind is *centrifugal force*. This is a force dependent upon the speed and direction of the wind; in a word, the wind's *velocity*. As an air flow deviates from a straight line to follow the curve of the earth it must accelerate to maintain a constant speed since it must travel a greater distance. This might be illustrated by the analogy of the children's game crack-the-whip, where the person at the end of the line must run much faster to keep the line straight as it goes around the center pivot. In such motion there are two opposing forces; one pulling toward the inside of the curve, the other toward the outside. The one pulling away from the curve is the centrifugal force. For large wind systems covering large areas the curve is slight and the centrifugal force fairly insignificant, but for small whirling systems such as dust devils and tornadoes the curve is greater and the centrifugal force very large. The importance of these various forces is quite different for vertical and horizontal motions, with Coriolis effect and centrifugal force being of little relative importance in the vertical.

The most important driving force for horizontal winds is the pressure gradient. Meteorologists plot barometric pressure readings from various stations on maps and connect all the points with the same reading with a line. They call such a line an *isobar,* a word derived from Greek *iso,* meaning "equal," and *bar*, a shortened form of "barometric pressure." Ideally, a wind should blow in the direction from high isobar readings to low isobar readings. In reality it does not. The Coriolis effect deflects the wind to the right until it counterbalances the pressure gradient force. The end result is that the wind blows at right angles to the pressure gradient if the isobars are parallel, there is no friction, and there is no acceleration to generate centrifugal force. Such a wind is known as a *geostrophic wind* and is seldom observable much below altitudes of 6000 to 9000 feet.

Examination of a weather map quickly shows that most isobars are curved; thus, the winds cannot be geostrophic and the effect of centrifugal force induced by the curved flow must be taken into account. When this is done the resultant wind is known as a *gradient wind.* When the gradient wind is flowing around a low-pressure system (cyclonic flow), the centrifugal force opposes the pressure gradient force and the resulting wind is weaker than theoretical geostrophic wind would be. On the contrary, anticyclonic flow around a high-pressure system is aided by the centrifugal force, and the resulting winds are stronger than the geostrophic wind would be.

Near the earth's surface friction is not to be ignored. It always opposes the direction of air flow and reduces the wind speed. The shape of the surface also may deflect the direction of the wind, locally changing the

62

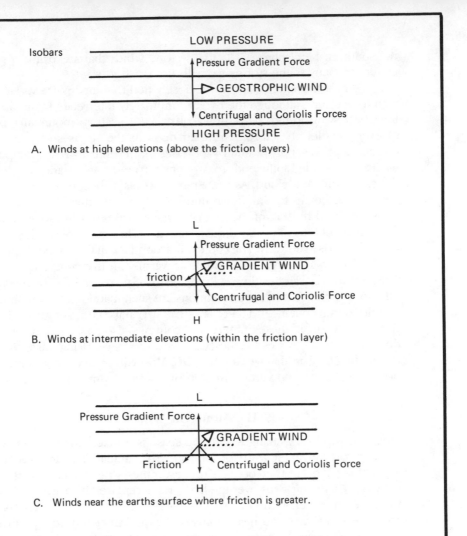

LOW PRESSURE

Isobars

↑ Pressure Gradient Force

⊳ GEOSTROPHIC WIND

↓ Centrifugal and Coriolis Forces

HIGH PRESSURE

A. Winds at high elevations (above the friction layers)

L

↑ Pressure Gradient Force

GRADIENT WIND

friction

↓ Centrifugal and Coriolis Force

H

B. Winds at intermediate elevations (within the friction layer)

L

Pressure Gradient Force ↑

GRADIENT WIND

Friction ↓ Centrifugal and Coriolis Force

H

C. Winds near the earths surface where friction is greater.

FIGURE 4.1. Pressure gradient and winds.

centrifugal force and creating local eddy effects. Or it may push the air upward, inducing a vertical component to the wind.

In middle latitudes, where most of the readers of this book will live, the major wind patterns are created by an ongoing series of eddies. Some of these break free from the large circular polar wind circulation and move generally southward and eastward. Some emerge in a northward and westward direction from the subtropical wind flows. Those that swirl around a cyclonic flow move counterclockwise, while those of anticyclones flow in a clockwise direction in the northern hemisphere. The pattern is reversed in the southern hemisphere. It is the cyclone winds that are primary generators of many of the storms we will discuss shortly.

Vertical movements are more closely tied to temperature variations than to pressure, although the two are intimately interrelated. Air can be lifted by flowing up and over a surface obstruction such as a mountain range, or over a cooler, therefore denser, air mass. As the air rises it cools. If it contains a good supply of water vapor, this may eventually reach the point where it has cooled sufficiently to condense around condensation nuclei in the air and form a cloud. As the air mass cools, it becomes denser and heavier and begins to sink down under the force of gravity.

Localized heating of the earth's surface may result in radiation and conduction of heat to the air directly above it. This parcel of warm air will expand and rise vertically. The cooler air around it will flow in beneath and pinch off the warm, creating a bubble of warmer air that continues to rise The invading cool air that flowed in will, in turn, warm, rise, and be pinched off into a bubble. Sometimes conditions are such that no pinching off into bubbles occurs, but instead there is a steadily rising column of warm air. As they rise, the air in these bubbles and columns also cools and eventually descends. This all creates a vertical circulation system of rising warm air and descending cool air that we call *thermals*. Most winds have some combination of horizontal and vertical motion over varying times and distances.

The Monsoon Winds

Monsoon wind flow changes with the seasons. Indeed, the very name is derived from the Arabic word for "season." The circulation pattern requires a combination of land and ocean. During summer, when the land is warmer than the sea, the air rises over the land and is replaced by warm moist air from over the water. As this in turn is warmed by the land, rises, and cools, its moisture condenses and heavy rains occur. In winter the flow of air reverses. The air over the water is warmer and rises to cool and flow landward, then to sink and flow back toward the sea. Since the descending air is dry, there is little rainfall during this time of the year. We generally think of monsoon in terms of southern Asia, and indeed it is strongest there, due to the highly mountainous land mass at right angles to the air flow. However, there is also a monsoon pattern in North America, in the southwestern United States. Here in summer moist warm air flows inland from the Gulf of Mexico and Caribbean Sea to be lifted by the western highlands. The geography is not as extreme as in Asia, however, and the monsoon pattern is weaker and often obscured by the the effects of cyclonic movements.

Land and Sea Breezes

Coastal areas often experience a similar type of reversing wind-flow pattern on a daily rather than seasonal cycle. Water gains and loses heat much more

64

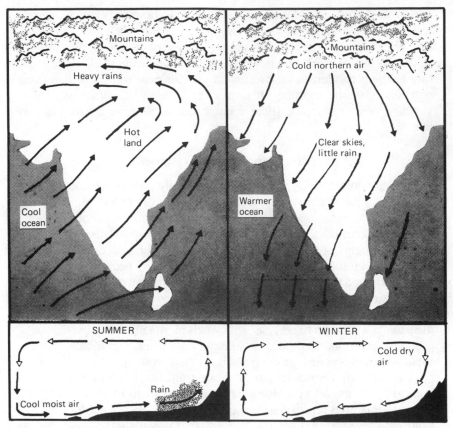

FIGURE 4.2. Monsoon wind flows.

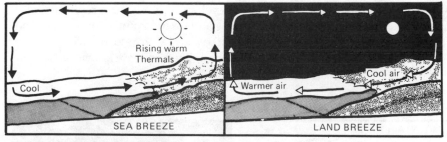

FIGURE 4.3. Land and sea breezes.

slowly than the land. Consequently, over a 24-hour period the water temperature will remain relatively constant, while the land during the day may be much warmer than the water and at night may be somewhat cooler than the water. In such cases air will rise over the land during the day, and the cooler air over the water will flow landward. At night the air over the water will be warmer and rise, and the cooler air over the land will flow seaward.

65

The daytime flow of wind from sea to land is called a *sea breeze,* its reverse a *land breeze.* In the tropics sea breezes may occur throughout the year, but in higher latitudes they are mostly a summer phenomena. Sea breezes seldom generate much rain but often create foggy conditions as the moisture in them condenses on meeting cooler air near the shore or inland, particularly in the morning. It is this sea breeze phenomenon that, in summer, often makes the shore a much cooler place to be than farther inland.

Mountain and Valley Winds

In mountainous and hilly regions look for a daily cycle of wind circulation powered by the diurnal temperature cycle. As solar radiation warms the valley floor and mountain slopes, they in turn warm the air above them, which rises, creating a wind flow up the mountain slopes. This upward flow generally begins somewhere around midmorning and continues until around sunset. It is called a *valley wind.* As the sun's heating effect is lost, the air cools and the wind lessens to near calm. By about midnight the air has cooled way down. The heavy air now flows down the mountain slope, creating a *mountain wind* that will blow until shortly after sunrise, when the pattern will begin to reverse again. Such mountain/valley wind circulation is most pronounced on clear summer days when prevailing winds are weak, and in valleys that are deep and have their mountain slopes facing the midday sun. Valley winds tend to generate cumulus clouds over the mountains that may grow to provide afternoon showers up in the mountains.

Mountainous areas often face other kinds of less regular local winds. Cold air masses over high plateaus often become even colder due to radiational heat loss and then will drain down the slopes to the valleys below. Such winds are generally gentle but can be accelerated to violent levels by wandering cyclones or anticyclones. In northern regions where the air passes over high-elevation snow and ice fields and cools rapidly, and the valleys the wind drains into are narrow and V-shaped, the winds can be exceedingly strong. Such downslope, drainage winds are known as *kataba-*

FIGURE 4.4. Mountain and valley winds.

66

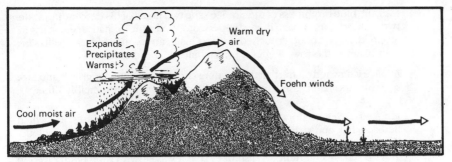

FIGURE 4.5. Foehn winds.

tic winds, and in regions where they are fairly frequent and fierce they may receive local names (many unprintable!) such as the *bora* that brings cold air down from the Austrian Alps to the normally warm Adriatic Sea region, or the *mistral* that drains from the Alps to the French coast of the Mediterranean.

Perhaps the winds most dreaded by humans are *foehn* winds. When these warm, dry winds blow for days they tend to generate extreme irritability and irrational behavior. Foehn winds are generated when warm, moist air is blown against a mountain. As it is deflected upward on the windward side, the moisture cools, condenses to clouds, and precipitates. The change of water vapor to liquid rain releases the latent heat of condensation, and the air is now warmer and drier. This warm, dry air now descends on the lee side of the mountain. This air tends to evaporate moisture from the surfaces it passes over, drying forests and creating dangerous fire hazard, or melting snow packs and creating flood hazards below. *Foehn* is a German term and such winds are common there in the Alps. In the Rocky Mountains of North America such winds are called *chinooks*. The Native Americans of this region called the winds "snoweaters," and it is not unusual for a chinook to consume a 2-foot snow layer in a single day. In California, a similar type wind is known as the *Santa Ana* wind. It flows from the high plateau of Nevada down through the mountain passes, bringing heat and often choking amounts of fine dust that sift into every crack and cranny. The wind is named for Santa Ana Canyon through which it reputedly flows most fiercely, but it often blows severely all the way to Los Angeles.

We usually associate storms with rain or snow, but wind-generated dust storms can be as awesome and frightening, if not more so. Wind-driven sand can frost car windshields, totally strip the paint from the vehicles, make breathing difficult for those caught in such storms, and clog all sorts of apparatus, making them inoperable. Ornithologist George Miksch Sutton has written a vivid description of being caught unawares by a dust storm. He had just tracked down a wren whose song he had earlier heard:

> I watched the little bird as he lifted his head to sing. I saw him clearly, for he was perched at the very edge of the rock above me. All was blue-bright back of

67

him, the blue brightness of the sky. He sang two notes of his descending scale, two bold, ringing notes, then stopped. Stopped as if he had been stricken. Stopped, faced about, crouched, turned his head to one side as if following with his eyes the towering of a prairie falcon, and darted into a crevice. . . .

At once it dawned on me that the evening chorus of the mockingbirds and lark sparrows too had ceased, that the world had grown unaccountably silent. . . .

I looked once more for the wren. He had disappeared. Above the spot at which he had sung, and sharp against the sky, was the bright edge of a thick cloud. That this was an unusual cloud I sensed immediately. It looked solid, like a grayish yellow wall hung with smoke. That it was slowly rising I perceived in an instant, for more and more of it showed above the rock.

To see more clearly I ran back a little and clambered up out of the cavern. Before me was such a scene as I had never beheld before: a vast brown cloud, the only cloud in the sky, stretching as far to the east and as far to the west as the eye could see, so dense and so low-hanging that it had completely obliterated the northern horizon. Its uppermost borders, which were eerily bright, were the grayish yellow wall I had first seen.

Slowly and gracefully the cloud bank moved, upward with the rolling effect of smoke from a great conflagration, and forward. I watched it spellbound. The beauty, the ineffable serenity, the horrible majesty of the thing! No wonder all the birds had ceased from their singing. As the wall advanced, it shut out more of the world to the north. Now even the purple dome of the Black Mesa was going. . . .

Suddenly, with a feeling of impotence that fairly buckled my knees under me, I realized that this opaque mass bearing down upon me had nothing to do with rain. That it was dust! That shelter in the caverns along the side of the hill would be no shelter at all from this! I looked once more at the advancing cloud, then back toward the highway. The storm would catch me long before I could reach the car.

Deciding to try for the car in any event, Sutton raced off, noting that his pursuer

no longer seemed brown, but was white instead. Its edges were feather-soft Behind and below the fluffiness of these nearest wisps was a darkness sullen and menacing. . . .

When I turned once more to look at the dust, it was upon me. No sky was visible now anywhere to the north. The vague blueness above me was plumed with gray and white. A mass of dust with the fluid appearance of muddy water slipped along the ground a little in advance of the high cloud, running between the trees and boulders like a wave about to break. There was no breaking of this queer wave. No ripple, no splash, no foam. Forward it slipped, always keeping just a little ahead of the cloud itself.

I saw the wave of dust flow about my shoes. I saw it grow deeper, shutting my knees from sight. Its thickness and its unexpected coldness struck new terror. . . . By this time the light was going, for the wave was engulfing me. The wind was not as fierce as I had expected it to be. It was strong, but not fierce. And it was cold. With it rose a hissing moan. I looked toward the south, toward the only light that remained. That light was weird, unearthly, reddish in cast. In

68

an instant it was gone—as if a huge curtain had dropped; as if a vast lid had suddenly been clapped on the world. "Awful! Awful!" I seemed to be saying, almost aloud. "Being buried alive must be like this. Drowning must be like this—drowing at the bottom of the sea! . . ."

For a moment I wondered if I could possibly survive. It was so dark that I could not see my hand or handkerchief no matter how close I held them to my face. My eyes did not pain me. I knew I had not been blinded. No, the light had simply gone. There was no light anywhere. The evening that had been so serenely bright had turned to utter darkness—the darkness of the tomb.

I realized that the dust was not choking me. I could feel dust on my lips and against my tongue and teeth, but I was not suffocating. I was surprised that breathing was as easy as it was. I kept my eyes shut and my face turned away from the blast.

With the passing of the first thick wave, the wind grew stronger and a trifle cooler. The complete darkness must have lasted twenty minutes. Then I thought I saw a dull red glow off to the north. Looking at my handkerchief again I could barely see it when I held it a few inches from my eyes. The worst was probably over.

Such dust storms are not infrequent in some of the more arid regions of the world and are as awesome in their own right as hurricanes, blizzards, and tonadoes.

Distinctive Winds

As cyclonic systems wander across the land, they may run into geographic situations that may alter their flow and create specific local wind conditions that the natives give special names. For example, cold air swirling southward from the back of a low-pressure system can be deflected much further southward by the barrier of the Rocky Mountain range. The cold air may reach as far south as Central America, even to the Panama Canal. Central Americans call these winds "nortes," and Texans call them "northers." In South America a similar condition exists when a cyclone over the South Atlantic has its northward-blowing sector deflect off the wall of the Andes and flow further northward than usual, even across the equator. Since these cold winds race across the pampas of Argentina they are called "pampero." In other parts of the world there are similarly created strong, cold winds and also some warm ones. Table 4.1 (page 70) gives their names and origins.

Cyclonic Storms

In the general circulation of air between the tropics and the polar regions, particularly in the middle latitudes, there regularly develop large horizontal eddies. Generally developing at the boundary between warm and cool streams of air, these clockwise-whirling masses, *cyclones,* tend to transport cold air toward the equator and warm air toward the poles.

The anticyclone parent air masses, those with counterclockwise rota-

69

TABLE 4.1

WIND NAME	WHERE FOUND	WIND TEMP. (Cold or Warm)
Norte	Central America	C
Norther	Texas	C
Pampero	South America	C
Buran	Siberia	C
Burga	Alaska	C
Boulbie	Southern France	C
Levanter	Southern Spain	C
Harmattan	West Coast of Africa	C
Sumatra	Malay peninsula	C
Sirocco	Sahara, Mediterranean	W
Khamsin	Libyan desert, Egypt	W
Simoon	Deserts, Africa & southwest Asia	W

tion, take on much of their temperature and moisture characteristics from the surfaces over which they pass. The more rapidly the air masses pass over a surface, the less change can occur; but when they move relatively slowly over a surface of fairly constant conditions of temperature and moisture, they tend to acquire similar temperature and moisture regimes.

Air masses are created primarily by clockwise, anticyclonic flow of polar and subtropical high-pressure belts. As indicated, they tend to take on a temperature/moisture regime, varying primarily according to whether they form over the ocean or the land. Consequently, air masses are classified according to their basic point of origin as *polar* or *tropical, maritime* or *continental*.

In winter, when North America has its worst storms, the major air masses are *continental polar* (abbreviated *cP), maritime polar (mP),* and *maritime tropical (mT)*. Each of these has its own source area where it acquires its basic characteristics. Northern Canada gives rise to our *cP* air masses, the north Pacific ocean gives birth to *mP* masses, and *mT* air derives from the semipermanent Atlantic anticyclone and gets its warmth and moisture from the Caribbean Sea and the Gulf of Mexico. As these air masses move away from their area of origin, they slowly acquire temperature characteristics of the land over which they pass. They are then classified as either warm or cold air masses in relation to the surface they are traveling over (that is, whether they are warmer or cooler than that underlying surface).

When two air masses of differing characteristics of temperature and humidity come together, their contrast forms a boundary or *frontal zone.* This is commonly abbreviated to simply *front.*) The struggle between the two masses, resulting in wavelike advances and retreats between the two, reminded Norwegian meteorologists of war-zone battle lines with their

70

FIGURE 4.6. Weather satellite photo (2:30, Oct. 13, 1983) shows layered clouds over southern Rockies and Great Basin associated with a frontal system and low-pressure areas. Clouds swirl about a storm centered over Iowa. Frontal clouds stretch from Florida northward across the Great Lakes. Widespread convective cloudiness east of frontal band covers eastern part of nation. Photo courtesy NOAA.

intermittent skirmish areas, so they applied the military term. The frontal zone always angles upward vertically, with the lighter, warmer air mass riding up over the denser, cooler air mass. No matter which air mass is pushing with greater force, there will be some uplifting of the warm air mass that often leads to cloud formation from condensation and precipitation along the front.

Cyclonic Birth

However, it is the wavy action along the front that gives birth to wave cyclones, which become the more potent storms. The physics behind the formation of the waves is complex, including *gravity waves, inertial waves,*

71

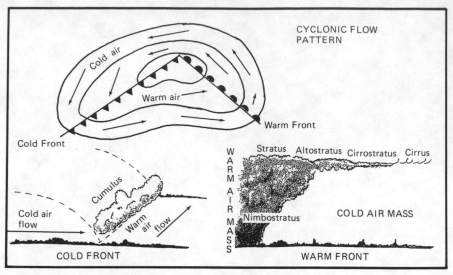

FIGURE 4.7. Cyclonic flow pattern and related clouds.

and *shearing waves*. Of import here is not how the waves form but that waves with lengths between, roughly, 375 miles and 1800 miles are unstable and may give rise to cyclonic whirls. As the wave develops along the front, a low-pressure area forms at its crest, and both cold and warm air currents flow around it in the cyclonic, counterclockwise pattern. There is a warm front riding over the cold, dense air, but in the circular pattern there is also a cold front pushing behind and under the warm-air sector. (See Figure 4.7.) We now have a wave cyclone.

If you are to the east of such an approaching wave cyclone, there is a generalized sequence of events you are likely to observe. The first sign of the approaching storm would be high cirrus clouds. As time passes these thicken and become cirrostratus clouds, often producing halo effects. Then the clouds lower and thicken as altostratus. The barometer falls, and the wind picks up and changes to a counterclockwise direction as the low gets closer. Then the temperature rises slowly as the frontal transition zone approaches, and shortly precipitation of rain or snow begins. Once the warm front passes, precipitation ends and the wind changes direction again to a clockwise flow. Pressure stops falling as the warm sector arrives. The weather therein depends upon the stability of that warm air mass and the surface over which it is moving, varying from showers to virtually clear skies. Then comes the cold front, and the weather it generates will depend on its speed, sharpness, and the stability of the warmer air it is forcing aloft. Towering cumulus and showers are the norm along the leading edge of the cold front, and in spring squalls are frequent. On the other hand, it is not uncommon for a cold front to produce a 50- to 60-mile-wide band of nimbostratus clouds with their attendant rain. Once the cold front passes,

72

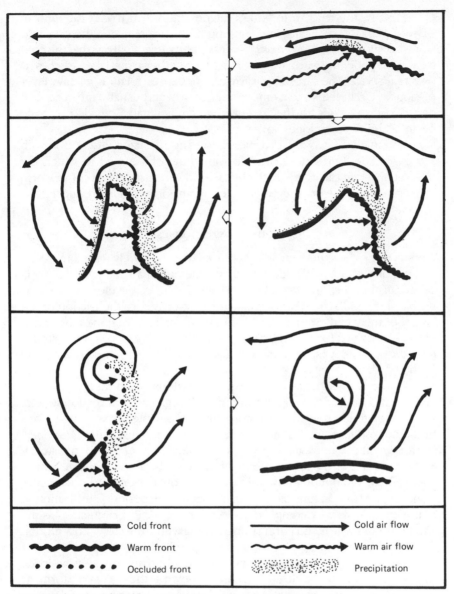

Cold front

Warm front

Occluded front

Cold air flow

Warm air flow

Precipitation

FIGURE 4.8. Frontal development and movement in cyclonic flow.

the wind veers again, and the pressure begins to rise, temperature falls, and visibility improves; all this is due largely to air descending behind the front. Particularly during winter and spring in midlatitude North America, when the contrast in conditions between air masses tends to be greatest, there may be periods of a continous sequence of three to five of these wave cyclones drifting eastward.

Wave cyclones remind one of a dog chasing a cat in a tight circle.

73

Occasionally, the cold front "dog" catches the warm front "cat" and in essence grabs its own tail. The resulting boundary between the two cold fronts is called an *occluded front*. What happens, essentially, is that the cold front dives under the warm front, forcing it up and away, and then catches its own rear sector. The forced-up warm air condenses, forming a heavy layer of clouds. Occluded systems move very slowly and usually mean several days of overcast skies for the area over which they stall. They do mean the death of the wave cyclone, however.

In actuality, few wave cyclones follow this idealized description with any exactitude. But it does provide something of a model to which the diligent observer can compare the behavior of any particular cyclonic storm sequence, for these wave cyclones are our major weather producers.

Cyclonic Powerhouses

Wave cyclones have fierce tropical cousins that are widely feared in inhabited regions. Although these tropical cyclones are spawned over the tropical oceans between the latitudes of 5° and 20°, once developed they may wander into midlatitudes and wreak great havoc before the friction of the land robs them of their force and dissipates them. Each region of the planet has its own word for them: in North America it's *hurricane;* in Australia, *willy nilly;* to East Asians it's *typhoon;* Indians refer to them as *cyclones;* and in the China Sea they are known as *baquio.*

These storms begin as tropical depressions. They then evolve the cyclonic motion that develops into a very well-organized convection system. It pumps huge amounts of moist, warm air, at rapid rates, to very high levels in the atmosphere. As the moisture in the air condenses, the latent heat released by the condensation process is added to the energy of the storm. Such storms have an enormous energy capacity; the average one generates about 300 to 400 billion kilowatt-hours of energy per day and precipitates some 10 to 20 billion tons of water in the same time period! The air motion of these storms is very complex; there is strong vertical circulation as the whole air mass whirls and is transported along within the circulatory motion of the larger air flow in which the storm is imbedded.

Seen from above in satellite photos, these storms appear as whirling rings of clouds around a clear center area, known as the *eye* of the storm. As one of these storms approaches and passes over an observer, the following generalized pattern of activity is likely to be experienced: High clouds will be seen approaching for some 200 to 300 miles ahead of the storm proper. Pressure will begin to fall slowly, and winds pick up above normal (that would be somewhere above the usual 10 to 20 miles per hour of the average trade winds). Winds will continue to increase, and pressure will begin to fall more rapidly. When the storm center is within about 100 miles, winds will have reached 50 miles-per-hour or more, and the clouds will be

74

FIGURE 4.9. Hurricane Diana (Sept. 12, 1984). Note dimplelike eye in center of cloud mass. Photo courtesy of NOAA.

low and menacing. At about 70 or 60 miles from the center the rain begins; it reaches torrential levels from 30 to 20 miles from storm center. At this point in the storm winds may be as strong as 125 miles per hour. If the eye of the storm passes over the observer, he or she must be prepared for a surprise. The winds abruptly die down to somewhere around 20 miles-per-hour; rain ceases completely and the clouds thin; the sun may even shine through. Storm eyes average somewhere around 15 miles in diameter and are surrounded by towering walls of cloud ranging in height from ½ mile to nearly 8 miles. The calm of the eye is short-lived and, when it passes over, one reenters the maelstrom, experiencing the same kind of weather as earlier, only in reverse order and with opposite wind directions. Damage from these storms is caused not only by powerful winds and flooding from torrential rain, but by enhanced tidal surges pushed by the storm winds and circulation.

Fortunately, these tropical cyclonic storms are far less numerous than their more northern wave-cyclone cousins, only about 10 percent as abundant. They do not occur throughout the year but have regular spawning seasons, during which anywhere from two to twenty-one of these potent storms may be born. Table 4.2 (page 77) indicates ocean areas and their tropical cyclone season.

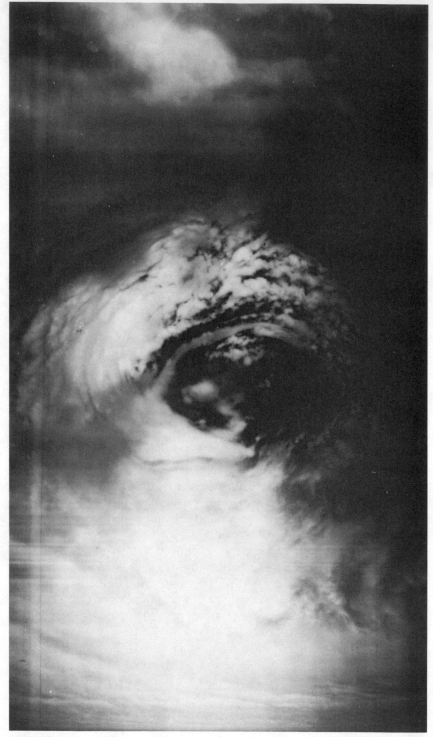

FIGURE 4.10. Viewed from 11 miles above earth, we look into the eye of Hurricane Betsy and view its towering cloud wall (Sept. 2, 1965). Photo courtesy U.S. Air Force Weather Service.

76

Table 4.2

OCEAN	SEASON
Northern Hemisphere	
Atlantic Ocean	June–November
Pacific Ocean (off Mexico)	June–October
Pacific Ocean (west of 170E)	May–November
Indian Ocean	May–November
Southern Hemisphere	
Pacific Ocean (Eastern coast/Australia)	December–April
Indian Ocean (northwest Australia)	November–April
Indian Ocean (Madagascar to 90E)	November–May

Dust Devils, Tornadoes, and Waterspouts

These phenomena share the fact that they are intensely whirling vortices around a nearly vertical core or axis. Dust devils form from thermal updrafts resulting from the intense heating of the earth's surface by the sun. They are most common over dry surfaces that can be heated to high temperatures, such as deserts, parking lots, and playgrounds. Normally, they are invisible, unless there is a supply of dust, dry leaves, or other debris to be caught up in the moving air. They begin as a bubble of hot air swiftly rising. The cooler air moving in to replace them begins to swirl like water going down a sink drain. That replacement air is also rapidly heated and, as it rises, centrifugal force causes it to spin even more rapidly, fueling the whole whirling process. Its behavior is similar to that of a figure skater who increases the rate of spin when he or she pulls in the arms and legs toward the body.

Many dust devils, particularly those that form in developed areas, are small and harmless and quickly dissipate after a life span of only a few minutes. In open desert, however, things may be quite different. Large dust devils can be quite powerful, more powerful indeed than about a quarter of all the tornadoes that occur throughout the world. They can do minor structural damage to houses and farm buildings. These large dust devils can persist for several hours, and there is a case on record of a dust devil forming over a railroad embankment that was under construction in Arizona and removing about a cubic yard of sand per hour from the site for a period of four hours. Like tornadoes, when dust devils begin to dissipate they often stretch their funnels up into very long, ropelike and contorted structures. Such ropes may extend 1000 feet into the air, yet be only a foot or so in diameter.

Tornadoes are included with the cyclonic storms because they are whirlwinds of cyclonic flow. However, they are born primarily from cumulonimbus clouds, which are not necessarily cyclonic in origin. They generally form in the area of intense cold fronts and squall lines, where there exists strong instability and special circumstances that lead to an intense low-pressure center. Once the strong spin is initiated, powerful convective action will sustain it until its energy is dissipated and the whirling

77

FIGURE 4.11. Tornado funnel over Plainview, Texas (May 27, 1978). Photo courtesy NOAA.

motion is stopped by friction. Winds in a tornado are too strong to measure with normal instruments. Their force must be determined by the evidence they leave behind in the form of damage to buildings and the impact force of flying objects, such as pieces of straw driven like nails into telephone poles. From such evidence, estimates are that wind speed ranges from 100 to 300 miles per hour and sometimes up to more than 500 miles per hour.

Tornadoes are characterized by a funnel cloud descending from the cumulonimbus. The difference in pressure between the inside and outside of the funnel ranges from 25 millibars of pressure to 200 millibars. This difference in pressure contributes greatly to the destructiveness of these storms. They cause damage in three major ways: by the enormous force of the wind; the sudden pressure difference between the inside and outside of a building (which causes the greater pressure inside to push the walls out); and the strong updraft currents that lift items in the tornado's path and deposit them later in odd ways (as in such occurrences as rains of frogs and fish). Stories about the freak occurrences caused by tornadoes are seemingly endless.

Tornadoes are relatively infrequent storms in most parts of the world, but some areas have more of them than others. They are most common over large continents where strong horizontal temperature contrasts exist. Tornado-prone regions include southern Australia, the southern and middle regions of the USSR, and the United States east of the Rockies, mostly in the central plains states. Usually late afternoon phenomena, tornadoes generally occur during spring but can appear at any time. Tornadoes are also often associated with hurricanes.

Tornadoes sometimes form over warm water, and because of the heavy moisture content of the air in such places, the funnels are so full of water drops that they look like a stream of water flowing from the base of the

78

cloud. Thus they are called *waterspouts*. The water increases friction; therefore, waterspouts are not as intense as tornadoes. But where the funnels touch down, the winds churn the water surface, generating waves and spray.

Thermal Storms

Thermal storms develop from the forces that generate cumulus clouds and may evolve within some cyclonic systems or completely isolated from them. The two thermal-storm formations—the cloudburst and the thunderstorm—are from cumulonimbus clouds of differing intensities. Both are produced from different stages in the life cycle of cumulonimbus formations.

Initially, the differential heating of the earth's surface induces the heating of a blob of air that then becomes less dense and rises through bouyancy. Cooler air coming in from below in all directions pinches off the rising blob, creating a rising bubble of warm, moist air. A new blob of warm air begins to form below and in turn becomes a rising bubble. (The effect is similar to that of gas bubbles rising in a glass of ginger ale.) The rising bubble cools, the moisture condenses, and a cumulus cloud forms. If the air is turbulent, the bubble mixes with the surrounding air fairly rapidly, and the puff of cloud degenerates and disappears. Horizontal winds aloft may cause the puff of cloud to drift downwind from its point of origin, only to be replaced by a puff of cloud from succeeding bubbles. This is typical fair-weather cumulus activity, as discussed in Chapter 3.

However, if the air is not too turbulent and horizontal winds are weak, the bubbles will emerge faster and faster until there is essentially a rising column of air—a *thermal*. Around the edges of a thermal there must be sinking cooler air, and this completes a vertical circulation. It is much like a coffee percolator, with its blobs of hot water that rise in the middle and drain down the outside. Cumulus clouds form at the top of each of these thermals, and the space between the clouds usually represents the downdraft areas. In unstable air the clouds expand more rapidly vertically than horizontally, and thus each cell begins to tower higher and higher. Air enters the clouds from all sides, and since the updraft is strongest near the top of the cloud, it continues to grow faster vertically than horizontally. This is because, as the water vapor condenses, its latent heat of condensation warms the air, causing it to continue to expand.

At its mature stage the cumulus cloud has become a towering cumulonimbus, and rain emerges from its base. The towering cloud has now reached altitudes such that it contains water in all its states—vapor, liquid, and solid. Its precipitation may be medium to large water drops or ice in the form of hail. A young cumulonimbus emerging from cumulus congestus (see page 80) may just dump torrential rain quickly, as a cloudburst, and then begin to dissipate, or it may continue to build its energy into a true thunderstorm with all its attendant thunder, lightning, and even hail.

79

FIGURE 4.12. Sequence of thunderstorm developing.

We will discuss these phenomena in detail in the sections on precipitation and luminous phenomena. Suffice it to say that thunderstorms contain enormous energy and may be quite violent, with plant-flattening winds, dangerous electrical discharges, and cutting, pounding hail.

Near the end of the mature stage the towering cumulonimbus reaches its greatest vertical development, usually attaining over 40,000 feet in altitude; sometimes even penetrating the tropopause and achieving altitudes in excess of 60,000 feet. In the storm there are strong downdrafts that reach the ground and spread away from the storm. As a thunderstorm approaches, you usually feel these cool, gusty winds a little before the storm hits. As the storm loses energy the downdraft enlarges and eventually cuts off the updraft. Without updraft the precipitation diminishes, and then the downdraft is subdued. The storm is dying out. Soon, all lightning stops, and the cloud begins to dissolve, often spreading out in a limited stratus formation.

These relatively brief but often awesomely powerful storms—with their gleaming white sails as they approach and glowering black bottoms trailing thick skirts of rain upon arrival, announced in advance by the low menacing rumble of thunder and searing flashes of lightning—may arrive singly or in small fleets if their formative air was forced aloft by mountain range or frontal clashes. They tend to form rather quickly under proper conditions and to survive in their mature stage for only a quarter to half an hour before beginning to dissipate. In some areas they seem to form almost on a daily schedule in appropriate seasons and to follow regular tracks. You can almost set your watch by the afternoon thundershower. In such areas the alert observer can regularly watch the whole life history of the storm, from the first cumulus puffs to the final dissipation of the cumulonimbus.

THE NATURE OF PRECIPITATION

The magic of precipitation is tied to the wondrous nature of water, the power of winds, and the vagaries of temperature. Within the normal temperature range of the planet, water is unique in being able to assume liquid, gaseous, or solid form. It most commonly exists as liquid, but when energy is added to the liquid sufficient to raise its temperature to 212° F (100° C), the individual molecules take on a dollop of extra energy and fly from the liquid state to the more energetic, gaseous form of water vapor; a form in which the water becomes invisible. When water turns from gas to liquid, it gives up that extra energy it took on to become a gas and releases it into the air. At the other end of the spectrum, as liquid water is cooled to 32° F (0° C), it gives off an extra dollop of heat and assumes either an amorphous or crystalline structure as a solid that we recognize as ice or snow.

When liquid water vaporizes, the water vapor molecules must occupy existing spaces between other gas molecules of the air. When a mass of air is cool, its molecules are closer together, and there is less space between them

81

for water vapor. A warm air mass has its molecules farther apart, and thus there is more space to be filled by water vapor molecules. For the same volume, warm air can hold more water vapor than cool air. If all the spaces available in an air mass are filled with water vapor, it is said to be *saturated*. When we talk about relative humidity we are actually indicating what percentage of the available space in an air mass of a given temperature is actually occupied by water vapor. Since the temperature of the air mass can change rapidly due to daily fluctuation in heat from the sun, or to being elevated by flowing over surface features, or to being given a ride on a thermal, the relative humidity of the air mass changes rapidly as well.

As a surface air mass that has a relative humidity of, let's say, 50 percent is elevated and becomes cooler, there is less and less space for water vapor and, with no additional vapor added, the relative humidity nonetheless becomes higher and higher. At some height temperature will be such that the air mass is saturated. Something has to give. To condense back to its less dense, less space-consuming liquid form, the water must have a solid particle, called a *condensation nuclei,* to cling to. This can be dust, salt crystals, or similar substances. When these are present, the vapor does condense and form a visible water droplet that remains suspended in the air. In the process of condensing the vapor gives off that extra dollop of energy it took on before vaporizing. However, in very clean air condensation nuclei may be absent or very scarce; condensation cannot occur. If the rising air continues to get colder and denser and the vapor cannot condense, there is a real squeeze play, and the air mass becomes supersaturated, with the motions of all molecules increasingly constricted. And if a rising air mass gets to points of temperature where its water droplets would normally become solid and there are no condensation nuclei, the water droplets become supercooled. It is not unusual for small drops of liquid water to exist in high clouds at a temperature of $-4°$ F. It is such conditions that scientists try to exploit to produce precipitation when they seed a cloud with silver iodide to serve as condensation nuclei.

Under normal conditions, however, condensation nuclei are available, and the water or ice particles form. They are very tin,y however, and remain suspended in air. This is not precipitation. To precipitate, the droplets or ice particles must get large enough and heavy enough for gravity to pull them down. This means that the average droplet may have to increase its size by a factor of a million before it can fall. One way this happens is that the droplets, of slightly varying sizes, get moved about in the cloud by convection currents, and they collide and coalesce to form larger drops. When they get large enough, drops may splinter on collision to form other drops that hit and coalesce. In many clouds the upper layers are primarily ice crystals, and lower ones contain supercooled water drops. As internal convection increases, the ice crystals and water droplets mix, and the drops

82

adhere to the ice crystals. These then increase in size; as they are pulled down by downdraft, they melt and become large drops that go on to grow through collision and coalescence. When they are large enough, precipitation can occur. As pedantic as all this seems, it is a stage setter for some almost magical sky phenomena. It is not so much that the forms of precipitation are magical, but that the impressions they leave in our minds are, the moods they evoke: fresh clean rejuvenation from a warm, spring rain; peace and serenity from whirling snowflakes; depression and discomfort from a soaking 3-day rain; soggy misery from the pelting rain of a torrential thunderstorm downpour, heightened by a touch of fear of the lightning; unhappiness and irritation at the stinging bite of wind-driven sleet; or awe at the power and destruction of a wave of hail. A wide range of impressions, all caused by a diversity of forms of one simple substance—water.

Liquid Precipitation

Rain is the most common form of precipitation; indeed, it's so common that we often do not stop to appreciate some of the variety that it displays. Often the rain comes down warm and gentle. In such cases the drops are usually quite small and are not pulled to earth with the acceleration force of larger ones. When the precipitation is so slow as to be hardly noticeable, it may be referred to as *mist* rather than rain. Some storms begin with a few large splats of water from drops so large they seem less like drops than like the contents of small shot glasses. Smaller, but still relatively large, drops are often cold even on a summer day, an indication of their birth high in the icy layers of the upper clouds.

Raindrops have formed around condensation nuclei and have often picked up other solids suspended in air as they hurtle to earth. When the drops evaporate, they leave this baggage behind. It is not unusual for there to be red rains from the inclusion of desert dust; black rain from industrial soot and some volcanic ash; and even yellow rain from pollen. It is often interesting and instructive to examine a clean polished surface after a rain to learn what the air was carrying and what the raindrops utilized as their rallying point for condensation. For the greatest information, microscopic examination of the surface is necessary.

SKY WASH

Our civilization's thirst for energy has generated massive air pollution. The sky also is endowed with wind-borne, eroded soil, the result of the careless practices of some farmers and agribusinesses. As a result, the sky has become increasingly loaded with particulates and gases. The varying ten-

83

dencies of these to transmit, scatter, reflect, and refract light has caused considerable reduction in visibility in many regions of the earth, particularly around, and downwind from, major urban and industrial regions. Of course, such particulates do occasionally contribute to more colorful sunsets and they do provide some condensation nuclei to stimulate precipitation.

It is precipitation that functions as a cleansing mechanism for the sky because the particles, around which the water gathers, will be removed along with other material with which the falling rain or snow comes in contact. Since everything must go somewhere, the materials rinsed from the sky return to earth to create a whole new set of problems.

It has been easy to believe that we could get rid of unwanted gas and soot by tossing it into the air and letting the wind disperse it. If it tended to come aground too soon, we could always build bigger, taller smokestacks so that the material would travel farther before it came back to earth. But as forests of smokestacks grew, this strategy no longer fooled anyone. The more responsible industries installed devices to remove particles and some gases before they left the smokestack. Laws were passed to force other industries to do the same. Smokestack scrubber technology, in concert with the laws, helped reduce the problems but is far from eliminating them. However, sulpher dioxide emissions have been declining since the inception of The Clean Air Act.

Exhausts from motor vehicles contribute their share of gaseous and particulate junk to the sky, and laws to reduce this load of "sky junk" has had some positive impact. Indeed, U.S. automobile emmissions of nitrogen oxides, carbon monoxide, and hydrocarbons in the 1980s are less than half what they were between 1957–1967. However, the net result is that unacceptable amounts of sky junk are still generated daily, although considerably less of it than if these laws were not in effect.

Our burgeoning numbers continue to generate demands that result in vast amounts of sky junk, even though *per capita* generation of such material has somewhat decreased. There are just more and more "capita." Like the Red Queen of "Alice in Wonderland" we have to run faster and faster just to stay where we are. Voluminous expanses of smog still form over most of Earth's great cities, and under the right conditions this sky junk is widely dispersed to other areas.

The sky wash system is throwing many of our pollutants back in our face in the form of acid rain. Particularly the gases of combustion—sulphur dioxide (SO_2), and various oxides of nitrogen (NOx)—dissolve in the rain and snow and form acids. These change the nature of our precipitation. Normal rainfall has a pH of 5.6. Understand that pH readings are based on a logarithmic scale, so a pH of 4.6 is ten times more acid than pH 5.6, and pH 3.6 is one hundred times more acid. In some storms in the eastern United States, rainfall is recorded that is one thousand times more acid than normal

84

rainfall! Such acid rains eat away at our statuary and the paint on our cars and houses; acid waters leach some metals from the pipes our drinking water flows through, they leach aluminum from our soils into our ponds and streams, choking our fish to death in the process, they make lakes and ponds acid, increasingly to the point where these no longer can support a diversity of living things; and they contribute to the death of forests, particularly in mountain areas. The National Academy of Science estimates that acid rain alone causes at least $5 billion in damages annually in the United States. Much of this is the price we pay for some 26 million tons of sulphur dioxide American industries dump into the air each year; two-thirds of this comes from coal-fired power plants. This is the shorter-term environmental bill that we pay, but there is a delayed billing for future generations, particularly if we don't find the will and the ways to reduce acid rain in the near future.

Frozen Precipitation

Raindrops, or melted snowflakes, that freeze while traversing a cold air layer near the ground form ice pellets that we call *sleet*. Freezing rain, on the other hand, is rain that freezes on contact with objects, such as tree limbs and electrical wires, or the ground. Technically, freezing rain is not a type of precipitation but rather a description of what happens to liquid rain precipitation under special conditions.

Sometimes we see a somewhat lumpy-looking pellet that is soft and tends to form a white splat of powdery snow when it hits a surface. These pellets are, not uncommonly, conical in shape. They represent a mass of frozen cloud droplets that are clinging together. They may form around some snow crystals initially, but they are not really crystalline in nature. They are somewhat like very soft hailstones, and indeed, they do form in strong updrafts as hail does. Some may even go on to form the core of a hailstone. These pellets are known as *graupel* and are usually associated with violent thunderstorms, blizzards, and "lake effect" snowstorms. Graupel itself may be highly electrified.

Hail is a special phenomenon associated with towering cumulonimbus formations of high energy and powerful internal updrafts. Droplets ride the updrafts and are cooled to become ice. As ice they drift downward, meet supercooled droplets which coalesce to them, and enlarge and fall faster. In the internal turbulence of the cloud they reach an updraft before they drop low enough to reach warmer zones, where they most likely would melt to large raindrops. The updraft rides them aloft again, and they may gain some more moisture on the way which will freeze to their surface. Again they will descend and grow through accretion to their surface. This yo-yo trip in the cloud will continue until the ball of ice is heavy enough that the pull of gravity exceeds the force of the internal updrafts. At such time the pellet of ice will rush to the earth as a hailstone. Hailstones may be of very odd shapes, due to the peculiarities of their pathways in the cloud and whether or not they have struck and fused with other, smaller hailstones-in-making during their joy ride in the cloud. A hailstone cut in half may look something like an onion in cross section because of the successive layers of moisture that it acquired in its up and down travels. Hailstones may be only $^2/_{10}$ inch in diameter or up to 3 inches, roughly the size of a baseball. Reports of even larger hailstones are on record but are much less common.

For reasons not completely known, hail may fall in patches rather than from throughout the base of the cloud. This is revealed in the patchy damage to crops that seems to show up as strips of damage roughly parallel to one another. Perhaps they reflect the areas outside the strongest updraft zones.

Snow can be the most beautiful of all the forms of precipitation, although we don't always see it at its best. Snow is essentially ice in its crystalline form, which is characterized by a six-sided crystal pattern of infinite variety but of fewer design families. Essentially, there are seven such families: *plates, stellars, columns, needles, capped columns, spatial dendrites,* and *irregular crystals* (see Fig. 4.13). The first five families are all symmetrical crystals and are the most beautiful and least common snow forms. Rarest are the stellars and plates, which require reasonably still air to develop their perfection. Search for them at night or shortly after dawn, although they can occur at other times. Columns, needles, and capped columns are more frequently found, particularly during prolonged snowfalls. Look for needles during the warmest snow conditions; they usually are not mixed with other crystal types, although they may accompany sleet or graupel. Heavy falls of needle snow are often accompanied by atmospheric electrical activity, including occasional lightning. If the snowstorm has been preceded by a 22° halo and the temperature is below 12° Fahrenheit, be alert for columns and capped columns. Capped column crystals are usually considerably larger than ordinary column crystals, in part because they represent a fusion of columns and plates.

The other families of snow crystals are asymmetrical in shape and are the most abundant forms in most snowfalls. Spatial dendrites are much more three-dimensional in form than the stellars and plates they somewhat resemble. The latter are essentially formed in one flat plane only. Spatial dendrites form when abundant, concentrated cloud moisture is available. The lifting of air over mountains, along with the presence of multiple cloud layers, tends to favor their formation. Irregular crystals form due to disturbances in the clouds that prevent the slower development needed to achieve symmetry. The presence of such conditions in the sky is usually much more prevalent than the absence.

A fall of rather rare occurrence, but one to be alert for, is that of "diamond dust." These are microscopic, asymmetrical particles of clear ice, essentially platelike in form, with several prismatic arms. Look for such a fall on very cold and clear mornings shortly after sunrise. It will be of very short

86

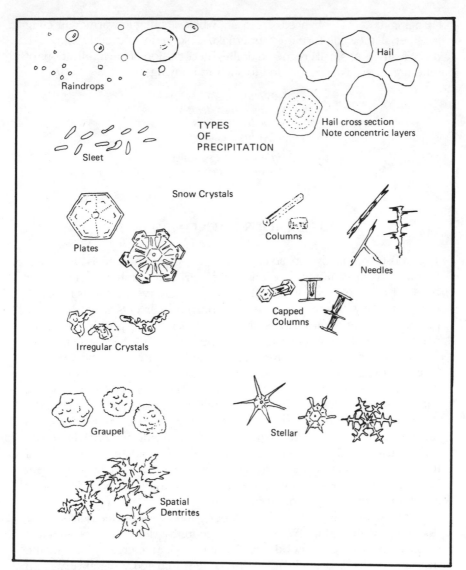

Raindrops

Hail

Sleet

TYPES
OF
PRECIPITATION

Hail cross section
Note concentric layers

Snow Crystals

Plates

Columns

Needles

Capped
Columns

Irregular Crystals

Graupel

Stellar

Spatial
Dentrites

FIGURE 4.13. Types of precipitation.

duration, and there will be no appreciable accumulation on the ground. The presence of these crystals in the air may help create a *sunstreak* or *sunpillar,* a streak or column of light apparently emerging in one plane from the sun.

When air is cold, snow crystals tend to be small and are unlikely to melt and turn to rain. When a storm arrives under such conditions, it is likely to be long-lasting. In warmer air the flakes can acquire more moisture and become larger, and the likelihood of the storm disintegrating and probably

87

changing to rain is enhanced. Often, snowflakes falling in warmer air cling together as they fall, forming "superflakes," sometimes even looking like down feathers or small crocheted doilies. Recognition of the implications of differing snowflake size has led to such folk sayings as:

> Snow like meal
> Snow a great deal;
> Snow like feathers,
> Softening weather.

> Little snow, big snow;
> Big snow, little snow.

LUMINOUS PHENOMENA

The most frequently observed luminous phenomenon is lightning. Cumulonimbus clouds are great natural electrical generators, and it is their behavior that creates most of the lightning we observe. Scientists have still not completely determined how the churning currents in such clouds produce the electrical charges and then separate the positive from the negative ones in different regions of the cloud. However, whether we understand why or not, positive charges do concentrate near the top of the cloud and negative ones near the bottom. The earth itself has a negative charge. As a cumulonimbus storm matures, it builds great electrical potential differences within the cloud and between the cloud and the earth. The difference in potential between positive and negative electrical charges is measured in volts. Just before a lightning discharge, the potential difference is in the nature of 3000 volts per centimeter along a gradient from the top of the cloud to the bottom. Resulting lightning flashes therefore may represent hundreds of millions of volts, with the average thunderstorm dissipating about a million kilowatts of electrical energy.

Air is a good insulator—that is, a poor conductor of electricity—but it does have its limitations. When the voltage in the cloud reaches sufficient strength, in the neighborhood of a million volts per meter, it overcomes the insulating effect, and an electrical discharge is initiated. Several very rapid leader strokes of negative charge initiate a path in the sky and are instantly followed by a ground to cloud streamer carrying a positive charge. These flows continue until the electrical field is reduced below the level needed to override the insulating property of the air.

The electrical current in a lightning stroke is enormous, and that causes temperatures to rise to millions of degrees along the lightning path. It also results in an explosive expansion of air, with a corresponding rush of cooler air crashing in to replace the hot air that was driven away. This generates the air vibrations that we hear as the crack of lightning and the rumble of thunder.

We see the light of lightning essentially instantaneously, but, although the thunderclap occurs at the same time, it takes longer for sound waves than for light waves to travel the same distance. This fact gives us a crude way of judging the distance of the storm from us. If you count the number of seconds from when you see a flash of lightning until you hear the resultant thunder, and multiply that by the speed of sound (roughly 1088 feet per second) and divide by 5280 (the number of feet per mile), the result will be the number of miles away the lightning flash occurred. Practically, this process can be shortened to dividing the number of seconds by five. If you do this calculation in five or ten minute intervals, you can determine if the storm is moving toward or away from you. If the flash and the crash are simultaneous, the storm is upon you!

It is estimated that somewhere around 1800 thunderstorms are operating over the earth's surface at any given moment and that lightning strokes strike the earth about 100 times per second. It is no wonder that so many people fear the lightning storm. The death toll from lightning each year is greater than that from hurricanes or tornadoes, and property damage is high. Persons struck by lightning receive a powerful shock and may be burned. They do not retain any charge, however, and can be safely handled immediately afterward. A lightning victim may appear dead but should be immediately treated by cardio-pulmonary resuscitation (CPR) techniques. Under such care many have revived and survived; most recover completely, others have impairment or loss of sight and hearing. Lightning commands respect. Its pathways are often apparently frivolous, but by avoiding taking shelter under the tallest trees or in isolated tall structures you are unlikely to be struck. If you are caught out in an open area, crouch down so that you are not the most direct pathway between cloud and ground. Lying down will make you even less elevated than crouching but gives more contact with potentially wet ground; that could increase your chances of a burn from a nearby lightning strike.

The pyrotechnics of lightning are fascinating to watch, for lightning may appear in a number of forms. It may be a single streak between cloud and sky, or it may be forked into several channels. *Bead lightning* is occasionally observed; in this the streak is electromagnetically constricted into a series of beads of light. Perhaps the rarest and most controversial form is *ball lightning*. Science cannot fully explain how this occurs, for it seems to be an electrified bubble of gas that may be very small or very large and persists for a short time moving in strange and unpredictable paths. Some suggest it may be initiated in ways similar to those which cause bead lightning. Ball lightning often drifts about a while, then disappears with a bang. Though generally spherical in shape, it has been seen as a rod or other asymmetrical shape.

Although lightning usually follows the shortest path of least resistance between the cloud and the sky, under the right atmospheric conditions it may make some long horizontal detours. At least one observation was made

FIGURE 4.14. Lightning. C.E. Roth photo.

in England of a bolt that started earthward from its cumulonimbus cloud and then veered sharply to the horizontal, striking down to the ground again about 5 miles from its cloud of origin.

Most lightning is white or yellow in color, but other colors, though less common, are far from unknown. The color depends upon the atoms and molecules in the discharge path, which are activated by the electrical discharge to emit light energy of their own characteristic wavelengths. Pink, orange, and red are to be observed and even, on occasion, bluish light.

Almost all lightning is generated by cumulonimbus clouds, but there are rare occasions when there is truly a "bolt from out of the blue;" that is, a lightning flash from a clear, cloudless sky. This may happen when different density thermal layers ride across one another and their molecular friction generates differences in electrical potential. However, no one knows for sure.

There is also thunderless lightning, which is generally known as *heat lightning* because it is usually observed in hot, muggy weather. It may simply be the reflection of lightning from storms below the horizon and too distant for the sound of thunder to reach the viewer. Often, it is low-energy, cloud-to-cloud electrical discharges too diffuse to create the hot-air channels that result in audible thunder. Displays of heat lightning can often be quite spectacular, even though their clouds produce neither thunder nor rain.

90

An uncommon lightning form to be alert for is *rocket lightning,* which is a discharge from the top of a cloud up toward the stratosphere. The scientific explanation of how this type of lightning occurs is very tentative and incomplete as well. It is usually accompanied by a colored flash of light below the cloud.

Luminous, Slow Discharges
of Electricity

Lightning is the category of rapid, powerful electrical discharges. But, although rarer, slow discharge of natural electrical currents does occur and creates beautiful luminous effects. These discharges usually extend into the atmosphere from tall projections, such as tall trees, ship masts, radio antennae, mountain peaks, or even small projections, such as human fingers, hair, and parts of clothing. The collision of solid particles in powerful snowstorms and sandstorms may generate electrical currents between sky and ground that will generate this phenomenon. Under such conditions a luminous glow may occur at the tips of such projections. On a human this can be positively eerie, for the fingertips, or a beard, or a moustache may glow. The phenomenon is known as *St. Elmo's fire* when it occurs on relatively small objects. When slow luminous discharge occurs from some high mountain peaks for similar reasons, it is usually known as *Andes glow,* from the mountain region where it is seen with some frequency.

Auroras

Auroras are among the most spectacular sights in nature, particularly when they are at their peak and sending sheets, streamers, and curtains of luminous light shimmering through the northern sky. They work much like neon lights, as the gas molecules are excited by electrons smashing into them so that they radiate light waves. With auroras it is primarily oxygen and nitrogen atoms in the upper atmosphere that are excited.

The exciting electrons come from storms on the sun expelling clouds of gas so hot that the hydrogen atoms are split into widely dispersed protons and electrons. These primary particles make up the so-called solar wind which reaches peaks during periods of heavy sunspot activity. When the solar wind reaches the region of earth on its path to outer space, some of the particles are deflected by the planet's magnetic field. They then pour into the big radiation belts of the exosphere, where some leak downward and poleward. At the same time the charged layers of the ionosphere swell in size and rise in altitude. More electrical currents course through the ionosphere, and a weak current is induced within the solid earth itself. At such times auroral lights flare up, primarily in polar regions but sometimes into midlatitudes; occasionally, they can even be seen in tropical regions. The auroral show most often occurs in the low and middle ionosphere at

91

altitudes of 60 to 150 miles, but the luminous display may reach to 500 miles. The lower-level auroral displays occur at about the region where radio waves are reflected earthward. It should therefore be no surprise that during auroral displays radio transmission may be severely disrupted.

Auroras are most frequently observed in a broad elliptical belt around the earth that ranges from about 70 to 60 degrees of latitude. In the northern hemisphere they are called *aurora borealis;* in the southern hemisphere, *aurora australis.* There are two main types of auroras, those with rays and those without, but within these categories there is variation to stagger the imagination—glows, streamers, curtains, bands, arches. Most common are the nonrayed auroras with wavy, pulsing glows, arcs, and bands. Rayed auroras send rays and streamers arching from the horizon toward the zenith in bursts and pulses of often vivid color that then shrink back and form again. The range of colors that may appear runs the spectral gamut. In weak auroras, white predominates; in stronger ones, yellows abound; while in the brightest auroras, reds are dominant. A range of pastel colors—blues, lilacs, and pinks—are often part of the curtain formations of some auroras. These provide great beauty to a night sky. Auroras do exist during daylight hours, but their light is too weak to be seen then, just as is the light of the stars.

The sky is a vast treasure trove of visual treats and dynamic events. From almost any point on the globe there are beautiful and interesting things to observe. They are always there for all who will take the time and effort to look on a regular basis. Again, Thoreau points the way. As he wrote in his *Journal* of January 17, 1852: "As the skies appear to a man, so is his mind. Some see only clouds there; some, prodigies and portents; some rarely look up at all; their heads, like brutes', are directed toward earth. Some behold there serenity, purity, beauty ineffable. The world runs to see the panorams, when there is a panorama in the sky which few go out to see."

SKY-OBSERVER ACTIVITIES

• Explore local air currents and similar air movement using bubbles and balloons. Gentle air currents can be studied using regular bubbles generated by dipping a wire frame in a soapy solution and then whisking the frame and soap film through the air. Different sized bubbles can be made by using different sized frames; the more uniform the bubble size, the more reliable will be the information you gather on speed of travel. Extra tough, long-lasting bubbles can be created for your studies by mixing equal amounts of glycerine, white corn syrup, and concentrated liquid detergent. The detergent provides the film-forming properties, the syrup contributes toughness, and the glycerine makes it all long-lasting. With such a formula and coat-hanger frames you can produce bubbles 1 to 2 yards in diameter. Use a compass to determine the direction of air flow, and time the passage of individual bubbles over measured distances. Record all your findings in your sky log.

• Check the size of raindrops at various times during a storm, and compare raindrop sizes of different rainstorms. A fairly simple way to do this is to prepare a pan of finely sifted flour. Expose the pan briefly to the rain, and then examine and measure the flour-coated droplet. Keep track of the percentages of the various size drops. How does this percentage change throughout the course of a storm? Your task will be somewhat easier if you mix dry, water-soluble methylene blue into the flour. This will turn blue wherever there is a drop of rain, easing the job of differentiating a drop from a flour lump. For more advanced techniques of measuring raindrops, see Shaefer and Day in Further Reading.

• Preserve snow crystals, and make a collection of the various types. Preserving the crystals is most easily accomplished with one of the clear plastic aerosol sprays such as Krylon. Formulas vary slightly, so it may take some experimentation to get the best one. You will also need glass slides, either the type used with microscopes or the 2 inch × 2 inch ones used to mount photographic slides. The latter allow you to protect your finished products if you wish.

Precoat the glass with a clear plastic film at room temperature. Then refrigerate the prepared glass in the coldest part of your refrigerator. When snow is falling, take the chilled slide out and expose it to the falling flakes. When enough of the crystals have landed on your slide, spray it again until the surface is moistened. Don't get the spray can too close or the force will damage the crystals. Once you stop spraying, the solvent quickly evaporates, and the crystal shape will become fossilized in the plastic. The slide can then be taken inside and warmed for inspection or even projection.

Not all crystals in a storm are perfect and worth preservation. There is a way to select only the crystals you want for preservation, but it takes more hunting to get the right chemicals to do the job. You will need to prepare a 1-percent solution of Formvar. This involves mixing 1 gram of polyvinyl Formvar resin (Resin 15-95E, produced by Monsanto Chemical Corp., Springfield, MA) into 100 milliliters of ethylene dichloride. In addition you will need a piece of black velvet mounted on a stiff backing such as cardboard and a toothpick or equivalent. You also need the glass slides, chilled.

During the storm expose the velvet to the snow. Now dip the toothpick into the Formvar solution which you have prechilled to 23° F ($-5°$ C), and let a drop drain to the tip of the pick. Let the drop fall onto the glass slide. Next, gently touch the damp tip of the pick to a snowflake you want to preserve, and transfer it to the drop on the slide. It will drop from the pick and sink into the drop and be preserved. Again, Shaefer and Day describe still other methods of preserving snow, frost, and ice crystals for those who get hooked on this activity and wish to pursue it further.

93

• Compile photographic records of building and approaching storms and their activity and dissolution. You will use the basic information given under the activities section of Chapter 3, but there are some tips for storm photography.

\# Watch your exposure carefully. Early stages of a storm often reflect a broad range of lighting conditions from very bright to very dark. Expose for the middle range. As the storm approaches, light tends to diminish very quickly, so you must frequently adjust your exposure, perhaps even the speed of the film you are using.

\# Precipitation directly in front of the lens, particularly snow, tends to appear as unpleasant blobs. To photograph the precipitation, do it from inside through a window or door so that none of it is falling too close to the lens.

\# Lightning is most easily photographed at night by means of a time exposure. Set the camera on a tripod, aim it in the direction of the storm, set distance for infinity, sit back, and wait. After a lightning flash close the shutter, advance the film, and try again. You can, of course, record several lightning flashes on one frame. Daylight shots of lightning are a gamble. Take a meter reading of the sky, and set your camera diaphragm to its smallest opening. Aim the tripod-mounted camera toward the storm, and open the shutter for a period of time about twice that called for by the meter reading. If you didn't catch a lightning flash in the time period, advance a frame and try again. If you overexpose the film by keeping the shutter open longer, your lightning flash, if you should catch it, will be barely visible.

\# Time-lapse photography of storms can be exciting and dramatic. This is worth a try if you have the equipment.

• Maintain a weather log, which is simply a variation of a general sky log. Keep track of directional wind shifts over time, changes in air pressure (a good barometer is a good investment), changes in wind speed, sequence of cloud form changes, changes in humidity. Be sure to log in the time of each of these observations. Instruments to measure these changes may be bought or constructed at home. For directions on making equipment see Hillcourt or Spilhaus in Further Reading. For special weather equipment see *Handbook of Meteorological Instruments*.

FURTHER READING

AKASOFU, S.I. *Aurora Borealis: The Amazing Northern Lights*. Forest Grove, OR: Hydra Book Co., 1980.
BENTLEY, W.A., and W.J. HUMPHREYS. *Snow Crystals*. New York: Dover Press, 1962.

94

BERNARD, HAROLD W., JR. *Weather Watch: How To Make The Most of America's Changing Weather.* New York: Walker and Company, 1979.

BROWN, SLATER. *World of the Wind.* New York: Bobbs-Merrill, 1961.

BROWN, TERRY, and ROB HUNTER. *Weather Lore (2nd ed.).* New York State Mutual Book and Periodical Service, Ltd., 1981.

CAMPBELL, TIM. *Progressive Farmer's The Do-It-Yourself Weather Book.* Birmingham, AL: Oxmoor House, Inc., 1979.

CORLISS, WILLIAM R. *Handbook of Unusual Natural Phenomena.* Garden City, NY: Anchor Press/Doubleday, 1983.

DABBERDT, WALTER. *Weather For Outdoorsmen.* New York: Charles Scribner's Sons, 1981.

EDINGER, JAMES. *Watching For The Wind.* Garden City, NY: Doubleday and Co., 1967.

FORRESTER, FRANK H. *1001 Questions Answered About The Weather.* New York: Dover Publications, 1981.

Great Britain Meteorological Office. *Handbook of Meteorological Instruments.* (For surface and upper air observations.) New York: British Information Services, 1956.

HILLCOURT, WILLIAM. *New Field Book of Nature Activities and Hobbies.* New York: G.P. Putnam's Sons, 1970.

LA CHAPELLE, EDWARD R. *Field Guide to Snow Crystals.* Seattle: University of Washington Press, 1969.

LONGSTREET, STEPHEN. *Storm Watch.* New York: G.P. Putnam's Sons, 1979.

LUDLAM, F.H. *Clouds and Storms: The Behavior and Effect of Water in the Atmosphere.* College Park, PA: Pennsylvania State University Press, 1980.

NAKAYA, U. *Snow Crystals: Natural and Artificial.* Cambridge, MA: Harvard University Press, 1954.

SCHWOEGLER, BRUCE, and MICHAEL McCLINTOCK, *Weather and Energy.* New York: McGraw-Hill, 1982.

SHAEFER, VINCENT J., and JOHN A. DAY. *A Field Guide To the Atmosphere.* Boston: Houghton Mifflin Co., 1981.

SLOAN, ERIC. *The Book of Storms.* New York: Duell, Sloan and Pearce, 1956.

SPILHAUS, ATHELSTAN. *Weathercraft.* New York: Viking Press, 1953.

WATTS, ALAN. *Instant Weather Forecasting.* New York: Dodd, Mead, & Co., 1968.

————. *Instant Wind Forecasting.* New York: Dodd, Mead, & Co., 1968.

Periodicals

Weatherwise: The Magazine About Weather (bimonthly). Weatherwise, Inc., Box 230 N, Princeton, NJ 08540

GWYNNE, PETER. "Looking Into Tornados." *Audubon,* March 1982.

IDSO, SHERWOOD. "The Wild Wind of the Desert." *Arizona Highways,* August 1981.

95

CHAPTER 5

THROUGH THE SKY AND BEYOND

Ask almost anyone what are the brightest objects in the sky, and the reply is sure to include the sun, and the moon, and perhaps one or more of the bright stars, or the planet Venus. In truth the answer should be a large meteor or a towering cumulonimbus, for both these objects provide their light within earth's atmosphere—the meteor as it ignites due to atmospheric friction and the cloud as it reflects the sun's light. All the objects listed in the traditional answer exist beyond the sky as objects in space.

Because of the limitations of our sensory receptors, the ways in which our brain creates images from incoming sensory messages, and the vast, almost incomprehensible distances at which moons, stars, and planets exist from us, we tend to perceive them as if they were all in the same plane on the surface of a flattened dome above us. Indeed, that dome forms the illusory upper surface of the sky. It has been the "reality" for most of human existence, due largely to the physical limitations of our eyes. Only in the past century have we developed the tools to measure the actual distances of such objects from us and to send still other tools beyond the sky to get a less distorted view of them. In one sense, we should not include such objects in a book on the sky, but we will bow to our ancestral perception of sky and present some limited information on astronomical objects.

Our discussion will focus on what we can see from earth with the naked eye, binoculars, or small telescopes. We will examine the objects of greatest interest and beauty and those with greatest impact on the sky itself. Your exploration of modern cosmology, the origin of the universe, the nature and structure of stars, pulsars, quasars, black holes, and the like must come from other sources. This still leaves the avid sky watcher with much to seek and absorb in both the day and night skies. The clear night sky is ablaze

96

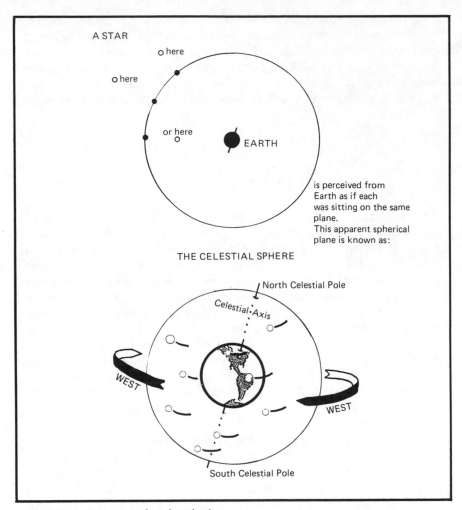

A STAR

○ here

○ here

or here
○

EARTH

is perceived from Earth as if each was sitting on the same plane.
This apparent spherical plane is known as:

THE CELESTIAL SPHERE

North Celestial Pole

Celestial Axis

WEST

WEST

South Celestial Pole

FIGURE 5.1. Perception of a celestial sphere.

with pinpricks of light of varying sizes and brightness, to say nothing of varied color. Many appear stationary, while others move about in predictable pathways. What actually are random distributions of stars and star clusters in space appear to the human mind to form distinctive and stable patterns, and the changing apparent shapes of the moon and planets have fascinated and absorbed individuals throughout human existence. As modern civilizations have evolved to spend less time under night skies, with people sleeping indoors or wandering brightly lit streets that overwhelm their perception of distant starlight, we have, as a people, been losing our appreciation of the night sky. It is a tragic loss, for as Ralph Waldo Emerson noted over a century ago: "If stars should appear one night in a thousand years, how men would believe and adore and preserve for many generations the remembrance of the city of God which had been shown."

97

Instead, stars are continuously about us, day and night, and we come to take their presence for granted. The most important of these stars to life on earth is the sun, whose visible presence separates our daily revolution about the planetary axis into periods of day and night. During the day the emission of light energy we receive from "Old Sol" is so powerful that it drowns our capacity to distinguish the lesser volume of light arriving from its stellar relatives.

OUR NEAREST STAR

The sun is relatively so near to us that we perceive it as much larger than it really is in comparison to the billions of other stars in the universe. Actually, it is only a medium-sized star in a medium-sized galaxy—the Milky Way galaxy. It was born in that galaxy about 5 billion years ago after a gestation period of around 5 billion years. Its address is toward the outer edge of the whirling galaxy, some 30,000 light years from its center. The galaxy itself is about 80,000 light years in diameter. (A light year is actually a shorthand term for the vast number of miles, roughly 6 trillion of them, that light travels The sun itself has a family of nine planets, tethered to it by invisible gravitational forces and which orbit it in a variety of more or less eliptical pathways. It is also host to the planetary moons, assorted asteroids, and a cloud of comets. Most of these are visible, at least periodically, through earth's sky window.

Like all heavenly bodies, the sun not only was born but will die. Best current estimates are that after a long period of ageing, death may come in about 5 or 6 billion years, give or take a few million. It is of no moment to us, probably not even to the human species, for both will probably have seen their demise much sooner. But, as author Robert Ardrey has noted, "We cannot even look on the sun as our proprietor, for—though it provides us with the light to see by and the shadows that regularly enfold us, the seasons that annually transform our ways, the evaporation of waters and the clemency of rain, the winds that bring us the cool breath of evening or the rain of hurricanes, though the sun's potent energies provide distinction between the lichen and the ledge it clings to, between life and death—still the sun itself must someday die as all stars die."

Untold generations of humans have been aware of the vital importance of the sun in their lives, indeed in all lives, even though they could not detail it in modern scientific terms. They intuitively knew what Walt Whitman so eloquently expressed when he wrote: "I believe a leaf of grass is no less than the journey-work of the stars." Culture after culture seeking religious explanations for worldly events turned to the sun as the major or sole deity. As deity the sun has been known as Re, Ra, Shamash, Tane, Itzamma, Ahura, Quetzalcoatl, Helios, Apollo, Balder, Mazda, Lugh, and

98

Dazhbog, among others. The respect and fears these people had for our nearest star are well summed up in a simple Native American prayer:

Thank you Sun.
Thank you for your warmth and light.
Have mercy on us human beings.
Come again tomorrow.

While the sun no longer is a deity to most modern people, it is no less vital to our lives than to those of the ancients, and we need not worship the sun to celebrate its existence. It will repay our closer acquaintanceship.

Taking a Closer Look

The sun is our day star and the only star we can see as an orb of glowing gases. All the others are so distant that we can perceive them only as points of light. But that very closeness makes the power of the radiant energy so great that it can permanently destroy the sensory receptors in our eyes if we look at it directly, particularly through a clear sky. Sometimes we can get away with a short peek in the early morning or late evening when the sun appears low in the sky and the clouds and haze filter out or scatter much of the radiant energy. However, *at no time should the sun be stared at directly.* The risk of partial or complete blindness is far too great.

How then shall we take a closer look at the sun? Indirectly. That is, we project the sun through a pinhole aperature, or a small telescope, onto a paper and view only its reflected image, as illustrated in Figure 5.2. We focus the apparatus by trial and error adjustment and never by looking through a view finder. To be sure, there are some specially designed, and expensive, filters that can be purchased and placed over the front lens of a telescope to provide reasonably safe direct viewing, but these are only for the most seasoned and knowledgeable amateurs and professionals.

FIGURE 5.2. Sun viewing setup.

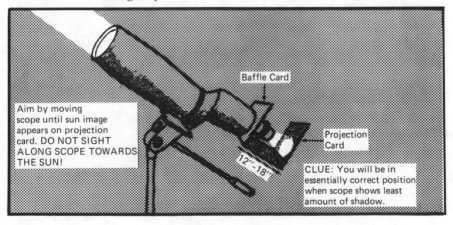

99

But why bother looking at the sun in any case; what may be seen? Periodic viewing of the sun reveals that it is more than just a homogenous gaseous sphere aglow from the nuclear fusion activity that is its basic nature. It is a seething, stormy body that sends fiery fountains arching thousands of miles above its apparent surface and shows its magnetic storms as dark spots of relatively less intense heat. These storms show up more or less regularly on the face of the sun, and as the sun rotates (about 25 days per rotation) appear to move across that face. The number and intensity of the storms vary in a fairly consistent 11-year cycle. The next peak of solar storms, or sunspots as they are commonly called, is predicted for 1990, with the fewest around 1985.

A number of sky watchers regularly project the sun onto paper and trace the outline of the orb and the various sunspots that appear. Under good magnification, these spots will appear to be two-toned, with a dark inner *umbra* and somewhat lighter *penumbra*. A series of such tracings compared or overlaid will reveal the changes in size and movement of these solar storms. Sunspot activity results in solar winds of charged particles that stimulate auroral displays here on earth and may disrupt the charged layers of the ionosphere and the radio transmissions they permit. Sky watchers recording sunspot activity will want to turn to the night sky in search of auroral activity when sunspot activity has increased.

Solar Eclipse

Solar eclipses are red-letter events for sun observers. These occur when, as the sun, moon, and earth rotate and orbit each other, the moon enters a position in which it casts its shadow on the earth. From an earthly viewpoint, the disc of the moon passes in front of the sun, virtually blocking it from our view. The area of earth where such an event is viewable is always limited, so that only a small portion of the human population can see it. Modern prediction skills and the availability of good transportation now permit more people who so wish to visit the best sites to see a particular eclipse event. Today, people seek to view eclipses, while not many generations ago our ancestors were given to grave panic at the onset of a solar eclipse, fearing that the life-giving sun might be disappearing forever. These people did not travel far, and although solar eclipses are not rare, the chances of a person seeing more than one total eclipse of the sun occur in his or her area in one lifetime was slim. They had only their oral histories to tell about other times the sun went dark.

Although the moon is about 400 times smaller than the sun, they appear to be about the same size when viewed from earth, since the sun is also 400 times farther away from the earth. Thus, the moon can appear to blot out the sun. However, the moon orbits the earth in an elliptical rather than circular path and is sometimes farther from earth than at other times. When the solar eclipse occurs at a time when the moon is at its greatest distance from earth, the lunar disc will not completely obscure the solar disc, and the moon will appear to have a thin, bright circle of light around it, an *annulus* in the astronomer's terms. This creates what is known as an *annular eclipse* as opposed to a *total eclipse*. If you are not in the exact path of the moon's shadow, you will see only a *partial eclipse;* that is, part of the solar disc will be obscured but not all of it. For the average person a partial eclipse is a more common event.

Total or partial, eclipse-viewing rules are the same as for any other sun viewing. *Do not look directly at the sun,* even briefly, without a proper filter. Do your looking with the indirect method. Proper noncommercial filters would include several layers of exposed and developed black and white film negatives. They have silver crystals which color film lacks; similarly exposed color firm *is not adequate.* Nor are any normal photographic filters or sunglasses, no matter how dark.

As the moon disc reduces the sun to a mere crescent, it is possible to spot small beads of light along the edge of the sun which have been named *Bailey's beads.* Due to a valley on the moon, the last of these beads to appear glistens brightly like a diamond, creating what is known as the "diamond ring effect." This lasts for 3 to 5 seconds, and then there is totality. Darkness prevails, except for a glowing corona around the moon. The coronal gases are always present but are overpowered by the intensity of the main orb of the sun. This corona is irregular in shape, and streamers from it reach millions of miles out from the main solar orb. Also during totality, if you look at the horizon sky in any direction, you will see a pinkish, sunsetlike glow. Unfortunately, North Americans and Europeans will have to travel to view total eclipses until essentially the next century, but it is an awesome spectacle worth the trip.

Sun Path

More practical sun observations involve recording, on a regular basis, the points at which the sun breaks above the horizon in the morning and sets in the evening. These points change slightly each day due to the tilt of the earth's axis and the changing orientation of the planet to the sun as it makes its annual orbiting trek. In the northern hemisphere the sun appears lowest to the horizon in winter and highest above it in summer. The distance between the high and low points of the sun's elevation above the horizon creates the so-called solar window, which is critical for orienting either active or passive solar energy—collecting devices. The solar window is that area of the sky from which solar collectors receive the most direct sunrays. The actual sun elevations above the horizon vary with latitude, so it is best to calculate the solar window for your property by active observation of sunrises and sunsets—activity as good for the soul as its results may be for the pocketbook.

The amateur sun watcher is limited in what he or she can observe. But the professional astronomer with expensive scientific equipment analyses the radiant spectrum of the energy from the sun, measures the speed of that light, computes the precise distances from earth to sun, investigates the energy-production process, measures changing magnetic forces, and in

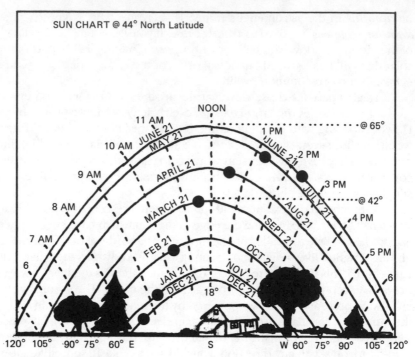

FIGURE 5.3. Sun path map.

myriad other ways reduces the mysteries of the sun to constructs the human mind can contemplate and apply to further understanding of the origins of the universe. Lacking such equipment, the amateur awaits announcement of the findings of the scientists but need not be cheated of experiencing the influence of this celestial body on the sky and living things. We feel the heat directly on our skin, experience the passing breezes and winds generated by unequal heating from solar input, see clouds formed by water evaporated by solar energy and lifted aloft to condense by the winds, enjoy the colors of the sun's visible light spectrum refracted by water drops and ice crystals or scattered by the molecules of air. The actual shape of the sky is molded by the solar winds, which also contribute to the ionization of the upper sky. Though it lies beyond our sky, the sun, in many ways, is an integral part of it.

SUN RELATIVES

For us the sun is a tyrant. During the day, when we can see it, its light is so bright it drowns out the light from its more distant relatives. It is only when earth rotation or solar eclipse blocks our view of the sun that we can see its relatives. Actually, many of the other stars are far larger and brighter than the sun, but their light must travel such far distances that its intensity is greatly reduced by the time it reaches our spot in the universe. Each photon of starlight that reaches us is not only radiant energy but fossilized time, for,

102

depending on its stellar source, it has been traveling in space for years, even thousands or millions of years. When today we spot the "sudden" brightening and enlarging of a star, an object we call a *nova,* we may be finally seeing an event that really occurred in the days of the dinosaurs or even earlier.

Although the unfolding story of the universe, its origins, and all the fascinating objects that compose it is a captivating one, we will limit ourselves to those celestial objects readily seen with the naked eye or simple binoculars and telescopes. By imposing this discipline the reader/observer is brought closer to the night scene of our ancestors than to the mind boggling perceptions of modern astronomy, but the sky is our focus here rather than the realities of the objects that lie actually beyond our sky.

There is nothing quite so awesome yet peaceful as a clear, moonless night with its star-studded canopy. Aside from the fact that cloud cover, air pollution, and increasingly, urban light pollution diminish the spectacle, it is common enough that we take it for granted. The ancients, lacking our modern technological distractions, watched the night sky more regularly, noting and naming outstanding stars and apparent star patterns. They used many stars and star patterns as mnemonic aids for spinning their myths and legends, with different stars in a pattern representing different aspects of a character, and different patterns representing different characters. These patterns came to be called *constellations,* and they are clusters of stars that seem to be located in a particular sector of the sky. Different, isolated cultures perceived somewhat different patterns which represented different legendary objects, but those cultures with some contact often shared their perceptions, and for much of Western culture, a fairly consistent cast of characters emerged. It is these ancient Western-culture constellations, with some additions made in the 1800s, that were finally compiled into a list adopted by the International Astronomical Union in 1928 and codified in 1930. This was more or less necessary to bring consistency to star mapping, and it did simplify matters greatly. Today the entire sky is divided into 88 regions, each with its characteristic constellation pattern.

Today's scientists examine the sky seeking answers to different problems than those explored by the ancient peoples. They give little attention to the old stories and legends, not only of our western society but of the Native Americans, Asians, and Australian aborigines. However, many of these stories are still fascinating, and it behooves the earnest sky watcher to look up some of the sources in the *Further Reading* in Chapter 8 and to become familiar with at least a few of these stories from around the world. Similarly, they should use the stars themselves as mnemonic aids in passing these myths and legends along to others. Today we can also use the constellations as aids to help us locate special stars or other celestial objects.

Mapping an Illusion

As mentioned earlier, we perceive all stars to be in one plane. Although it's an illusion, for practical purposes we prepare maps of the night sky that illustrate the stars all on the same plane, using different-sized dots to represent the apparent brightness of the stars. Again, modern information reveals that many stars, apparently very dim, are actually many times brighter than some that appear bright to us, but since they are very many times more distant they appear smaller and dimmer. However, these star maps prove useful to those who would explore the night sky and become familiar with some of its "skymarks." Unfortunately, there are so many millions of stars scattered through space that even those we can see with the naked eye create confusing maps. The first time one sets out with the proper star chart for the season and latitude, frustration can quickly gain the upper hand, leading to abandonment of the whole project.

It pays to unravel the confusion, slowly learning only a few key stars and constellations at a time and using those as skymarks to locate still others. You have a lifetime to get acquainted with the night sky. Savor it, don't rush it, and it will continue to be a joyous experience. For those in the northern hemisphere midlatitudes, the best two constellations to seek and learn are the Big Dipper (Ursa major) and Orion the Hunter. Using stars in these two constellations as pointers and a simple distance-judging set of hand measurements to be described shortly, you can soon learn to locate many of the other major star groupings and the brightest stars. These two star patterns are the most prominent in the sky, and the Big Dipper can be seen in any season and at any hour. Once you are secure in locating and using them to find some of the other constellations and bright stars, you will be able to use the more complicated star charts with much less frustration.

In reality, stars do move relative to one another, but the distances involved are so great that it takes many many human generations before even slight changes are perceptible to naked-eye observers. For all practical purposes, the positions of the stars are fixed in the sky, and their apparent distances from each other are likewise fixed. These distances are calibrated in the degrees of an arc. A sextant can be used to make the measurement, but there are a number of simple, rough estimates based on the human hand at full arm extension that are quite satisfactory for basic night sky orientation. They are illustrated in Figure 5.4

Once you are familiar with the different measures, study the diagrams of the Big Dipper and Orion, and use them to locate the various other stars

FIGURE 5.4. Guide to hand measurements relative to degrees of arc.

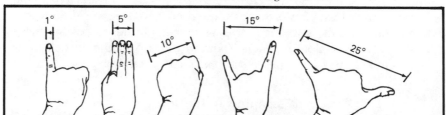

104

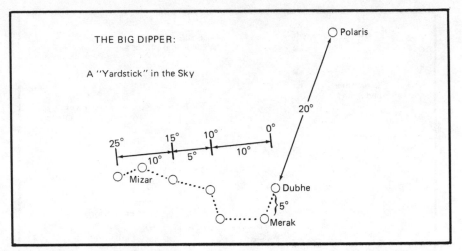

FIGURE 5.5. Big Dipper—yardstick in the sky.

FIGURE 5.6. The night sky clock. The regular movement of the Big Dipper around Polaris permits its use as a kind of sky clock. For each 15° of arc it moves from the time of your first observation, one hour of time has passed.

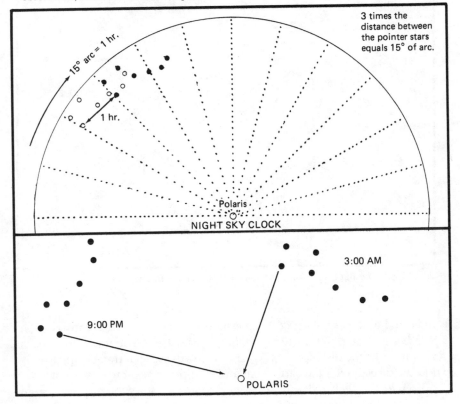

105

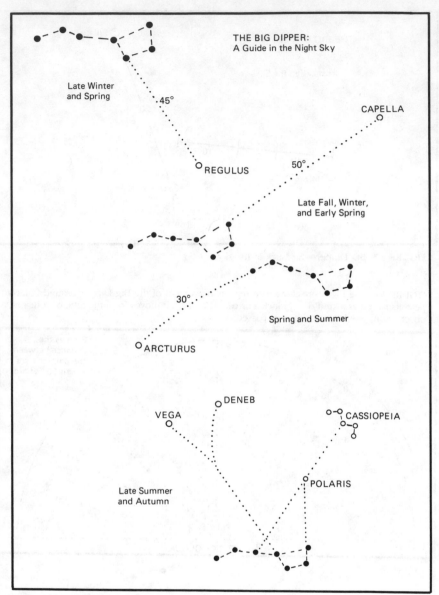

THE BIG DIPPER:
A Guide in the Night Sky

Late Winter
and Spring

45°

CAPELLA

50°

REGULUS

Late Fall, Winter,
and Early Spring

30°

Spring and Summer

ARCTURUS

DENEB

VEGA

CASSIOPEIA

POLARIS

Late Summer
and Autumn

FIGURE 5.7. The Big Dipper—as a seasonal guide to some bright stars.

indicated in the sky. Each of these stars is located in another constellation and is a starting point for learning that constellation. The first star to learn after locating the Big Dipper is Polaris, the North Star. It is the star apparently located directly over the earth's axis and so appears never to move. Polaris is not a particularly bright star, so it often requires use of the pointer system using the Big Dipper and the rough measuring tools illustrated. Polaris is also the last star in the handle of the Little Dipper (Ursa minor).

106

The importance of this faint star is that it is the pivot point for the apparent turning around us of the sky. Actually, of course, it is we who rotate, giving us a changing view of the various sectors of space with the stars that occupy each area. In general, the stars appear to move from east to west as does our day star. Stars in the north appear to circle about a point near Polaris. If you point a camera at Polaris and take an all-night exposure, the resultant photo will reveal curved tracks of light that illustrate the apparent motion of the nearby stars.

This nightly motion is not the only movement to be noted. As earth travels in its annual orbit, viewers on its surface are gradually exposed to different regions of space with different stars. Thus, we annually parade through a fixed sequence of constellations, each with distinct seasons of visibility. A dedicated all-night star watcher actually has the opportunity to see some of three seasons' worth of stars. In early evening a few of the previous season's stars are still visible, by late evening the view of the current season's stars is excellent, and by predawn one can get a brief preview of some of the next season's stellar attractions.

This nightly changing parade has its own distinct cadence. Any particular star you choose to observe will rise and set about four minutes earlier each day than it did the day before. This small amount adds up. Each week the star will rise about a half hour earlier than the previous week, and on a monthly basis that means approximately two hours earlier than the prior month. Of course, one full year later the star will be rising at the same time as when you first observed it. Rising and setting times, of course, are a mere convenience to make a point. If you see a star anywhere in the sky, it will be in that same sky location four minutes earlier the next night, and so on.

With the Big Dipper and Orion to point the way, the basic hand measurement system in mind, and an awareness of the regular progress of stars across our sky window into space, the charts of the night sky will begin

FIGURE 5.8. Orion as a guide to bright stars in the winter sky.

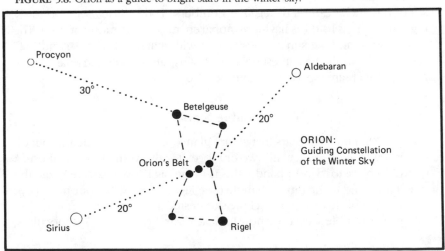

107

to make some sense, helping you to locate some of the more interesting events to be noted there. A listing of some of the sources of star charts and other astronomical events is provided at the end of this chapter.

Among the things to find are some of the colored stars. Most stars appear white or yellow, but there are some that are red, such as Antares and Betelgeuse; some blue-white, like Vega and Sirius; and some are bluer yet, such as Spica and Rigel. I have noted only some of the brighter, more obvious ones. Star viewing with binoculars and telescopes will reveal that many of the stars show this range of colors. Astronomers now know that star color indicates the heat of these bodies, with the blues being the hottest and the reds the coolest, and that temperature is a major clue to a star's age and its life cycle.

You will also quickly note that there is great variation on how bright stars appear to be. Some are very bright and quickly attract our attention, while others are very dim, in fact so dim that we can barely discern them with the naked eye. Use of a powerful telescope reveals that there are millions more stars well beyond the limits of our unaided vision. There is no necessary correlation between the apparent brightness of a star and its actual size and energy production. Light intensity dimishes relative to the square of the distance traveled, so that many stars that appear dim to us are actually much brighter and larger than those that appear bright, often only because the latter are so much closer.

Astronomers, aware of the incomprehensibility of the numbers that describe the differences in brightness between stars (for example, the day star at midday is some 16 trillion times brighter than the faintest stars visible to the naked eye), have developed a more comprehensible scale of values. This *apparent magnitude* scale is based on logarithmic rather than arithmetic relationships. Thus, for every apparent magnitude difference of 5 between two stars the brightness differs by a factor of 100. The scale was originally established with the brightest stars given a magnitude of 1, but in modern times better measurements have caused a reassessment, and the scale now includes 0 and negative numbers. Today Sirius, our brightest nighttime star, is listed as having an apparent magnitude rating of -1.4. The planet Venus and the sun are designated with magnitudes of -4 and -27 respectively, while the faintest stars most of us can see with the unaided eye are rated with an apparent magnitude of 6.

Double Stars

There are a number of stars that at first glance appear to be one star but on closer observation are actually two or more. It is always fun to locate these. A good first place to try your hand at this is in the Big Dipper. Locate Mizar, the star at the bend in the dipper handle (see Figure 5.5). With your naked eye you may be able to distinguish a little star beside it known as Alcor. Together they form a double star. If you now look at Mizar through 7×50 binoculars,

108

you will discover that that "star" itself is actually a double star. You are now ready to search the sky for more doubles. Many star charts, field guides, and atlases will guide you to other doubles. Most are only apparent through a powerful telescope.

Star Clusters

Some stars occur in clusters and are more or less gravitationally bound to each other. Individuals in a cluster have the same composition and apparently were born at the same time from the same cloud of interstellar material. Astronomers recognize *open star clusters* and *globular clusters*. Perhaps the most famous of the open star clusters, one that has intrigued many cultures, is the one we know as the Pleiades located in the constellation of Taurus. Six or seven of its stars are usually visible to the normal naked eye, and they are arranged in the pattern of a small dipper. Some individuals with acute vision can see as many as nine to eleven stars with their unaided eyes. The ability to see at least the seventh star was a basic eye test for young Native Americans. Binoculars will reveal many more stars in this cluster, and a small telescope will bring more than 100 stars into view. Nebulous wisps of light surround the cluster and are especially bright near the more luminous stars. Another open cluster found in Taurus is the Hyades, which outlines the bull's face. There are fewer stars in this cluster than in the Pleiades, and they are somewhat further apart. A few are visible to the naked eye, but binoculars or telescope reveals a great many more. In nearby Perseus there is a double cluster visible in part to the naked eye.

Globular clusters appear as single points of light to the naked eye, but when viewed with powerful binoculars or telescopes they show up as tight aggregations of many stars.

Galaxies

The largest aggregations of stars are *galaxies*. Most are so distant that most appear to us only when viewed by powerful telescopes, but one is very visible. It is the galaxy to which our solar system belongs, a galaxy we call the Milky Way. It is one of the spiral galaxies, with several arms seeming to unwind from a central nucleus (that is, it would look that way if you could look down on it from another distant galaxy). The location of the solar system in the galaxy is on one of the spiral arms toward the outer part of the galaxy such that we can only look at the rest of the galaxy on edge. This gives the impression of a luminescent stream across the sky, a sort of thin, milky white path across the sky from which the galaxy derives its name. View this path with binoculars, and it is seen to be composed of thousands of stars (actually it's about a trillion), and glowing gases and dust.

Galaxies are essentially islands of matter in the vastness of space, and except for our own Milky Way, they exist at incomprehensible distances from us. Scientists tell us also that they are all moving steadily away from us. The nearest galaxy to ours is the Great Galaxy in Andromeda, and its center is just visible to the naked eye. If you view it, the light you see left the galaxy 2.2 million years ago! And there are millions of other galaxies in the universe; spiral ones, elliptical ones, and irregular ones, all much more distant. All require telescopic aid if you are to see them.

FINDING YOUR WAY IN THE NIGHT SKY

You have already learned some simple tricks to get you started finding objects in the night sky, but there are so many things to look for once you get hooked, and such a big area to cover, that you need a map and you need to know how to read that map. Astronomers, who make the maps, have some different terms than we use on earthly maps, and you will need to gain some familiarity with them. For locational purposes the sky is modeled as if the earth were a globe suspended in the center of a larger globe called the *celestial sphere.* All the stars are conceived as if they were painted on the inner surface of that celestial sphere. At any given time you can only see half of that sphere.

Figures 5.9 and 5.10 illustrate the celestial sphere concept and some of the imaginary lines that are projected upon it, similar to those used on an earth globe—the *celestial equator* and the *prime meridian.* You will also note a dashed line that represents the solar orbit and is referred to as the *ecliptic.* Note also the *celestial poles* and the *ecliptic poles* created because of the tilt of the earth's axis. You will notice that the height of the ecliptic above the celestial equator at its high point equals the degree of tilt of the earth's axis.

To locate a star on this imaginary sphere a set of equatorial coordinates are used, equatorial in this case referring to the celestial equator. The north-south coordinate, comparable to latitude, is called *declination* and is measured in degrees north or south of the celestial equator. In the astronomical chart it will be listed by the abbreviation *Dec.* or the lower-case Greek letter delta Δ. The east-west coordinate is called *right ascension.* Although sometimes measured in degrees, it more commonly is stated in terms of hours, minutes, and seconds. This is based on the degrees of an arc. Earth turns 360° in 24 hours; thus, in 1 hour it turns through 15° of arc. In the same logic, 1 minute of time is 15′ of arc, and 1 second of time equals 15″ of arc. Sometimes, instead of the symbols just used, letters will be indicated, such as 3H45m15s. Another reference sometimes used is *celestial longitude.* It is similar to right ascension except that it is measured along the ecliptic. Since planets move close to the ecliptic, it is particularly useful for locating them.

More useful to the more casual observer are *horizontal coordinates.* To use these you assume there is a celestial dome with your horizon line as

110

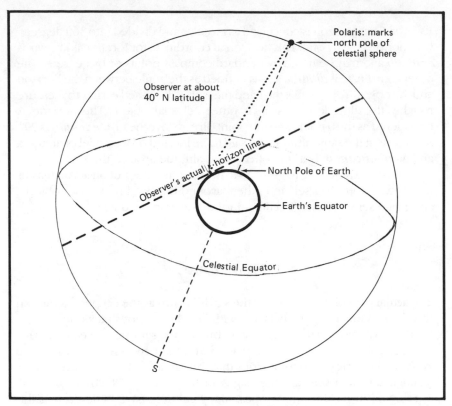

FIGURE 5.9. The celestial sphere illustrating derivation of hemisphere depicted in Figure 5.10.

FIGURE 5.10. Celestial hemisphere with key orientation lines.

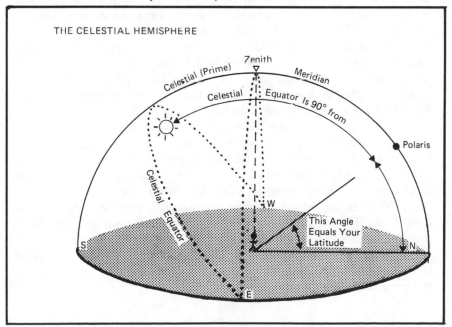

111

its floor. That horizon is conceived as circular and divided into 360 degrees, with north as the 0 point. This horizontal coordinate for location is known as *azimuth* and may be noted by standard compass points or by degrees. The other coordinate is *altitude* and is defined as the angle between the horizon and the object. You can use the hand measures discussed earlier to measure roughly the altitude of a star or other celestial object. The horizon is considered as the 0 point, and the point directly overhead, the *zenith,* is 90°. All objects at the same altitude are said to be located on a parallel of altitude, and an *almucantar* is a line of constant altitude around the sky.

It takes a little time to get used to the terminology, but once you master it, you can direct yourself and others around the sky, find various objects, and make sense of the directions in the sky charts and atlases.

THE ZODIAC

The actual path of the sun across the sky is known as the ecliptic. As the sun travels, of course, its planets go with it. They follow paths across the backdrop of the stars that are close to, but not the same as, the ecliptic. This broader pathway of the flock of planets and their moons is known as the *zodiac.* The series of constellations that the sun and planets appear to pass through during a year are the "signs of the zodiac," which are used by astrologers in making horoscopes. Many cultures have believed that the daily affairs of people are determined by the positions of the stars. There is no scientific verification of such a hypothesis, but people continue to believe it anyway. Astrological horoscopes and predictions are to be found in many daily newspapers and for sale in many stores. For sky watchers, the signs of the zodiac are more useful for quickly orienting themselves to those sections of the sky where planets may be observed. The constellations of the zodiac are Aries, the Ram; Taurus, the Bull; Gemini, the Twins; Cancer, the Crab; Leo, the Lion; Virgo, the Virgin; Libra, the Scales; Scorpious, the Scorpion; Sagitarius, the Archer; Capricornus, the Sea Goat; Aquarius, the Water Carrier; and Pisces, the Fish.

On the clearest, darkest nights you may be able to spot a faint glow along and near the ecliptic. This is called *zodiacal light* and is caused by reflection from dust grains that are part of the matter of the solar system, deriving primarily from comets. The glow is brightest nearest to the sun and fades away as we glance away from that direction. However, directly opposite the sun a fainter counterglow, or *gegenshein,* may be seen as a blob of light. Zodiacal light is best seen by viewers in midnorthern latitudes a little after sunset in March and April and just before sunrise in September and October. During the early part of the night you can usually also perceive a basic sky glow caused by upper atmospheric gases excited by solar radiation angling past the curvature of the earth.

112

THE MOON AND THE PLANETS

The positions of the stars relative to each other are for all practical purposes fixed. The actual changes that do occur are at such great distances from earth that it takes the accumulated observations of many, many human generations to reveal even minor perceptual changes. But the near motion of the planets does produce regular and perceptible change in their positions in relation to the stars. Indeed, the word *planet* derives from the Greek word for "wanderer."

Neither the moon nor the planets produce any light of their own as the stars do. They are all essentially mirrors moving through space, invisibly tethered by gravity to the source of the light they reflect. Since planets have different sized and shaped orbits and move at different speeds, they are never all viewable at the same time. This is due to the fact that planets rise and set in relation to the horizon as do the sun and moon but on their own schedules. Sometimes only one will be visible; at other times several will be on view at the same time. Those usually visible to the naked eye are Mercury, Venus, Mars, Saturn, and Jupiter.

Mercury and Venus are classified as *inferior* planets because their orbits lie between earth and the sun. The rest of the planets are *superior* planets whose orbits lie beyond that of the earth. The superior planets are seen by us on earth as illuminated discs, but the shape of the illumination of the inferior planets and our moon change as they change position relative to earth and sun. Of course, the planet doesn't change shape at all; what changes is the amount of the illuminated surface that we can see. In some positions we see the whole disc illuminated and say that the object is in its *full phase.* When it is in the opposite position, it may appear almost totally dark because we can view only its nonilluminated side. This is called its *new phase.* In the in-between positions the object appears as an increasingly larger crescent shape until we see half the illuminated surface. Then, more and more of the surface is illuminated until it finally reaches the full phase. The view is then slowly reversed, proceeding to half phase and then smaller and smaller crescents until the new phase is reached again.

Mercury

Mercury is the planet closest to the sun and thus, in the sky, never appears far from the sun, which makes it difficult to observe. Look for it during a short period after sunset and before sunrise. Best viewing is usually on those days when it rises before the sun. Use a binoculars or telescope for best viewing.

Venus

The only planet bright enough to cast shadows, Venus is the third brightest appearing object beyond the sky, bowing in brilliance only to the sun and

113

moon. When it appears shortly after sunset it is known as the "evening star," and when it rises before sunrise it becomes the "morning star." The apparent size of Venus changes as it goes through its phases. In its crescent phase it is between the earth and the sun; it is thus closer to earth and appears at its largest. During its full phase it is on the other side of the sun from earth; it is thus most distant from us and appears much smaller. In its half phase its apparent size is midway between the two extremes. It is during the ten weeks before and after it reaches its most distant point from from us that Venus switches from appearing as an "evening star" to appearing as a "morning star."

Mars

Mars is the rusty planet. Indeed, its own sky is pink due to the iron-rich dust in its atmosphere. This gives it the distinction of reflecting more reddish wavelengths, giving it a reddish hue to the eyes of the earthbound viewer. Mars is close enough to earth that we can see some of its larger features through binoculars and telescope. Look for the white patches at the poles that are its ice caps and which change in size with the Martian seasons. Several good astronomy guides will help you locate some of the larger surface features and give you clues to observing the seasonal dust storms on the planet.

Jupiter

Jupiter is far and away the largest planet in the solar system, but its distance from the sun means that it does not appear as bright as does much smaller, but closer Venus. Its apparent size, like Venus's, depends upon whether it is on a direct line with the sun but on the far side of the sun from earth, the point at which we say it is in *conjunction* with the sun, or whether it is on the same side of the sun as earth but at its furthest point from the sun, at which point we say it is in *opposition* to the sun. Since the planet appears largest to us when it is in opposition, that is the best time for viewing it. It will be in opposition in August of 1985 and in each successive year of the 1980s will be in opposition one month later.

Through a small telescope you can view the light and dark bands around the planet which are gaseous clouds pulled out into streaks by the rotation of the planet. These often show subtle colors under good viewing conditions. Sometimes you can observe a large reddish area known as the Great Red Spot. Today we know that it represents a very persistent storm area of the planet. Through the telescope you should also be able to see the four brightest of Jupiter's sixteen moons. These have been named Io, Ganymede, Europa, and Calisto after some of the mythical lovers of the god Jupiter, after whom the planet is named. The persistent observer should be able to see shadows of these moons across the planet from time to time, and note the passage of the moons behind the planet.

114

Saturn

Saturn is the planet with the hula hoops; that is, its main body has a set of concentric rings that can be seen through a small telescope, and with good viewing conditions you will be able to discern a bright inner ring, then a dark ring, and finally a less bright outer ring. These rings give the planet a unique beauty and a special place in the affection of sky watchers. The planet also has the second largest moon in the solar system, named Titan. Unfortunately, Saturn is so distant from the sun that it does not appear brighter than an eighth-magnitude star. But it can be seen as a pinpoint of light near the planet. It has many other moons, but these are visible only with powerful telescopes.

Uranus and Neptune

These two planets, though much larger than earth, are so distant that they appear only as tiny bluish or greenish dots in binoculars and telescopes. You are fortunate to locate them. The even more distant Pluto is reserved for those with quite powerful telescopes, and even professional astronomers know little about it.

Viewing Tips

You will get the best look at the planets when "seeing conditions" are good. This may not be when the air is most transparent! If the stars are twinkling a lot, even though the air seems transparent, the image will not hold steady in your viewing instrument. Celestial objects always twinkle near the horizon as their light passes through layers of more turbulent air; the higher the object is in the sky, the less likely it is to twinkle. This is particularly true of the planets, which are reflecting rather than emitting light. Often, nights with a bit of haze turn out to be better for seeing because the conditions that create such a night also create less air turbulence. Your viewing will also be best at greater altitudes, because the amount of sky you are viewing through is reduced; you are also further away from the lower-sky glow caused by the scattering of city lights. When looking for the less bright objects in the sky, choose nights when the moon is new or in crescent stages. Bright, moonlit nights have their own magic but make seeing all but the brightest stars very difficult, if not impossible.

METEORS AND COMETS

Wishing on a "falling star" is one of the charming mystical rituals that many still enjoy. It truly helps drain away tensions to lie on your back under the heavens in hope of seeing one or more of these bright streaks of light cross the sky. On an average night it is possible to see upward of ten of these random meteors if you remain alert and have a little luck. As we have stated earlier, meteors are truly among the brightest objects in the sky.

The best time for viewing meteors is after midnight. Meteors, which are actually streaks of light, are created when *meteoroids,* small chunks of matter, mostly dust to pea-sized, strike the atmosphere and are heated by friction with the air molecules. Occasionally, much larger chunks enter the atmosphere and are very bright as they burn. These are known as *fireballs.* Sometimes fireballs explode with an audible popping sound. Most meteors are totally vaporized before they get anywhere near the earth's surface, but some are large enough that only part of them is vaporized, and pieces actually reach the earth's surface. These stony or metallic remnants of the meteoroids are then known as *meteorites.*

Many meteoroids occur in the orbits of comets and are like a stream of tiny pebbles trailing after the comet. When the orbit of earth intersects one of these comet orbits, the odds of some of these meteorites striking the atmosphere and creating a meteor greatly increases. In such instances the meteors seem to be originating from one point in the sky and radiate outward from an area known as the *radiant.* Such situations are known as *meteor showers.* Meteor showers are named for the constellations in that segment of the sky where their radiant occurs. For example, the radiant of the Perseid showers is to be found in the area of Perseus, the radiant of the Lyrids in the area of Lyra, and so forth. Table 5.1 lists some of the major annual meteor showers, the date when they are at peak, their average duration in days, and the number of meteors likely to be observed per hour at peak. Numbers will be less on either side of the peak day.

Table 5.1

NAME	PEAK DATE	DURATION	METEORS/HR.
Quadrantids	January 4	2.2 days	40
Lyrids	April 21	4 days	15
Eta Aquarids	May 4	6 days	20
Delta Aquarids	July 28	14 days	20
Perseids	August 12	4.6 days	50
Orionids	October 21	4 days	25
South Taurids	November 3	?	15
Leonids	November 16	?	15
Geminids	December 13	5.2 days	50
Ursids	December 22	4 days	15

Comets have somehow become confused in the public mind with meteors. People expect a comet to be a fast-moving streak of light. Although they are traveling in their orbits at great speed, they are distant enough that their apparent motion is relatively slow. Indeed, we can usually follow the

116

passage of a particular comet for several weeks or more. Comets are actually masses of frozen matter traveling in eccentric, elliptical orbits around the sun. The head of a comet is a ball of ices mixed with rock and dust. As the comet approaches the sun, however, usually when it gets nearer than the orbit of Mars, the solar energy converts the ices to gases. This also frees some of the dust particles. These reflect sunlight and give a hazy glow or *coma* around the head. As the comet continues to approach the sun, more of the gases and dust are freed and pushed away from the head by the solar wind. This creates the glowing *tail* of the comet. As the comet circles the sun, solar wind keeps the tail always pointing away from the sun, so that as the comet is heading away from the sun its tail precedes it. When the comet gets beyond Mars, it refreezes as it continues on its long elliptical journey. Although comets are not uncommon, most are seldom seen except by professional and dedicated amateur astronomers. Most do not follow paths that bring them close enough to the sun to become bright and visible to the average viewer. Perhaps once a decade a bright one appears.

THE MOON

No celestial object is held in greater affection than the moon, with the possible exception of the sun, which after all is the source of the moonlight. This bright orb captures human imagination in many ways. We have been inclined to see vague, facelike features in the light and dark patterns of the full moon; we watch it go through its various phases and find beauty in all of them; we have discovered the effect of the lunar gravity in causing the twice-daily ocean tides. Agricultural cultures have long used the phasing of the moon to guide planting and harvesting, and some believe that at times the moon can affect human behavior and cause some to become insane.

The same lunar gravitational force that generates ocean tides also generates tidal effects in the sky, causing the atmosphere always to bulge slightly in the direction of the moon. There is increasing evidence that minitidal effects, with resultant changes in air pressure, affect the fluids in living creatures as well. In some situations this effect may be enough to cause subtle changes in behavior, making the old belief that the moon could make people mad more plausible. Shakespeare wrote that "it is the very error of the moon; she comes more near the Earth than she was wont, and makes men mad." Such lunar-generated madness gave rise to the term *lunacy* for physiological craziness. The reproductive cycle of many species, including humans, is linked to lunar cycles also. It is little wonder that the moon is linked to romance in our culture. Of course, there are those who see a strong link between romance and lunacy.

With the naked eye it is easy to follow the changes in the moon through its 29½-day *synodic period.* That is the time it takes to travel from one conjunction with the sun to another. The actual time it takes the moon to

117

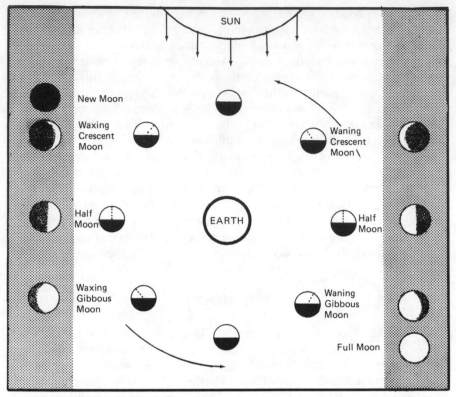

FIGURE 5.11. The phases of the moon.

orbit the earth is only 27⅓ days, but because of the relative motion of the earth in its orbit it takes the longer period to achieve a return to conjunction. It is the synodic period that is used in calculating lunar calendars. At the *new* phase the moon is between the earth and the sun. The far side of the moon is illuminated, but we can't see it. (Actually, we often do see the dark side as being faintly illuminated. This occurs because of *earthshine,* the reflection of light from the sun off earth to the dark side of the moon.) After new moon the amount of illuminated surface that we can see steadily increases, or *waxes.* First we see crescent moons up to the point of half the moon being illuminated. Beyond that point more than half is seen, and the shape of the growing illumination bulges. At this stage it is called a *gibbous* moon. When the earth is between the sun and the moon, the full lunar disc is illuminated and is called a *full* moon. The cycle then reverses itself from gibbous, to half, to crescent phases, back to new moon. In this half of the cycle the moon is said to be *waning.*

You may well wonder how you know whether the crescent or gibbous stage you are seeing is waxing or waning if you have not been following the pattern. With crescent phases, observe the direction the horns of the crescent are pointing. If they point left, the moon is waxing; if right, it is waning.

118

The horns of the crescent always point away from the sun. The waxing half-moon will have the straight side on the left; the reverse is true for the waning half-moon. Similarly, the bulge of a waxing gibbous moon is to the left and of a waning gibbous moon to the right.

The moon rises at a specific time each night depending upon which phase it is in. This is because the phase is determined by the angle between the moon, the earth, and the sun. A full moon rises when the sun sets, while a new moon rises when the sun rises and sets when the sun sets. The moon rises about 50 minutes later each night. The half-moon that occurs about one week after the noon moon will rise about noon and set about midnight. That puts it at its highest point in the sky about sunset. It is fun to sketch the moon each night for a month or more, noting the phase and its position in the sky at that hour. You will, in time, learn where and when to look to find the moon. The moon can often be seen in the daytime, and once you familiarize yourself with its traveling habits, you will know where and when to look for the moon in daytime as well as at night.

The rotation period of the moon is such that it always keeps the same side toward earth. With binoculars or telescope you can see a great deal of the detail of the lunar surface. It is pocked with craters and has broad, flat plains. These have all been mapped and named, and there are good field guides to help you identify the various named features. It is these features that cause the irregular, changing shape of the *terminator,* that line that separates the lighted surface from the dark surface of the moon.

At the time of full moon the earth is casting a shadow in the direction of the moon. There is a dark inner shadow or *umbra* and a less dark outer *penumbra.* At times the moon's orbit takes it inside the shadow, causing a *lunar eclipse.* If the moon passes through only the penumbra, it will only seem to grow dim. This is a *penumbral eclipse.* If it passes into the zone of the umbra, either a partial or total eclipse is possible, depending upon how completely it enters the umbral zone.

When the full moon rises, it often seems much larger than it does in the evening when it is higher in the sky. The setting or rising sun may similarly appear much larger. But it's all an illusion. You can prove this to yourself with an aspirin. An aspirin tablet is only a little larger than the apparent size of the moon when you hold the tablet between thumb and forefinger at arm's length. Even when the moon seems enormous on the horizon, the aspirin tablet will still cover it. Explaining the illusion is what creates the headache. At one time it was believed that the phenomenon was caused by atmospheric refraction, or by the orientation of the eye in its socket, or by the comparison of the relative sizes of objects near the horizon with the moon. The real explanation lies in how our brain interprets what enters through the eyes. The two diagrams in Figure 5.12 help clarify the explanation. The first shows how our brain interprets objects inside two parallel lines that appear to converge at the horizon. Block A and Block B are the same dimensions, but we perceive B as larger. The second diagram illustrates the arch of the celestial sphere as we actually perceive it. To

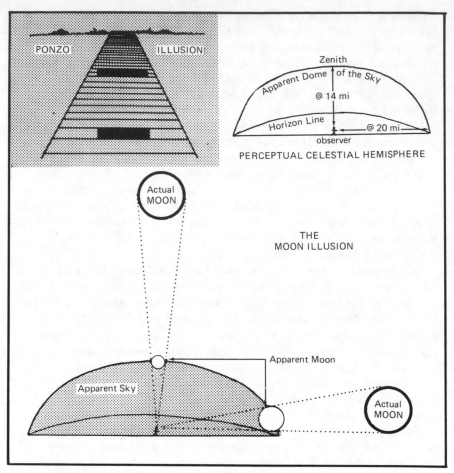

PONZO ILLUSION

Zenith
Apparent Dome of the Sky
@ 14 mi
Horizon Line
@ 20 mi
observer

PERCEPTUAL CELESTIAL HEMISPHERE

Actual MOON

THE
MOON ILLUSION

Apparent Moon

Apparent Sky

Actual MOON

FIGURE 5.12. The moon illusion.

us it appears to be a greater distance to the horizon than to the zenith. We perceive a rather flattened dome rather than the true hemisphere that illustrators usually draw. The lower diagram shows how this deludes us into believing that the moon near the horizon is actually larger.

Large or small, the moon remains a beautiful object worthy of an observer's attention throughout the year. The night sky as a whole is filled with interesting objects and events to delight the eye and puzzle the mind. Our space shots have generated mountains of data about our neighbors beyond the sky, and we have even had men walking on the moon. In one sense this has removed some of the mystery, but in true scientific fashion almost every mystery solved generates several new ones. However, knowing data about the various celestial bodies in no way diminishes their beauty from one generation to the other. No matter how much we learn about the

120

origin of the universe and its long-term future, the mass of twinkling stars on a clear night will still make the pulse tingle, stroke our aesthetic sense, and provide a stimulus to our spiritual side no matter what set of specific beliefs we hold.

SKY-OBSERVER ACTIVITIES

• If you find tracking sunspot activity particularly intriguing, you may want to become active with the solar group of the American Association of Variable Star Observers, which keeps track of sunspot activity. (American Association of Variable Star Observers [AAVSO], 187 Concord Ave., Cambridge, MA 02138.

• Set up a telescope or pinhole viewer as in Figure 5-2, and project the sun so you can locate sunspots. Draw the sun and the spots on the card, and redo the setup each day for a week or more. Use a different color to mark the sunspots each day, and you will be able to graphically follow their movement across the face of the sun for the period of time of your observations. The American Association of Variable Star Observers (187 Concord Ave., Cambridge, MA 02138) has a special group that keeps track of sunspots. You may want to contact them and share data.

• Get out and observe meteors, particularly during one of the showers. Find a comfortable place, away from city lights, where you can lie back the sky. Then count, and record, the number seen in an hour; during a good shower you may do better to count the number seen in 15-minute periods. If you develop a strong interest in meteors, you may want to report your findings to, or even join, the American Meteor Society, Department of Physics and Astronomy, SUNY, Geneseo, NY 14454, or the British Meteor Society, 26 Adrian Street, Dover Kent, CT17 9AT, England.

• Familiarize yourself with the major objects in the night sky through the season. Begin with the circumpolar constellations. When you have mastered them, gradually expand your recognition of major patterns season by season. Locate the zodiac, and follow the movements of the brighter patterns as they move along this pathway.

Start with some simple star charts, and become familiar with how they work. Once you are comfortable with these, take on some of the more complex ones. Do some observing of stars with binoculars; use at least 7× magnification. You may become interested enough to graduate to a small reflector or refracting telescope.

• Amateur sailors, and others, may want to learn how to use a sextant to locate star positions, and/or to use the simpler but less accurate hand references to do the same in order to use stars for navigational purposes.

121

FURTHER READING

BUDLONG, JOHN P. *Sky and Sextant.* New York: Van Nostrand Reinhold, 1981.

CHARTRAND, MARK R. III, and HELMUT K. WIMMER. *Skyguide—A Field Guide for Amateur Astronomers.* New York: Golden Press, 1982.

DICKINSON, TERENCE. *Nightwatch, An Equinox Guide To Viewing the Universe.* Ontario: Camden House Publishing, Ltd., 1983.

GALANT, ROY A. *Our Universe.* Washington, D.C.: National Geographic Society, 1980.

KALS, W.S. *How To Read The Night Sky.* Garden City, NY: Doubleday & Company, 1974.

MENZEL, DONALD H., and JAY M. PASCHOFF. *A Field Guide To The Stars and Planets.* Boston: Houghton Mifflin Co., 1983.

MOCHE, DINAL L. *Astronomy, A Self-Teaching Guide.* 2nd ed. New York: John Wiley & Sons, Inc., 1981.

MOORE, PATRICK. *Astronomical Telescopes and Observatories for Amateurs.* New York: W.W. Norton & Company, 1973.

———*The Picture History of Astronomy.* New York: Grosset and Dunlap, 1972.

MUIRDEN, JAMES. *Astronomy With Binoculars.* New York: Harper and Row, Thomas Y. Crowell, 1979.

RAYMO, CHET. *365 Starry Nights: An Introduction to Astronomy for Every Night of the Year.* Englewood Cliffs, NJ: Prentice-Hall, Inc., 1982.

REY, H.A. *The Stars—A New Way To See Them.* Enlarged World Wide edition. Boston: Houghton Mifflin Co., 1976.

SHERROD, P. CLAY, and THOMAS L. KOED. *A Complete Manual of Amateur Astronomy.* Englewood Cliffs, NJ: Prentice-Hall, Inc., 1981.

WHIPPLE, FRED L. *Orbiting the Sun, Planets and Satellites of the Solar System.* Cambridge, MA: Harvard University Press, 1981.

Periodicals

Sky and Telescope (monthly). 49 Bay State Rd., Cambridge, MA 02238.

PART II
BIOLOGY OF THE SKY

CHAPTER 6

LIFE
IN THE SKY

Sitting on a windswept rocky promontory along the Kittatinny Ridge on a November day, eagerly anticipating the appearance of the next migrating hawk or eagle, can be a chilling but exhilarating experience. All the ridges in the area form a chain curving from northeast to southwest. As the prevailing northwesterly winds of fall sweep into these ridges, they are deflected upward, creating updrafts that these handsome birds skillfully ride on their annual journey southward. It really stirs the adrenalin of the gravity-bound observer to watch a majestic eagle riding free on the wind only a few hundred yards away. You may see the keen eye turned to take in both you and the vast panorama spread out below it and you feel a flush of envy, perhaps even jealousy. As you watch it drift by on outstretched wings, its biofeedback systems automatically maneuver the tail or trim the secondaries (a set of wing feathers) to optimize the opposing forces of lift and gravity as the bird first rises, then glides downward to the next area of updraft. The great bird seems perfectly adapted to a life in the sky.

On the other hand, one might ask whether the eagle is adapted to life in the sky or the sky is adapted to the life in the eagle. We might even ask if the sky could be adapted to the life in all of us. Absurd questions? Not at all. The answer is that both are true. The sky around us today is made up of quite different gases, in markedly different percentages, than existed in the primordial sky prior to the appearance of life; a sky then rich in methane, ammonia, hydrogen, and water. In those days oxygen was rare, and its triatomic form, ozone, even rarer. This meant that there was very little shielding layer in the stratosphere to reduce the life-threatening ultraviolet rays. The earliest life forms, according to best current evidence, were anaerobic, single-celled organisms that dwelled in muds and soils to avoid

124

FIGURE 6.1. Eye to eye with the eagle. Jack Swedberg photo.

the direct powers of incoming radiation. But the very processes of life utilized methane and ammonia metabolically and released oxygen, and the nature of the atmosphere changed as new life forms evolved to utilize carbon dioxide and oxygen. As oxygen increased so did ozone, and the increased stratospheric shield allowed life to come out of hiding and expose itself more safely to the sky. A whole set of interlocking cycles of the utilization of gases and minerals from earth, seas, and sky evolved. This established a self-regulating system dependent upon life to use and excrete those gases and minerals. The increasing diversity of life forms adapted to a seemingly infinite set of opportunities. These life forms shifted the details of life in any given era or place but not the gross systems of cyclic material flows. It appears as if our sky was shaped by life and new life adapts to conditions and opportunities of the sky. On earth, the sky and life coevolved and coadapted. The eagle and the human and the sky are one. At first glance they seem to be separate, unrelated entities, but in reality they are only

125

separate components of a living megasystem. Scientist James Lovelock, who developed the hypothesis of this megasystem, has called it *Gaia*. In essence, his hypothesis is that "the entire range of living matter on Earth, from whales to viruses, and from oaks to algae, could be regarded as constituting a single living entity, capable of manipulating the Earth's atmosphere to suit its overall needs and endowed with faculties and powers far beyond those of its constituent parts." Central to Lovelock's thinking is that the atmosphere, our sky, is today really an extension of the biosphere, the realm of life.

The increasing evidence for this point of view comes from the study of the atmospheres of other planets and the radical ways in which our atmosphere differs from those. Lovelock states that his experiments and those of his colleagues have

> convinced us that the composition of the Earth's atmosphere was so curious and incompatible a mixture that it could not possibly have arisen or persisted by chance. . . . The chemical composition of the atmosphere bears no relation to the expectations of a steady-state chemical equilibrium. The presence of methane, nitrous oxide, and even nitrogen in our present oxidizing atmosphere represents violation of the rules of chemistry to be measured in tens of orders of magnitude. Disequilibria on this scale suggests that the atmosphere is not merely a biological product, but more probably a biological construction: not living, but like a cat's fur, a bird's feathers, or the paper of a wasp's nest, an extension of a living system designed to maintain a chosen environment. Thus the atmospheric concentration of gases such as oxygen and ammonia is found to be kept at an optimum value from which even small departures could have disastrous consequences for life.

SKY DWELLERS

Other than truly aquatic creatures, almost all the plants and animals you are most familiar with are sky dwellers. To be sure, they live *on* the land because of the forces of gravity, but they live *in* the sky. The sky has much more moment to moment impact on their lives than does the land. So finely adjusted is the internal counterpressure of our cells and organs that we do not feel the roughly fifteen pounds of pressure from the sky on every square inch of our bodies unless we make a rapid ascent to places of less pressure or descend rapidly in a mine shaft where the pressure is greater. Normally, we are not conscious of the ongoing rhythmic breathing in and out of chunks of sky during which we mine it for oxygen and dump our waste carbon dioxide. Nor are we normally aware that with every step we are pushing ourselves through the sky. Only in the teeth of a strong wind do we become conscious of that fact and of the effort that moving through the sky may take. The sky transmits the sound waves our ears and brains are adapted to hear, and at the same time it is the dumping ground for many of the wastes of our metabolism—water dumped through lungs and skin, volatile oils from perspiration, and the digestive gases we discreetly refer to as burps and flatulants. Actually, though we tend to think of many of these bodily wastes as socially embarrassing, they are actually important contributions to

126

POGO'S SOLUTION

FIGURE 6.2. "Pogo's Solution" from *Impollutable Pogo* by Walt Kelly. Courtesy Mrs. Walt Kelly.

the nature of the sky and contribute, en masse, to the self-regulating, life-sustaining mechanisms of Gaia and its sky organ. I have spoken in this paragraph primarily of humans but all is true, in general, of other living things as well, although they may have different adaptations to achieve the same ends: intake of vital materials and dispersal of metabolic wastes.

The sky is our most intimate environment, the one with which we are literally in constant contact. It is this constancy and intimacy which cause us to take it so much for granted. We also generally take the broader Gaian role as transporter and disperser for granted, except for our envy of those creatures that have adapted to moving freely in the sky with only intermittent contact with the earth. From earliest times humans have envied bird, bat, and butterfly the gift of flight. We have also observed, and eventually emulated, some of those creatures that take to the sky with something less than sustained flight; witness the development of the parachute and the balloon.

THE DRIFTERS

Sustainable, controlled flight is clearly not the only way organisms move through the air. Perhaps as many species are drifters at some time in their lives as are true fliers. And drifters are found across a broader spectrum of living things. Viruses and bacteria attach to motes of dust, and once blown aloft on the wings of the winds may remain airborne for long periods of time

127

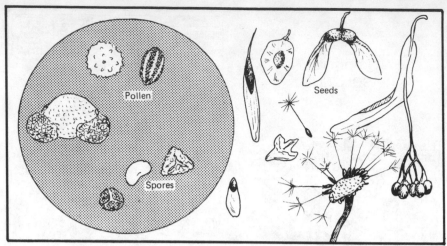

Pollen

Seeds

Spores

FIGURE 6.3. Drifters.

until, as components of condensation nuclei, they find themselves at the heart of a snowflake or raindrop en route back to earth. The pollen of many plants depends upon the wind for dispersal. The ride is usually relatively short but on occasion may be quite sustained, involving high roller coaster rides in growing cumulus clouds until it is eventually washed from the clouds in rain; a rain so full of pollen that it appears yellow or at least leaves yellow rings around the evaporating puddles. The seeds of many field flowers and trees of open areas have adapted to the drifter's life, with specialized structures such as cottony tufts that catch the breeze and resist the downward pull of gravity for some time; winglike protrusions that cause the seed to whirl, sideslip, and drift away from the parent; and those that mechanically launch their seeds into the air, more like bullets or rockets than parachutes or gliders. The spores of many of the fungi are so minute that they drift for long times and distances, like the pollen. The large ranges of many fungal species, often spanning several continents separated by oceans, are possible only because of the long sky flights of their motelike spores. These tiny life forms are extremely tough, for they must survive dessication, rapid changes in temperature (sometimes dropping very low), and increased exposure to potentially deadly radiations.

The animal realm also includes a variety of drifters. Among the more obvious, particularly in late summer or fall, are the spiders. Anna Botsford Comstock wrote:

> If we look across the grass some warm sunny morning or evening of early fall, we see threads of spider silk clinging everywhere; these are not regular webs for trapping insects, but are single threads spun from grass stalk to grass stalk until the fields are carpeted with glistening silk. We have a photograph of a plowed field, taken in autumn, which looks like the waves of a lake; so completely is the ground covered with spider threads that it shows the "path of the sun" like water.
>
> When we see so many of these random threads, it is a sign that the younger spiders have started on their travels, and it is not difficult then to find one in

128

FIGURE 6.4. Spiderling ready for liftoff.

the act. The spiderling climbs up some tall object, like a twig or a blade of grass, and sends out its thread of silk upon the air. If the thread becomes entangled, the spiderling sometimes walks off on it, using it as a bridge, or sometimes it begins again. If the thread does not become entangled with any object, there is soon enough given off for the friction of the air current upon it to support the weight of the body of the little creature, which promptly lets go its hold of earth as soon as it feels safely buoyed up, and off it floats to lands unknown. Spiders thus sailing through the air have been discovered in midocean.

Most spider species go through this ballooning activity as a sort of "rite of passage" to adulthood. It certainly has a weeding-out effect on the population of young spiders, for they face many life and death trials: extreme temperatures, capture by birds and insects, prolonged hunger, and landing in inappropriate habitats. But some do survive, land in suitable habitats, and proceed to produce a new generation of ballooning adventurers. The challenge of such a way of life has not been entirely lost upon our poets. Walt Whitman wrote:

A noiseless, patient spider,
I mark'd where on a little promontory it stood isolated,
Mark'd how to explore the vacant vast surrounding,
It launch'd for filament, filament, filament out of itself:
Ever unreeling them, ever tirelessly speeding them.
And you O my soul where you stand,
Surrounded, detached, in measureless oceans of space,
Ceaselessly, musing, venturing, throwing, seeking the spheres to connect them,
Till the bridge you will need be form'd, till the ductile anchor hold;
Till the gossamer thread you fling catch somewhere, O my soul.

Spiders are not alone in spinning threads to launch themselves adrift to unknown landings. A number of caterpillars, such as those of the gypsy

129

moth, follow this behavior. Most are quite fuzzy, which adds to their buoyancy while they are very young and have not yet gained much mass from foraging upon the leaves. Once aloft, they drift until they reach a hill which the wind tends to override. Then, on the other side, the downdraft deposits the voracious little caterpillars. Thus, advancing infestations of such creatures often start near the tops of hills and work their way downhill. Their distribution follows the prevailing winds of the season in that area.

THE GLIDERS

A variety of vertebrate animals have evolved adaptations that increase their surface and thus their air resistance, permitting them to glide from heights to some lower surface. There is the Borneo flying frog, and other members of its genus *Rhacophorus,* with enlarged toe webbing that acts like a parachute when the frog leaps. There are snakes of the genus *Chrysopelea* that can flatten their ribs out for a similar purpose, and some lizards, such as flying geckos and the flying dragon of the genus *Draco,* with flaps of skin along their sides that can be unfolded outward by elongated ribs to create a gliding surface. Several mammal groups have species capable of regular gliding locomotion. These include the marsupial gliding possums of the genus *Petaurus,* the colugos or flying lemurs of the order Dermoptera, and the flying squirrels of the genus *Glaucomys,* with which some of you may have at least a nodding acquaintance, as they are not uncommon in the wooded areas of much of North America. All of these mammals have folds of skin along their sides which can be extended by various cartilaginous rods at wrist and ankle.

Most of these gliders have only a minimum of control over their glidepath once they have launched. However, some, such as the flying squirrels, can perform some midglide course corrections by maneuvering one or the other of the leg pairs to cause sideslipping (that is, tipping the resistance more to one side or the other). Their flattened tails also provide some rudderlike maneuverability. In general, we can say, however, that the effective "wing" area of gliders is small and the loading on that wing large, so that all have a rather steep glide angle and high landing speed. Lift is small in relation to gravitational pull, although it is greater than in those animals that have no such gliding adaptations. Gliding is an early step toward the evolution of sustained flight.

There are also the various flying fishes, which are somewhat intermediate in their ability between gliding and true flight. They are water creatures, not sky creatures, but have adapted to retreat into the sky temporarily to avoid aquatic predators. There are two major groups of such fishes: the flying gurnards (Dactylopteriformes) and the flying fish (Exocoetidae). The flying fishes have an elongation of the lower half of the tail fin that helps accelerate them with a swimming motion even after the

130

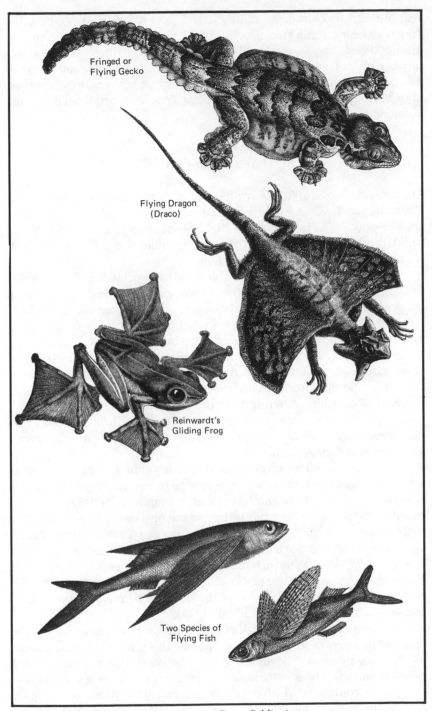

Fringed or
Flying Gecko

Flying Dragon
(Draco)

Reinwardt's
Gliding Frog

Two Species of
Flying Fish

FIGURE 6.5. Cold-blooded gliders. Courtesy Dover Publications.

rest of the fish is airborne, and they have greatly enlarged pectoral fins (the ones near the gills) that provide the flight surface. Their pelvic fins are also modified to act somewhat like the elevators on an airplane. These fish are capable of controlled glides of over 150 feet and may actually flap the pectoral fins much as a bird flaps its wings. They are sea creatures, however, and their respiration depends upon the sea. True sustained flight thus must continue to elude them.

SUSTAINABLE FLIGHT

Only insects, birds, and bats are biologically capable of true sustainable flight. Humans have gained the power of true flight only by first understanding the principles that make such flight possible and then designing and building mechanical structures that compensate for our physical and physiological limitations relative to flight.

Although the specifics are complex, the basic principles that underlie flight are relatively simple. To fly, an object moving through the air must continue to generate more upward-directed lift forces than the downward-directed pull of gravity. A rock thrown, or a bullet fired, passes through the air continually encountering frictional air resistance that slows it down until its forward momentum is increasingly less than the pull of gravity. It angles downward until friction slows it completely and gravity finally claims it for the earth. The distance it is airborne is a function of the initial thrust it received. This is little different from the situation of the gliding animals, except that they are adapted to provide a bit more lift, which keeps them aloft longer than could be expected from the limited thrust they can generate with their leg muscles.

To generate lift an object should be fairly thin and smooth, with a rounded forward surface that will cause the air to pass easily over and under it. Preferably, it should be *cambered;* that is, slightly arched. This shape is called an *airfoil* and is the typical shape of the bird or airplane wing. As an airfoil passes through the air, it encounters two major aerodynamic forces: *drag,* which is resistance to forward motion and tends to slow the object down, and *lift,* which is the upward force. The amount of both these forces is dependent upon the angle of the airfoil in relation to the direction of the air flow. This angle is referred to as the *angle of incidence,* and as it increases so, too, do both drag and lift.

Air passing over an airfoil does so in layers, with the molecules in the various thin layers moving at different speeds. This is referred to as *laminar air flow.* Air flow over the airfoil is deflected downward both above and below it, and so there is an increase in pressure from below and a decrease in pressure from above which results in a general upward force. (See Figure 6-7.) As the angle of incidence increases, the upward force increases, but more of the surface of the airfoil is presented to the air flow so that resist-

132

Pterodactyl

Rhamphorhyncus

Archaeopteryx

Petrel

Kestrel

Bat

FIGURE 6.6. Sustained flyers, including some long-extinct pioneers. Courtesy Dover Publications.

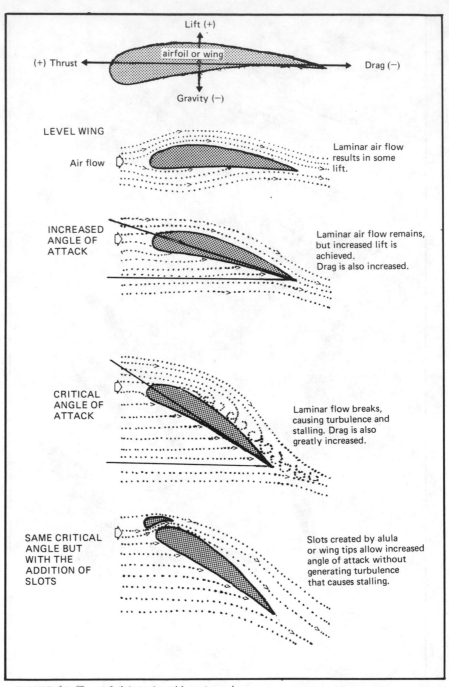

Lift (+)

airfoil or wing

(+) Thrust

Drag (−)

Gravity (−)

LEVEL WING

Air flow

Laminar air flow results in some lift.

INCREASED ANGLE OF ATTACK

Laminar air flow remains, but increased lift is achieved. Drag is also increased.

CRITICAL ANGLE OF ATTACK

Laminar flow breaks, causing turbulence and stalling. Drag is also greatly increased.

SAME CRITICAL ANGLE BUT WITH THE ADDITION OF SLOTS

Slots created by alula or wing tips allow increased angle of attack without generating turbulence that causes stalling.

FIGURE 6.7. The airfoil (wing) and how it works.

134

ance, or drag, is increased as well. Generally, the lift forces are ten or more times greater than the drag forces. However, with large wings at high speeds the amount of increased lift with increased angle of incidence does not continue indefinitely. Rather, at certain critical angles drag forces increase sharply, and air molecules flowing over the wing separate from the top surface of the wing, causing turbulence and a great reduction in lift. This creates the situation known as a *stall,* and the object will fall until the wings can be brought once again into a situation where the angle of incidence generates laminar air flow over the wing, and appropriate lift is restored.

With large wings, angles between 5° and 10° may induce a stall, but with smaller wings and slower air speeds it is more difficult to generate the turbulence that precipitates a stall. Some insect wings continue to give useful lift at angles of incidence as high as 45°. As you might imagine, the challenge lies in being able to adjust the angle of incidence to the air speed. This means dealing not only with the speed the flier generates in a forward direction but also with the oncoming speed of any winds. This is where dealing with the simple principles becomes complex. The object is, of course, to continue to generate enough lift to equal the animal's, or airplane's, weight. For each creature there is a minimum thrust or ground speed that must be attained to achieve minimum lift for flight, and angles of incidence which must be avoided or adapted for if unwanted stalling is to be prevented. Some species deliberately invoke stalling angles of incidence as part of their landing technique and/or as a device to permit rapid changes of direction while airborne.

Birds have evolved physical and behavioral adaptations to reduce stalling speeds and thus increase their range of options for remaining airborne. There is the *alula,* sometimes called the *bastard wing,* which can be extended as a small leading edge flap to delay the breaking away of the air flow into turbulence, thus allowing greater than normal angles of incidence. The birds may lower their secondary wing feathers, thus increasing the camber of the wing to create more lift, or they may depress and fan the tail or separate the primary wing feathers so that each forms a smaller wing with lower stalling speed. Bats have considerable flexibility in changing the camber of their wings and may use the tail membrane in a manner similar to the way birds depress and fan the tail feathers. Some bats have a wider flap of skin running from shoulder to thumb that may be used similarly to a bird's alula. Insect adaptations will be looked at in more detail a bit farther along in this chapter.

All creatures that have developed sustainable flight—even those that spend much of their time aloft, soaring rather than flapping—have a wide range of anatomical and physiological adaptations that allow them to make the rapid adjustments of their airfoils that sustain lift and power them forward when desired. Flight is a high-energy enterprise, and fliers must have ready access to supplies of energy or the ability to store it in a

Swift	Grackle
RAPID FLAPPING FLIGHT WING	GENERAL PURPOSE FLIGHT WING

FIGURE 6.8. Silhouettes of flapping wing shapes.

lightweight fashion. Large fliers have generally developed the soaring habit whereby they can get the most lift at the least expenditure of energy. To the sky watcher it is soaring flight, with its apparent effortlessness, that stimulates the imagination, although flapping flight is the most common mode.

Flapping Flight

Even those birds that soar for hours must be capable of flapping flight at some times, particularly at takeoff and in calm air. Whereas soaring flight depends primarily on maintaining lift and preventing stalling, flapping flight must simultaneously achieve lift greater than the animal's weight and forward thrust greater than drag.

Downstroke of the wing provides thrust as the resultant force of the forward movement of the animal and the downward movement of the wing. In essence, for a brief moment the creature is acting as if it were in a downward glide. If the upstroke were equivalent to the downstroke, an opposite and equal force would be generated and would, in essence, cancel out the advantage gained by the downstroke. Obviously, this does not happen. Wings have joints and are essentially hinged. Thus, they can be folded or twisted to reduce the wing area on the upstroke, or change the angle of incidence, or alter the spread of the primaries so that the counterforce on the upstroke is somewhat less than the downstroke force. There are some species, however, that can achieve little more than preventing greater loss on the upstroke than is gained on the downstroke.

In normal flapping flight the downstroke has a high angle of incidence which produces considerable lift and some drag. This results, overall, in a large upward movement and a small forward one, while on the upstroke the angle of incidence is reduced so the wing produces some lift and drag but no thrust.

Flapping flight is energy-intensive, and those that use it are limited in the duration of their time aloft because they must always be near a refueling supply. Those that migrate long distances over areas bereft of suitable energy sources must be able to store concentrated energy supplies in the form of relatively lightweight fat that can be carried with them.

Some species of birds, bats, and insects are capable of *hovering* flight,

136

which means that they are able to generate sufficient lift without thrust. To achieve this they must be able to twist their wings considerably to produce essentially symmetrical figure-eight strokes that have a positive angle of incidence at both halves of the stroke. This produces lift on both halves of the stroke.

The basic anatomy of most flying species is such that the limbs move up and down. Those that hover generally do so by changing the angle of their bodies from horizontal to vertical while hovering and then orient themselves back to the horizontal, and use asymmetrical wing strokes, for forward flight. Hovering generally requires more power than forward flight and creates the problem of how to generate enough steady air flow over the wing surface to generate adequate lift. In the figure-eight stroke the wing moves through only about a 120° arc before reversing and thus does not generate as much lift as it would in forward flight. Most hoverers compensate for this by clapping the wings together at the top of the stroke; then they rotate them apart before pulling them downward. This generates air flow around the wing before the effective stroke begins and allows considerable additional lift. Some nonhovering birds use a similar *clap-fling* maneuver at takeoff for an initial boost to the lift.

Some of the most skilled and spectacular fliers among the birds are primarily flapping fliers, and many of them spend many hours on the wing. Swifts and swallows fall into this category, as do nighthawks, whippoorwills, and others of the goatsucker clan. These birds are all adept at rapid aerial pursuit and capture of their insect prey and are capable of rapid twisting and turning flight maneuvers to follow their often elusive prey. So fully adapted are many of these species to life in the sky that their movement on the ground, even their perching ability, is severely limited. Swifts in particular seem almost to be part of the daytime sky.

Soaring Flight

Soaring flight is great to watch. The birds, with outstretched, almost motionless wings, rise on updrafts as effortlessly as humans riding an elevator and then glide downward to the next thermal updraft, often remaining aloft for hours with almost no flapping of the wings. Or they circle within the diameter of a thermal circulation where upward air flow is sufficient to support their weight. If they use a smaller circling radius, centrifugal force will cause them to sink faster because a soaring bird is always falling, even when updrafts make it appear that they are rising. Most proficient soaring birds are large, and flapping flight used to keep their relatively large weights aloft is very expensive in terms of an energy budget. Soaring is an adaptation that allows sustained flight on a lower-than-normal energy budget.

Effective soaring demands creating maximum lift and minimum drag, so the soaring species are generally well streamlined in body and keep their legs tucked tight to the body to reduce the drag. Larger wings produce more lift and less drag than smaller ones, which is another reason why the smaller

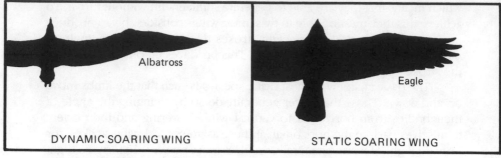

Albatross — DYNAMIC SOARING WING

Eagle — STATIC SOARING WING

FIGURE 6.9. Silhouettes of soaring wing shapes.

birds don't soar well and rely more on flapping flight. Large wings can essentially be either relatively short and broad, like those of many hawks, eagles, and vultures, or long and slender, like those of the albatrosses, shearwaters, and a number of other sea birds. It is the long, slender wing pattern that produces the very best gliding abilities, and it is the one humans have adopted in designing sailplanes. Broad wings lend themselves to static soaring; narrow ones to dynamic soaring.

The wing shape affects the aerodynamic properties that control gliding performance. As air passes over the wing, air pressure is reduced there, and there is a tendency for air circulation around the wing tips. As the birds move forward, this sets up a spiral of air movement behind the wing tips. The large, broad-winged soaring birds are able to spread and angle the tips of their primary feathers to take advantage of this spiraling movement to generate some forward thrust. By contrast, with a long, slender wing a smaller proportion of the lesser overall lift is lost to such wing-tip vortices, which makes these wings more efficient for overall gliding speeds.

Most of the broad-winged soaring species are essentially land-based species. Their flight is slower and covers less distance per unit time than that of the narrow-winged species, which are primarily sea birds that must regularly cover more area to find sufficient food to meet their energy needs.

Perhaps no bird is more efficient at sustained, dynamic gliding flight than the wandering albatross of the southern oceans of the world. Robert Cushman Murphy tells us that "this great bird, capable of encircling the world in its normal cruising, possesses an instinctive knowledge of meteorology, aerodynamics and applied mechanics, combined with split-second reactions to constantly changing aerial conditions." Its mastery of the sky is awesome. Perhaps no one has described and explained it better than William Jameson, in his classic monograph on the species. He describes spotting one of the birds flying about 55 feet above his ship and to windward of the ship's wake:

> The bird is overtaking us rapidly, but as I watch it turns downwind across the wake, "reefs" its wings into a shallow W and dives rapidly to leeward. Moving fast through the air and with the wind behind it, its speed over the water is very

138

high and in a few seconds it is well to leeward; turning south and vanishing in a trough between the waves as it banks steeply just above the sea. A few seconds later it emerges several hundred yards away on the port beam, facing the wind on fully extended wings and rising. This leg of its flight-track, against the wind, takes rather longer, but the albatross has soon crossed the wake again, turned south onto the same course as the ship and is back in its original position 55 feet upon the starboard quarter. For over an hour I watch the albatross, flying on this same curved flight-path and returning at perfectly regular intervals to the same position. Not once do I see it flap its wings.

This is no mean feat, for the bird has to find a way to regain the lost height from the downswoop and forward speed. It was many years before an adequate explanation was presented of how this is done. There is some updraft from winds striking waves and being deflected upward but not enough, regularly enough, to account for the precision flight of the albatross. What has been discovered is that wind blowing over the sea is slowed down by friction with the water. This creates, in effect, a series of air layers moving at slightly different speeds, slowest at the water surface and more rapidly with elevation up to about fifty feet. As the bird begins its upward swoop, it turns into the wind, which is blowing at varying speeds. As it rises it is constantly encountering faster-moving layers of air, and when it dives it moves into slower-moving air layers. The speeds achieved using this phenomenon are impressive. Jameson provides the following example:

> At the highest point of its flight-curve the bird has an air speed of 30 m.p.h. It turns downward and dives toward the sea, descending at a steady angle of descent but gaining air speed rapidly because of the successively slower-moving layers of air into which it flies. At 20 feet its air speed is 46 m.p.h.; the wind directly behind it is blowing at 36 m.p.h., giving a ground speed of 82 m.p.h. to leeward. The bird now begins to turn across the wind, diving into a trough between the waves and finishes its downward trajectory with an air speed of 67 m.p.h., but moving to leeward at the same speed as the sea, 20 m.p.h. . . .

> The bird using any up-currents it finds on the flanks of the waves, flies for some distance along the trough, banks and turns rapidly into the wind, using the strong up-draught near the crest of a wave to gain considerable height—an initial kickoff, as it were, of 10 or 15 feet. Its air speed instead of dropping actually rises as, propelled by its own momentum, it suddenly meets the faster-moving wind, and it forges quite rapidly to windward as it begins its steady upward climb, moving continually into layers of higher wind speed. At 20 feet its air speed is still over 77 m.p.h. and its speed to windward is 41 m.p.h. At 30 feet its air speed is 75–76 m.p.h. and it is still moving steadily to windward or about 38 m.p.h. By keeping a fairly steady air speed the surplus energy accumulated in the dive is used again to gain height. It finishes the upward climb with an air speed of 65–70 m.p.h., still forging slightly to windward as it turns across the wind, and regains its position above the starboard quarter of the ship without having lost height or making any leeway.

Such impressive feats are not possible by the hawk, eagle, and vulture clans, but there is still an almost regal majesty to their slower, more deliberate,

139

FIGURE 6.10. Sketch of the soaring apparatus of a buzzard by Andrew Wyeth. Courtesy Museum of Fine Arts, Boston.

circling flight patterns while hunting. During migration they are more likely to use flight strategies more similar to those of the albatross and other sea gliders and achieve quite respectable flight speeds as they journey on. It is well worth the effort to visit one or more of the hawk migration flyways and viewing points to observe these great birds in passage. And it is always fun to lie on one's back on a summer's day and watch some of these birds circling ever higher in a cloud-breeding thermal until they virtually disappear from view.

THE FLIGHT OF INSECTS

Insects have possessed the power of true flight longer than any other group of animals. Our tendency is to think immediately of birds when flight is mentioned, which is grossly unfair to the highly diverse six-legged flying creatures. Structurally, the insects are radically different from the other flying animals, and thus their manner of flight is often significantly different

140

as well. They must deal with the same aerodynamic forces as the other fliers, but they have evolved some different approaches to dealing with them.

In the early days of understanding of aerodynamics, insects like bumblebees completely flabbergasted the scientists, because according to their theories such a bulky insect with such relatively small wing area could not possibly be capable of flight. Yet it was very obvious that the insects didn't believe the theory and flew quite well. Today we know more about the nature of insects and their different solutions to the problems of flight. Yet Stephen Dalton, a recognized authority on insect flight, writes: "Clearly, insect flight cannot be adequately explained in simple terms, as it is governed by such a vast range of interrelated and coordinated aerodynamics and biological factors. Furthermore, it is virtually impossible to follow, photograph, or measure the multiplicity of fluctuating parameters such as lift, drag and thrust, while insects are flapping through air in free flight." Actually, as fliers, insects greatly outclass birds and are capable of almost any flight maneuver, including loops, rolls, inverted flight, hovering, vertical ascent, and backward or sideways movement. Such maneuverability adds greatly to the difficulty of explaining just how insects accomplish it all. Within the context of this book we can only present a few of the unique aspects of insect flight and urge the interested reader to pursue the topic further in some of the references provided.

Bird wings have a classic airfoil shape with an essentially permanent camber that can only be slightly modified. Insect wings, by contrast, are more or less flat or somewhat wrinkled. Bird and bat wings have bone, muscle, tendons, and blood supply, while insect wings are essentially a lifeless sandwich of two layers of chitin strengthed by veins that have fluid in them at metamorphosis but lose it once the wings have been pumped out to a fully unfurled state. At that time the veins become more structural than conductive. Insect wings extend from the thorax as an aerodynamic surface to be controlled and powered by the walls of the thorax, part of the insect's external skeleton, and the muscles attached internally to them.

Insect wings seem at first glance to be simple, indeed primitive, flight surfaces, but in reality they are very complex. Every vein, hair, scale, and corrugation plays a part in the efficiency of the wing. Veins tend to be thicker at the leading edge of the wing where the greatest stress occurs. The various lines and furrows in the wing determine the camber and twist when the creature is in flight. The boundary layer, that layer of moving air in direct contact with the wing, is affected by the presence or absence of hairs and scales, although we don't always know how. We do know, however, that moths that have lost wing scales are able to generate far less lift than those with their scales intact.

Birds and bats have one pair of wings, but the basic insect pattern is two pairs. However, evolutionary insects seem headed toward at least functional operation of only one pair or the equivalent. The more primitive orders of insects still have both pairs operating on an equal plane, but more

141

FIGURE 6.11. Some flying insects. Courtesy Dover Publications.

advanced orders have developed structural ways of locking fore and hind wings together in flight so that they act as one pair, and many of these species have much-reduced hind wings. Flies have gone so far as to have only functional forewings, with the hind wings heavily modified into a pair of gyroscopic knobs that help the insects maintain flight stability. The beetles are the major exception to this trend. Instead, they use the hind pair of wings as the main wings while the thick, heavy forewings mainly serve as fixed airfoils for extra lift when in flight.

A number of insect species, particularly among the flies, bees, and wasps, are capable of exceedingly rapid wingbeats. A wing cycle is considered to be one up and one down beat, and for such insects 200 to 250 such cycles per second is not uncommon. Some of the midges are capable of 1000 cycles per second! Small wonder that their wings generate a buzzing sound. Such rapid motion exceeds the speed at which bio-electrical impulses can travel along the nerves, so it raises the issue of how the wings can be made to vibrate so fast.

A major part of the answer lies in the high elasticity of some of the wing and thorax material and the automatic contraction of special types of muscle tissue after it has been stretched. *Resilin* is the most perfectly elastic material known, a substance which to date has eluded humanity's ingenuity for synthesizing, and *fibrillar muscle* is the most active tissue in any living organism. They both contribute to the operation of the so-called *click mechanism* that lets the wings flap as if the animal were double-jointed. Once initiated by a nerve, the mechanism uses momentum to keep the oscillation going automatically between nerve impulses.

The click mechanism depends upon an articulation of the wings and

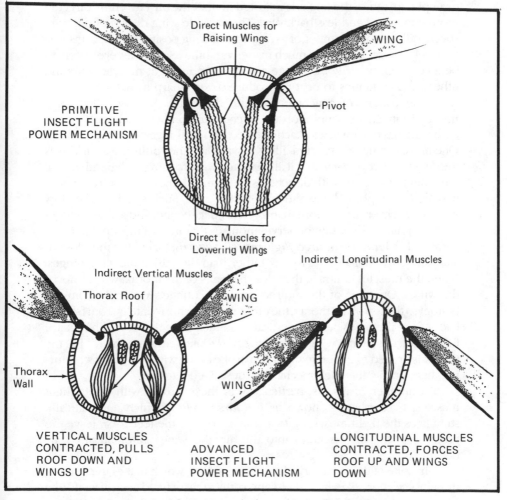

FIGURE 6.12. Cross section of primitive and advanced insect flight mechanisms.

143

fibrillar muscle and movement of the thorax wall. In essence, the mechanism acts as a switch with two stable positions—up and down. In the middle the switch is unstable. In the insect this is caused by the forcing out of the thorax walls at midposition. Their natural tendency to pull back in flips the wing to either the up or down position, whichever is the basic direction of wing momentum at the moment. This stretches the muscle, which then automatically contracts at the end of the stroke. This creates a symmetrical stroke cycle with equal lift and drag on up and down strokes.

Through the stroke cycle the insect wing pursues an elliptical or shallow figure-eight pathway. The stroke begins with the wing tips above and behind the thorax. They move forward at the same time as they move downward. The effect of this pattern of movement is to fan a current of air downward as well as backward to generate both lift and thrust. By adjusting the angle of the wingbeat they are able to affect the direction of flight. For example, to climb, the angle is adjusted so that the air current is directed more downward and less backward. The variable wing design of different species allows for a number of asymmetrical wing positions that, at insects' relatively low speeds, allow much maneuverability. Some flies even seem to be able to temporarily disengage a wing from its flight muscle while the other wing continues to beat to produce a very sharp turn.

The pattern of attachment of the flight muscles also affects maneuverability. In the simpler orders, such as dragonflies and grasshoppers, each wing has two muscles attached directly to the hinge point of the wings. One muscle, when contracted, lifts the wing; another pulls it down. This is the *direct muscle pattern,* and it allows each wing to move independently of the others. In species with direct muscle connections, front and rear wings may be out of phase by as much as half a cycle. Such species have slow wingbeats, never much more than 25 beats per second, and are dependent upon a similarly slow rate of nerve impulses that initiate movement. More advanced orders have *indirect flight muscle patterns;* that is, the muscles are attached to the walls of the thorax rather than directly to the wing hinges. When the muscles contract, they flex the walls of the thorax, which moves the wings. One pair of the indirect muscles connects vertically from the bottom to the top of the thorax; the other pair runs horizontally from front to back of the thorax. When the verticals contract, the sides of the thorax are forced out, raising the wings. When the horizontals contract, the roof of the thorax is arched to generate the downstroke of the wings. It is this structuring that permits the click mechanism described earlier.

A number of insects, particularly in those orders with direct flight muscles, have what is known as the *tarsal reflex,* which automatically stimulates the flight muscles into action as soon as the feet, *tarsi,* leave the ground. As the insects jump into the air, the wings automatically start beating.

In spite of their mastery of maneuverability, which makes the flight of most insects more like that of helicopters than that of fixed wing aircraft, few

144

species have mastered gliding at all, and none have the skill in this art possessed by a number of bird species. Some dragonflies flap the wings and then glide for a few seconds, and a few butterflies will flap and then lock their wings into a shallow-V position. Monarch butterflies in particular use this energy-saving maneuver during their migratory flights. Locusts are also known to rise in thermals on fixed wings and let the upper winds disperse them to new areas where food is potentially more available.

WATCHING LIFE IN THE SKY

Watching living things in the sky adds immeasurably to sky watching in general. Day or night, there is often life to be spotted in the sky, life that contributes to the overall mood generated by the sky itself. We have already referred to the pleasures of watching for migrating hawks from any of a number of appropriate promontories around the country where winds along the ridges foster their soaring mode. It is also fun to watch the flight of gulls along the coast as they deal with coastal winds. Sometimes they hang motionless, adjusting their wing angle of attack to the wind speed, then turn abruptly and speed away, riding the wind in its preferred direction. You may wish to lie on your back in an open field and watch the skilled movements of swifts and swallows twisting and turning overhead; you may even be lucky enough to watch swallows playing aerial tag with a drifting feather. Both groups are skilled hunters of insects, and swifts in flight collect in their throats balls of 300 to 1000 insects to feed their young or themselves. A pair of swifts may feed their young about 40 such balls a day. This says a great deal not only about the hunting skills of swifts but about the abundance of flying insects.

At dusk, as the evening kaleidoscope of colors deepens toward darkness, look for the early bats beginning their hunting with remarkable exhibitions of turning, twisting flight. You may soon be able to recognize the hunting routes of individual bats because they tend to fly the same pattern over and over as they search for food. Dusk is also the time to look for the darting, twisting flight of nighthawks and listen for their sharp *peenting* call above both city and farmlands. They are not hawks at all, but members of the goatsucker family, and feed entirely on insects caught on the wing. Their huge mouths, fringed with bristles, increase their chances of scooping up the insects they pursue.

Migrant birds provide sky spectacles each spring and fall. The stirring calls of high-flying migrant geese seem to seep into our very souls and urge us to wander, or at least foster confidence that spring is definitely on its way or that winter will soon be breathing down our backs. Such feelings are nothing new to humankind. For example, the Japanese poet Mitsune wrote around the year 900:

145

Since I heard
Faintly the voice
Of the first wild goose,
Upon mid sky alone
My thoughts have been fixed.

Rivers of blackbirds flowing toward night roosts, flocks of ducks, or the darting silhouettes of smaller birds across the bright face of a full moon are all stimulating experiences to be sought out in the sky.

Nor should anyone overlook the ballooning flights of the spiderlings in autumn or the pollen-rimmed puddles of spring. Pollen, indeed, is one sky-borne life form that gives millions of people serious problems, due to allergic reactions to certain pollen grains that lodge on our mucous membranes, causing so-called "hay fever." Of course, there is always the chance that you may spot one of the bizarre, storm-related showers of living things where it appears to rain little frogs, or other life forms, that were sucked up by violent winds elsewhere and deposited in your area.

Most importantly, although we focus attention on those creatures that spend much of their time aloft in the sky, we should never lose sight of the millions of other creatures that live on the floor of the sky—plants and animals alike. Reflecting the thought of Pueblo Indians, poet Nancy Wood sums up nicely the interrelationship between the sky-floor creatures and the sky itself:

The rain walked with long legs
Across the cracked-earth mesa
And the floor of the sky
Where the corn was dying.
The walking rain
Healed up the cracked-earth mesa
And wept on the floor of the sky
Until the corn stalks grew
Straight and tall enough to reach
The feet of the walking rain.

SKY-OBSERVER ACTIVITIES

● Spend time afield watching and recording the different flight patterns of the winged ones. Look for swallows over ponds and fields, swifts and nighthawks over urban areas, and gulls near the coast and inland around plowed fields, golf courses, and dumps. Keep alert for soaring hawks and at sea for petrels, shearwaters, and albatrosses. All these are particularly enjoyable birds to watch in flight, but don't ignore other species either. And don't overlook bats, butterflies, and dragonflies, all of which are fascinating fliers to watch.

● Make a collection of all the winged seeds in your area that depend upon the wind to help them disperse.

146

• Place glass slides thinly coated with petroleum jelly out in the open near your home. Leave them for several days; then examine them under a microscope and determine how many different kinds of pollen and/or spores have drifted onto them. (See Kapp in the *Further Reading* section.)

• On warm, sunny, early fall mornings or evenings be alert for the shining silk threads of ballooning spiders draped across the grass. These threads are largely the results of ballooning failures where the gossamer thread tangled in the weeds rather than taking the spiderling aloft. When you find the silks, begin looking for the spiderlings. When you locate some, watch them spin the silk and seek the breeze. Keep track of the successes and failures. What percentage of those you watch become airborne successfully?

• Keep track of migrating birds, butterflies, and dragonflies. Note carefully the sky conditions during the migration periods. Can you determine which weather patterns presage heavy migration flow and which retard migratory movement?

FURTHER READING

ARNETT, R., and R. JAQUES. *Insect Life: A Field Entomology Manual for the Amateur Naturalist.* Englewood Cliffs, NJ: Prentice-Hall, Inc., 1985.

DALTON, STEPHEN. *The Miracle of Flight.* New York: McGraw-Hill, 1977.

————*Borne On The Wind.* New York: Reader's Digest Press, 1975.

HEINTZELMAN, DONALD S. *A Manual for Bird Watching in the Americas.* New York: Universe Books, 1979.

JAMESON, WILLIAM. *The Wandering Albatross.* New York: William Morrow & Company, 1959.

KAPP, RONALD O. *How to Know Pollen and Spores.* Dubuque, Iowa: Wm. C. Brown Company Publishers, 1969.

KRESS, STEPHEN W. *The Audubon Society Handbook For Birders.* New York: Charles Scribner's Sons, 1981.

LOVELOCK, J.E. *Gaia.* New York: Oxford University Press, 1979.

PYLE, ROBERT MICHAEL. *The Audubon Society Handbook for Butterfly Watchers.* Charles Scribner's Sons, 1984.

SCHOBER, WILFRIED. *The Lives of Bats.* New York: Arco Publishing, Inc., 1984.

TERRES, JOHN. *How Birds Fly.* New York: Hawthorne Books, Inc., 1968.

CHAPTER 7

COPING AND PLAYING IN THE SUN

When people are carrying lots of troubles or are depressed we often say that, like Atlas, they are carrying the weight of the world on their shoulders. That would be quite a feat, of course, yet every day we all do something every bit as astounding, for we all bear the weight of the sky on our shoulders. On some days that seems to be a lighter burden than on others.

Ironically, it is during the times when the air pressure upon us is less that we tend to feel more depressed; when it is highest we tend to be more alert and have a greater sense of well-being. Our bodies become generally attuned to the overall pressure of the atmosphere at any given altitude but respond in various ways to relatively rapid changes, whether they be from rapid ascent or descent such as in a plane or elevator, or from wandering air masses of varying pressure. For most people there is that general sense of well-being and alertness during periods of high pressure; but low pressure has more variable effects not only on different individuals but on the same individual at different times. Sometimes it makes one sad, at other times irritable, drowsy, or contrarily, quite gay. Low pressure alone is seldom responsible for the depression that is frequently engendered; attendant high humidity from the accompanying storminess, plus the prolonged overcast, contributes heavily. However, all are attributes of the sky. Clearly, our physiological and emotional adaptations to sky phenomena contribute to our moods and sense of well-being. There is evidence that this holds true for many other creatures as well, with sky conditions affecting the behavior of living things in many ways.

148

A PRESSING SITUATION

At sea level the sky presses upon every inch of our bodies with a pressure of about 14.7 pounds. To prevent being crushed, our cells exert an equal pressure outward. But if sky pressure is reduced rapidly, outward pressure in our body cells is too great, and we perceive some discomfort. In particular, we are likely to have increased dehydration in our tissues which may result in aches in arthritic joints, old wounds, corns, bunions, and the like. Indeed, there are people who use their aches as indicators of rapidly approaching foul weather; and this has some validity, since such weather is usually associated with low-pressure systems.

If the air pressure changes are slower, the body usually has time enough to regulate its equalizing internal pressure, and a person will remain unconscious of this external sky pressure that is always with us. It is the equilibrium point between external and internal pressure that establishes the baseline for the pressure-sensing cells in various parts of our bodies. Our brains do not respond to the normal pressure, only to deviations from normal pressures. Skin, the largest organ of our bodies, is the organ in most direct and continuous contact with the sky around us and the one that contains most of our sensors for indicating pressure changes. Some body pressure sensors respond to pressure directly, as in the sense of touch; others are linked to hairs that vibrate under the pressure of wind or sound, both of which are sky phenomena, although wind more exclusively so than sound. Our eardrums and the tympanic membranes of frogs and some insects are essentially adaptations of skin for responding to rapid pressure pulses traveling through the sky as sound waves. Other sensory cells then transmit and interpret these pressure pulses. Of course, sound transmission is a phenomenon of only the lower, molecularly dense, regions of the sky; molecules are too sparsely distributed in the upper atmosphere to transmit such pressure pulses.

Most sky dwellers are adapted to the speed and intensity of sound pulses transmitted via the sky, and if they arrive through a solid or liquid they may prove to be painful. We tend to take such basic adaptations to life in the sky totally for granted. We are most apt to become aware, at least partially, of the existence of such basic adaptative mechanisms when the effects of a cold plug our Eustachian tubes with mucus so that they can no longer rapidly transmit air to the ear canal and so equalize normal pressure between the inner ear and the sky outside. The resulting stress on the eardrum can be almost unbearably painful. We similarly become partially aware when we have to yawn to equalize pressure upon takeoff or landing in airplanes, or even when driving up or down hills quickly.

149

COMMUNICATING WITH SOUND WAVES

Most of the creatures that are adapted to receive the pressure pulses we call sound waves are also capable of generating them as well. Some take the air they have inhaled from the sky and pass it over vocal cords or other structures that can be vibrated to create air pressure pulses of controlled variability. These sound pulses may then pass through a resonator, such as the throat sacs of many frogs and some birds, to amplify the pulses as they are released into the sky for transmission. Among many species the ability to generate sound and to receive it is a basic component of their system of communication. The sky is the primary medium of transmission of these pressure signals.

Perhaps the creatures that have best adapted to such a pressure-wave communication system for life in the sky are the various species of bats that utilize echolocation for navigating in the night sky. These animals generate sound pulses of varying wavelength and intensity and have evolved a variety of complex facial and ear structures to focus and receive the sound reflected back from objects in their path or from the ground below. Slower, longer wavelength sounds provide them with information on their relationship with the earth below them, while more rapid, shorter wavelength sounds help them zero in on fast-flying prey species. Some of their prey species among the moths have adapted to be aware of bat-generated pulses of the proper frequencies and drop immediately to the ground to avoid pursuit and possible capture.

Sound is only one of several things transported by the sky to the advantage of a host of living things. Chemical molecules are another. They are the basis of a complex world of scents which we humans can appreciate only peripherally. As chemicals are released into the sky from any source they are rapidly diluted. Many species are capable of discerning extraordinarily small concentrations of certain molecules and interpreting them in ways that have meanings for their lives. Normally, animals sensitive to scent messages are capable of orienting their movement toward increasing concentrations of any particular scent, which will ultimately lead them to its source. Flowers may generate and release such scents to lure pollinators, female moths release sexual pheromones that may attract males from over a mile away, and by contrast, the odor of an offended skunk riding the breeze may warn others to keep their distance and let the animal forage in peace. The world of scent lures and warnings is large and complex but intimately tied to the sky as its primary transmitter.

Those people particularly sensitive to scents can often tell something of the travels of a newly arriving air mass by the scents it carries. They may detect the odors of the sea, or the scent of apple blossoms from distant orchards, or the less pleasant aromas of industrial areas. But for most of us the evocative world of scents is largely a lost world, temporarily regained only when concentrations of scents are quite high. We are often aware of just

FIGURE 7.1. Migrants on the wing. C.E. Roth photo.

how much more sensitive many of our animal cousins are to this scented world. Those who track our mammal neighbors for hunting or other forms of recreation learn to keep downwind of their quarry so that scent messages are less likely to reach the quarry prematurely. Wild predators often use the same strategy and are ever conscious of the patterns of windflow.

The transparent nature of the sky means that it transmits light well except where dense cloud cover blocks it. Of course, some wavelengths of radiation are partially filtered or reflected by such phenomena as the ozone layer. Aside from the obvious variety of eye structures that animals have evolved to capture images from reflected light, or the leaves that plants have evolved to utilize sunlight as the energy source for food manufacture, living things have evolved other ways of coping with radiant energy from the sky and its consequences. The changing amount of daylight through the seasons stimulates hormonal changes in a number of groups of animals and plants that affect their behavior. Such *photoperiodism* affects the time of flowering of plants, the time of migration of birds, the time of spawning of fish, the seasonal change of color in some birds and mammals, and the seasonal development of sexual organs and the stimulus to reproduce.

The physiological mechanisms that are triggered by the changing levels of radiant energy have their focus in an area of the forepart of the brain called the *hypothalmus*. It triggers the pituitary gland to send chemical messengers coursing through the bloodstream to awaken dormant glands or suppress them. The mechanism is different in plants, but the effect is the same. Some plants bloom only under conditions when the nights are long, while others bloom only when nights are relatively short. Night is stressed

151

with plants because that is the time most growth occurs, since daylight hours are largely devoted to photosynthesis.

COPING THROUGH ARCHITECTURE
AND ENGINEERING

Although sky is a welcome carrier of sound and scent, it also brings rain, fierce winds, lightning, dust clouds, and other phenomena that can be unpleasant or devastating to a variety of living things, including people. Part of coping with the sky for many creatures includes seeking or making shelter from the various excesses of the sky. This process may be as simple as taking shelter under a leaf or rock, or may include construction of complex dens or tunnel systems below the ground or, in the case of humans, construction of elaborate, climate-controlled structures that drastically reduce the impact of weather events on people. Unfortunately, the comfortable environmental homogeneity of these structures tends to lull us into almost totally ignoring the sky, robbing us of the delights of the sky as the price of our comfort. A blandness is induced that debilitates our passions for the glories of the natural world about us.

We now have air-conditioned shopping malls, surrounded by parking-lot ovens; glassed-in walkways between buildings that keep us from the rain and also from even the balmiest breezes; rabbit-warren office buildings, climate-controlled (when the system is functioning), with even views of the sky limited to a lucky, high-ranking few. In all too many workplaces there is no such thing as a window that opens; the energy-consumptive central-climate system must meet all needs. When that system fails, and they all do periodically, a certain revenge for their continuing denial of the nature of the sky and its many moods is visited upon the inmates.

There are places, however, where human architects have learned to build in concert with the sky to make living more enjoyable. Proper orientation of buildings on tropical islands takes advantage of the constant trade winds to ventilate the structures, while the roofs provide protection from excessive sun and rain. Similarly, orientation can take advantage of onshore and offshore breezes and other such local wind patterns. It is notable that on islands such as Puerto Rico, shortsighted social aspirations have resulted in a vast decline in open structures, well oriented and naturally ventilated, and in the meteoric rise in construction of little concrete boxes that become ovens under the tropical sun and demand expensive air-conditioning systems to make them habitable. These in turn require environmentally damaging power-grid systems to provide the power to run them.

In northern climes many early homes were sited to take fullest advantage of solar gain in winter, with high, south-facing walls and low, earth-

152

sheltered, north-facing walls to minimize the chilling effects of prevailing northerly winter winds. Today, these environmentally sensitive buildings have become rare as row upon row of houses are set up facing any which way, ignoring the sky dynamics, depending instead upon central heating with declining, finite fossil fuels. The cartel-induced fuel shortages of the 1970s shocked some into rethinking the siting and design of new buildings and increased insulation installations and some solar retrofitting of old ones. But as those artificial shortages abated, so too did much of the enthusiasm of real energy conservation in siting and construction. People have yet to truly comprehend that the sky phenomena of weather and climate have a much greater life span than does the supply of fossil fuels, and that the consumption of these fuels, either directly or to generate electricity, has a heavy impact upon the sky itself and the weather it generates. Acid rain, smog, soot, emphysema, and lung cancer are all part of the consequences of the way we cope with the sky. Our strong tendency to overlook the sky and its daily impact on our lives in so many ways leads us to many shortsighted solutions to problems only partially comprehended. These solutions result in the generation of other, even more complex, often dangerous problems. It is necessary to ask, as did one of the potent folk songs of the 1960s: "When will we ever learn?"

POLLUTION: A HISTORICAL PERSPECTIVE

Since time immemorial, the sky has received belching inputs of dust and noxious gases from volcanic explosions, some so violent that their effluvia remained airborne, circumnavigating the planet for years at a time. Yet these events were geographically scattered and of fairly short duration for any given episode. In addition, there have always been fires, usually of lightning origin, burning at various points around the globe and pouring smoke into the sky: these too, have been relatively scattered and of short duration. With the birth of the Industrial Revolution in human history, something new was added to pollution of the sky: gases and particles spewing forth on an ongoing basis, in ever-increasing amounts, over increasingly larger areas of the globe. It was as if humankind had launched an undeclared war on the sky.

From the time that people first discovered how to tame fire, they have been increasing the amount of particles and some gases released into the sky. The quantity increased even more when people learned to burn large supplies of wood or charcoal to smelt metals from rock ores. Such burning resulted in the deforestation of large areas, and increased air pollution. But throughout history, human populations were relatively small, and the impact of the air pollution created was comparably small in relation to the input from volcanic activity. Since the sky also has innate cleansing

153

FIGURE 7.2. Mt. St. Helen spews dust and gases aloft. Photo courtesy U.S. Geological Survey.

mechanisms such as rainfall that tend to remove pollutants, the net result was, that until the Industrial Revolution, human activity had little more than local, short-term impact on the sky.

The Industrial Revolution had a twofold impact: the industries themselves began to burn more and more fuels to do their work; and the success of the revolution spawned both an increase in population and a concentration of that population in urban areas. People burned more fuel for their home needs. This all resulted, in effect, in an increase of artificial volcanoes spewing out gas and ash on a daily basis, year after year without respite.

John Ruskin, in his early writings, suggested that "God paints the clouds . . . that men may be happy in seeing Him at His work." Ruskin made that statement before the skies in his area were fouled from the industrial cities, but by the late 1860s changes took place that led to Ruskin's disillusionment. In the preface to a book written as a study of the Greek myths of Cloud and Storm titled *The Queen of the Air,* Ruskin observed: "I have seen strange evil brought upon every scene that I best loved, or tried to make beloved by others. The light which once flushed those pale summits with its rose at dawn, and purple at sunset, is now umbered and faint; the air which once inlaid the clefts of all their golden crags with azure is now defiled with languid coils of smoke, belched from worse than volcanic fires. . . ." Actually, what he saw was only a pale precursor of what was to come.

154

FIGURE 7.3. The sky—a convenient industrial dump.

Some viewed the growing pall of soot from the burning of coal and peat as the color of progress and the smell of profit. Others found it to be the color of oppression and the smell of sickness, even of death. Periodically, local sky conditions combined with the airborne garbage to create major disasters claiming hundreds of lives in places like London, England, or Donorra, Pennsylvania. Many other places had less dramatic, but no less deadly, incidents. For such cities, fresh country air took on new meaning and nostalgia.

Governments acted in a variety of ways to reduce the severity of the impact of such pollution of the sky, but with limited results. In general, local reduction was offset by overall growth. Fuel shifts away from peat and coal reduced some particulate matter but did little to affect amounts of noxious gases. By the twentieth century something new had been added—the internal combustion engine that powered new transportation devices made available and affordable to vast numbers of people by the Industrial Revolution. These cars, buses, and trucks increased urban pollution and allowed such pollution to be rapidly extended into the countryside. Airplanes further contributed combustion gases to the sky. Electricity became widely available in the twentieth century, virtually as a perceived right of every American. The generation of that electricity by fossil fuels, particularly high sulphur coal, across many regions of the nation added further to the burden. Generation of electricity added a burden of noxious gases and particulates,

155

FIGURE 7.4. Air pollution over Boston, 1969. Courtesy Massachusetts Audubon Society.

156

and lighting of the cities at night, with resulting light scatter. This all but shut off a view of the night sky, even to professional astronomers who have been forced to find ever more remote mountain locations for their observatories.

By the mid-1960s, deterioration of the quality of our skies had reached a point where almost no one could be unaware of the scope and magnitude of the problem, even if they did not understand completely what was happening and why. By the 1970s, political action to begin rectification of the situation occurred both in North America and Europe. It is not the intent of this book to explore the politics of the anti-pollution efforts, but it cannot ignore an examination of some of the things we have done and are doing in our inadvertent war on the sky and thus upon ourselves. With a better awareness of what the sky is, its phenomena, its role in our lives, and the nature of what we have done and are doing to the sky, you may be more willing and better prepared to fight to see that our skies are kept spacious, clean, life-sustaining, and aesthetically and spiritually uplifting.

THE GREENHOUSE EFFECT

One of the major products of combustion is carbon dioxide. This colorless, odorless gas is a normal component of air and is of vital necessity in the food-generating process of photosynthesis. Over the usual course of events, the plant life of earth utilizes almost as much carbon dioxide as is produced. Some of the excess is dissolved in the ocean and becomes part of carbonate rocks, and only a small surplus remains as a minor constituent of the atmosphere. Volcanic eruptions and extensive forest fires produce temporary surges in the amount of carbon dioxide in the atmosphere, but soon the natural processes bring the excess back down to the more or less normal background level. Throughout Earth's evolution, the precise amount of that background level has varied depending upon the amount of volcanic activity and the abundance of plant life. At times it probably was two to three times the present level.

Carbon dioxide is transparent to incoming ultraviolet radiation from the sun. Ultraviolet rays heat the earth in the form of infrared radiation, and would all radiate back out into space except that some of those rays are blocked by infrared-opaque molecules. Carbon dioxide is chief among those molecules in the atmosphere. The glass of a greenhouse is also transparent to ultraviolet and opaque to infrared so that solar heat is trapped inside. Since carbon dioxide helps trap heat in the atmosphere on a global basis, like glass does in a greenhouse, we speak of its action as the "greenhouse effect." Without carbon dioxide, Earth's climate would be a great deal cooler, probably too cold to support life. If, on the other hand, our atmosphere were some ninety percent carbon dioxide, like that of Venus, our climate would be too hot for life.

The problem is that, since the Industrial Revolution, human activities have been steadily increasing the background level of carbon dioxide in the

157

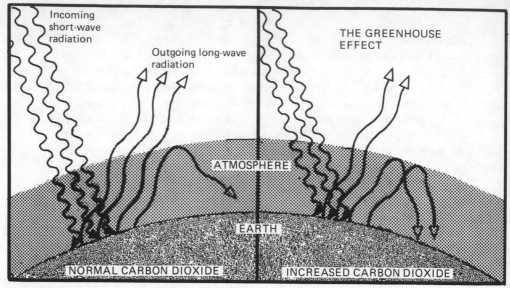

Incoming short-wave radiation

Outgoing long-wave radiation

THE GREENHOUSE EFFECT

ATMOSPHERE

EARTH

NORMAL CARBON DIOXIDE

INCREASED CARBON DIOXIDE

FIGURE 7.5. The greenhouse effect.

atmosphere. This comes from two major interacting activities—increased combustion, particularly of fossil fuels, and massive deforestation that reduces carbon dioxide consumption. Best estimates indicate that within the next fifty years, we will see a doubling of carbon dioxide in the atmosphere from turn-of-the-century levels. Today carbon dioxide represents around 330 parts per million of our atmosphere; by 2030 or 2040, according to Dr. Walter Orr Roberts of the National Center for Atmospheric Research, it is likely to reach concentrations of 500 to 600 parts per million. The net result of this will be an average increase in the planet's temperature. This change in climatic temperatures will be unequally distributed around the globe with some places much warmer, and some even cooler, than at present. Since the turn of this century, carbon dioxide increases have amounted to between 20 percent to 25 percent and there has been an average temperature increase of about 1.8° F. Based on Dr. Roberts projections, we can expect an average increase of about 5° F, with about an 18° F increase at the poles, and as little as 1.8° F increase at the equator.

Such an increase will be a mixed blessing. It will shift atmospheric dynamics and resultant rainfall patterns, and will increase melt of polar ice caps affecting sea levels upward, with potential flooding of low-lying coastal regions. It will thus be a blessing for some regions and a curse for others. Such an increase in global temperature will be unprecedented in the entire history of the human species.

Carbon dioxide is the primary, but not the only, contributor to the greenhouse effect. Unburned hydrocarbons, like gasoline vapor, and other gases may contribute between a third and a half of the blockage of infrared rays. Nonetheless, it remains a fact that human activity is the moving force behind all the factors of this long-term increase in global heat-up.

158

There are other impacts on the sky that can temporarily counter the warm-up. Volcanic eruptions, which generate high volumes of ash and dust, may create layers of dust in the stratosphere that reflect incoming sunlight, causing a cooling of some areas for a period of several years. Eventually gravity settles the dust out and the cooling effect is diminished, and eventually eliminated, until next time.

There has been a great deal of speculation on the impact the overall greenhouse effect will have on humankind and its civilizations. One thing is for sure—things will be different. In the meantime, we can work to reduce the demand for the burning of fossil fuels and to decrease the rapid deforestation of the planet through programs of reforestation and population control. This type of action can slow the rate of temperature increase created by the greenhouse effect, helping our species gain more time to better understand and adapt to the inevitable changes. It seems clear that our present society is creating huge environmental bills with payment due from future generations.

FUN WITH THE SKY

Life is more than just survival; it involves the spirit, and joy and fun. Increasingly, people have been turning to the sky for that as well. To be sure, since time immemorial people have gotten an aesthetic and spiritual lift from viewing sunrises and sunsets, rainbows and lightning displays, and the delights of cloud forms. They have also envied birds in particular the freedom and perspective granted by the power of flight. Many creative minds over the centuries have devised schemes to attain that power, but only in quite recent times has success been achieved, and only in the last half-century has that option been available to more than a mere handful of people.

In spite of myriad attempts to fashion wings of ingenious, but futile, design and attach them to the human anatomy, the first successful flight into the sky was undoubtedly accomplished accidentally by kite fliers. To most North Americans the kite is a children's toy, but in other parts of the world kite flying is a serious adult sport. This is particularly true in the Far East and has been so for many generations. There, flight competitions and kite fighting engage the attention of large numbers of people. The first recorded mention of kite flying goes back to literature of China written in 500 B.C., and there is mention of kite flying in Egyptian papyrus scrolls dated at 300 B.C.

It seems to be a universal tendency among people to try to build bigger versions of almost everything, and kite building has been no exception. In time the Chinese built kites so large that they developed enough lift to haul a small human into the sky with them. It must have been something of a surprise to the first people who got such a free ride, but before long

159

FIGURE 7.6. Kite aloft. Stock Boston, Inc. photo.

160

FIGURE 7.7. Sailboat. C.E. Roth photo.

such kites with human passengers were being put to practical use. It should come as no surprise that it was a military use. Kites with airborne observers could get a good bird's-eye view of enemy lines and fortifications. Use of this tactic spread, and by the sixteenth century it was employed throughout Asia and Europe. Of course, it could be employed only in situations where there were strong winds, and even then the observers had to be small and light (and fearless!). Human kite-borne flying went into eclipse essentially after World War I. It has been reborn in recent years as a sport.

In many resort areas the sport of water skiing has been combined with kite flying. The person is harnessed to the kite and skitters over the surface of the water on water skis, towed by the boat, until the kite lifts him or her into the sky. The person rides the sky until the boat slows its speed, the kite gradually loses lift, and the rider more or less gently returns to the water. It is exhilarating but still a long way from the free flight of the birds.

Of course, for centuries people have used the sky to move about on the water, for the sail is nothing but a device to harness some of the power of the wind. Until the invention of the steam engine and its offspring, wind and muscle power were the only sources of motive power for boats and ships. For a while it looked as if the romantic days of commercial sailing ships were gone forever, but recently concern for new sources of energy other than fossil fuels has led to sophisticated wind devices that greatly reduce, and in some cases eliminate, the need for conventional engines while the ship is on the high seas.

161

FIGURE 7.8. Windsurfer. C.E. Roth photo.

FIGURE 7.9. Hot-air ballooning. C.E. Roth photo.

FIGURE 7.10. Water skiing to the sky. C.E. Roth photo.

Of course, the romance of sailing remains in the form of recreation craft ranging from wind-driven surfboards to expensive yachts. There are even a number of the "tall ships" back in service for training, research, and some recreation. Whatever the size of these sailing devices, they require sophisticated reading and understanding of winds for proficiency in their use. The sailing sportsperson must be equally acquainted with sky and sea. Winds alone are not the limit of required sky knowledge. The sailor must be able to navigate with sun and stars, read the clouds for impending weather changes, and understand the potential impact of sky events upon the waters. Sailing, be it windsurfing or yacht racing, comes somewhat closer to flight, but the sailor is still anchored to the floor of the sky.

In 1782 Joseph Montgolfier, a French inventor, devised another approach to flight—the hot-air balloon. Joseph and his brother Etienne figured that if clouds could float in the sky, why not capture a cloud and enclose it in a bag? This, of course, proved impractical, but it sent their minds along the trail that resulted in the invention of the balloon. Based on the principle that hot air rises, this device demonstrated that if that hot air could be contained, it would provide considerable lift to anything attached to it. Unfortunately, it also produced a great deal of drag and had very little maneuverability. The Montgolfier brothers' first successful indoor attempt at trapping hot air in a silk bag was conducted in 1782, and the following summer they gave their first public outdoor demonstration. The balloon soared to 6000 feet and landed a mile away. A sheep, a rooster, and a duck were the first animals to be given a ride in such a device; the flight was eight minutes long. The first manned flights were in tethered balloons, but on November 21, 1783 John Pilatre de Rozier, a young physician, became the first free-flight balloonist. Unfortunately, only two years later he became the first aerial human fatality. Interestingly, Joseph Montgolfier, inventor of these balloons, only flew once in his life.

At first these balloons were used primarily on tethers much as the early manned kites were, for sky spying, but they were also to be seen and ridden on in fairs and other such social gatherings. Observation balloons were used briefly in the American Civil War and in the 1870—71 siege of Paris in the Franco-Prussian War.

There were, of course, bold adventurers who released the tethers and drifted with the winds where chance took them. Such flights were a serene but dangerous experience: If something went awry, it was a long way down.

The danger gave rise to invention of the parachute, essentially a circle of cloth attached by harness to the human which, when fully opened, would provide enough drag through the sky to permit a relatively soft landing. Early parachutes were all attached by their ripcords to the basket of the balloon so they would automatically open when a person went overboard. These early devices were very imperfect and prone to tangling and opening improperly, which left hot-air ballooning a very risky business.

Today, hot-air ballooning has become a stately pastime. The expensive balloons are designed with magnificent colors and patterns. They are a glory

163

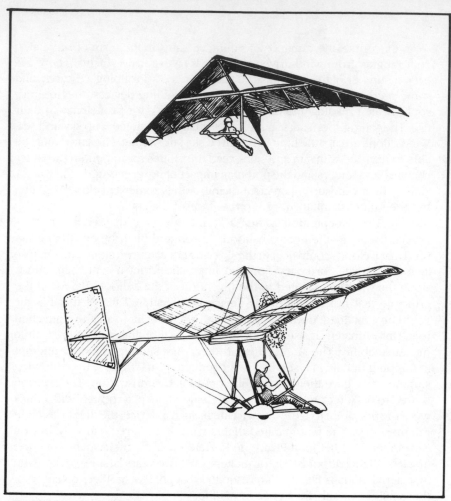

FIGURE 7.11. Hang glider and ultralight.

to behold as they drift across our view in silence or with the whooshing roar of the heat jets as their pilots heat some more air to keep them aloft. They remain at the mercy of the local air currents, with their captains able to control little more than their ascent and descent. Ground crews follow below in vehicles to pick up the passengers, gondola, and collapsed balloon when the time has come to return to earth. Hot-air ballooning is a heady experience that brings the passengers to closer union with the sky, but in ways more akin to those experienced by spiderlings than by birds.

For good hot-air ballooning, the air should be calm (or with only a very gentle breeze), clear, and cool. The latter is important because to assure good lift the pilot must be able to achieve a 100° temperature differential between inside and outside the balloon. Ballooning is a great activity for the early riser. It is also an activity that requires great team effort to get the bag unrolled and inflated to the point where it can carry the gondola and its passengers. Usually, the fliers stay aloft for only ten miles or so and then descend to trade places with members of the following ground crew. Ballooning is a very social, yet very peaceful activity.

The more adventuresome, and well off, may shift from hot-air balloons to helium-filled ones. These do not need the fuel supplies that heating the air for hot-air ballooning demands, and they can rise much higher in the sky, where they meet more consistent currents of air. This permits much longer trips and new insights about the nature of the sky; it also exposes fliers to much greater hazards, such as much more limited oxygen and much lower temperatures. Only with special equipment can people survive these longer, upper-tropospheric adventures. On the other hand viruses and pollen, even some seemingly delicate insects, are hoisted as far aloft in the updrafts of thunderstorms and survive their trip little the worse for wear.

Of course, what the kite, balloon, and parachute lack that birds possess is a means for providing sustained thrust. For people to achieve anything approaching the freedom of bird flight required development of the internal-combustion engine. Nonetheless, development of the self-propelled airplane began with kites. Wilbur and Orville Wright spent many years making and flying large kites. For a time they even made part of their living making and selling such kites. It was from what they learned from kites that they developed their ideas for powered flight. Indeed, the *Kitty Hawk,* their first successful airplane, was essentially a box kite with an engine and propeller. The Wright brothers were not trained engineers but self-taught mechanics whose empirical, trial-and-error, cut-and-paste experiments with large kites gradually led them to the successful aerodynamic designs for powered flight. Kites, like birds and insects, fly only because they balance the four forces that act on all flying objects—gravity, lift, drag, and thrust. By careful observation and observation of the opposing pairs (gravity/lift and drag/thrust) of the kites, they came to design the wings and elevators of the airplanes. With the airplane, for the first time, people could go aloft for sustained periods with the ability to choose direction and change speed much as birds, bees, and bats do.

The rapid evolution of powered flight from those early "powered kites" has been nothing short of phenomenal. In the span of one lifetime my own father-in-law went from the excitement of barnstorming in biplanes to piloting jet planes. I believe he always retained his love for the earlier planes with their open cockpits because they made him feel more in tune with the sky itself. Modern aircraft, by contrast, tend to isolate pilot and passengers from the dynamics of the sky, depriving us of the sense of wonder and the sensations of simpler flight. We become not the butterfly in free flight, but the chrysalis or cocoon tossed through the sky. Modern air travel is fast, efficient, but strangely unsatisfying.

I believe that it is a desire for real contact with the sky that has led to growing involvement with two related forms of flight: hang gliding and piloting ultralights. The hang glider evolved from an arrowhead-shaped, flexible wing called a *parasail* or *parawing.* It was designed by Dr. Francis

165

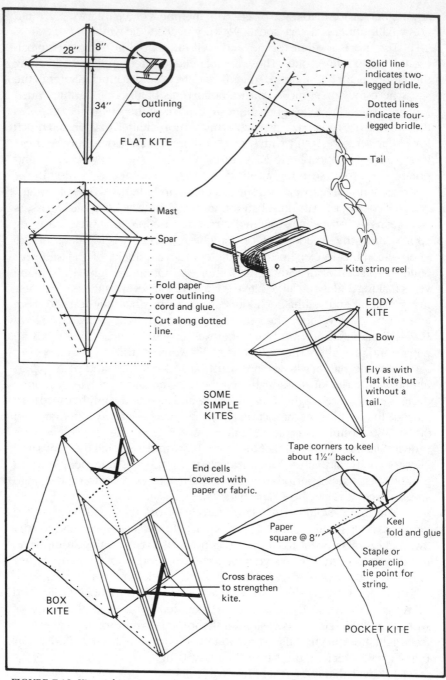

28" 8"

34" ←Outlining cord

FLAT KITE

Solid line indicates two-legged bridle.

Dotted lines indicate four-legged bridle.

Tail

Mast

Spar

Fold paper over outlining cord and glue.

Cut along dotted line.

Kite string reel

EDDY KITE

Bow

Fly as with flat kite but without a tail.

SOME SIMPLE KITES

End cells covered with paper or fabric.

Tape corners to keel about 1½" back.

Keel fold and glue

Paper square @ 8"

Staple or paper clip tie point for string.

Cross braces to strengthen kite.

BOX KITE

POCKET KITE

FIGURE 7.12. Kite making.

166

Rogallo for safely dropping large objects to the ground from heights up to 40 miles. The device had a number of uses. In essence, the parawing is a combination of a kite without a tether and a parachute. A daredevil named Bill Bennett is credited with adapting the parawing as a people's sport. He and his friends, who had been experimenting in various ways with large towed kites, added a pilot's harness and a control bar to the parawing, which allowed some control of the flight by shifting weight in the harness. The hang glider was born and, for the first time, lifted the story of Daedalus and Icarus from the realm of pure myth to partially achievable fantasy. A hang glider is fashioned from aluminum tubes, steel cables, a Dacron sail, and the harness, and weighs about thirty-five pounds. After proper training and instruction, people can launch from a cliff and soar like the ravens with which they may share the sky space. Alert to updrafts, they can rise and drift and stay aloft for hours if they so desire and are skillful enough. The sport has grown exponentially. In 1970 there was a world population of hang-glider pilots of only about two hundred; by 1976 some 16,300 were registered with the United States Hang Gliding Association alone. This comes as no surprise to anyone who has tried it, for the wind rushes around the skin providing a variety of sensations, you can view the creatures at the bottom of the sky from new perspectives, and within limits you can move reasonably freely in the sky.

But there are limits to hang gliding. It should be no surprise, therefore, that soon there were those who decided to add small gasoline engines and propellers to the hang gliders. They used a great variety of sources for their engines—chain saws, lawn mowers, snowmobiles, and many others. Such experimenting did remove some of hang gliding's restricted movement. These early experimental craft had no wheels but were launched by foot just as hang gliders were, and consequently they did not require registration with the Federal Aviation Administration. It didn't take long, however, before some users were adding tricycle-type frames and wheels to their experimental craft to make landing easier and safer.

By the end of the 1970s a considerable evolution had occurred in these crafts. Parasails had given way to very light ribbed and strutted wings, and an elementary fuselage with rudders and elevators had developed. The trapeze and harness had become simple seats, and the whole thing looked more like a tiny plane. Emphasis still was on minimal size, weight, and cost in conjunction with maximum safety, simplicity, and portability. They were of many styles, but all became known as *ultralights*. These planes were now more like those that are required to be registered with the FAA. That raised some serious questions about how they and their evolution should be handled.

The FAA handled the problem by defining the limits of unregistered ultralights. By that ruling no ultralight can be more than 254 pounds (115

167

kilograms) empty; can hold more than one person; can carry more than 5 gallons of fuel; can have a maximum speed above 63 miles per hour (55 knots); and can stall or lose its ability to remain in flight at any speed greater than 275 miles per hour (24 knots). Ultralights are also to be used only for sport and recreation. Although they are far less expensive than standard aircraft, they can hardly be called inexpensive. But they do offer increased numbers of people the freedom and excitement of a powered flight. Less in contact with the sky in an ultralight than on a hang glider, the flier still is heavily aware of the whims of the sky. No one should attempt to fly one without a solid training course that includes plenty of imput on dealing with local winds and weather.

Although both hang gliding and ultralight piloting are great fun and offer a unique communion with the sky, they present considerable safety hazards to the poorly trained or careless, and even the most skilled experience accidents. Both sports have their own associations and publications dedicated to assuring a high degree of safety, but injuries and fatalities have occurred and will continue to occur. Anyone contemplating involvement with the sky by these means must carefully and realistically assess the risks and take all necessary training to be prepared to both avoid and meet the inherent dangers.

Between the hang glider and the engined aircraft lies the sky experience of the sailplane. Like huge fiberglass and plexiglass imitations of the albatross, these sleek craft, once released from their launching tow, penetrate the sky at high speed while maintaining a very flat glide. Their pilots learn to read the sky for thermals like an eagle and to keep their craft aloft for from 30 to 150 miles or more. Sailplane flying truly pits the pilot against the elements, but it often truly gives a person the opportunity to "fly with the eagles." Unfortunately, sailplaning, like flying standard powered craft, is expensive and requires long hours of training and practice.

Perhaps the most heady experience with the sky derived from the development of safety measures designed to save pilots when their powered aircraft fail. Early experiments with parachutes dealt with tethered chutes that permitted escape from tethered balloons used in wartime. And there were the chutes whose ripcords were attached to the gondolas of balloons. In the early dogfights among World War I pilots, similar parachute arrangements were used with ripcords attached to the cockpit. These all proved highly unreliable, and many pilots died tangled in the chutes or around debris of the stricken craft.

It remained for one Leslie Irvin to design and test the first self-contained parachute. His first model was composed of a silk canopy 32 feet in diameter, with twenty-four 16-foot-long rigging lines linking the canopy to a harness on the user. At the apex of the main chute was attached a small pilot chute designed to open with a built-in wire spring and draw out the main chute and rigging line. The main canopy had a hole built in so that some escaping air would prevent excessive oscillation of the device as it descended. All of the material was carefully folded in a pack held closed by an elastic band and secured by two metal pins attached to a steel ripcord cable. The Air Force was interested in Irvin's invention and put him to work with another inventor, Floyd Smith, who had been working in a similar vein. Together they modified the initial design somewhat, reducing the canopy diameter to 28 feet composed of 40 sewn panels and making the vent hole expandable by sewing it to thick rubber bands. The final package was stowed in a back pack. On April 28, 1919, Irvin jumped successfully with the chute from 1500 feet, although he did suffer a broken ankle in landing. It was a daring feat; but soon others were eager to try, and the parachute proved its reliability. In a few months, 27-year-old Lieutenant Harold Harris became the first man to be saved by a manually operated parachute when his plane failed aloft.

For a long time it had been believed that a person falling in the sky would be unable to move the arms and so would be unable to reach for and pull a ripcord. Irvin disproved that, and in so doing set the stage for new experiences in the sky. Irvin went on to set up the first company to produce parachutes commercially, a company that, through a clerical error that he did not initially have the money to correct legally, became known as the Irving Air Chute Company. It provided most of the early parachutes for commercial as well as military aviation and for early sport jumping.

During World War II troops were trained to parachute into battle areas, and some soldiers learned to enjoy the jumping and pursued it as a civilian hobby. Some began to wait increasingly long periods of time before pulling the ripcord. They discovered that by controlling their bodies and arms they could even glide and maneuver a bit, somewhat like a flying squirrel, or do a variety of high-diving maneuvers. Thus was born the sport of sky diving. No other sky activity provides such intimate contact with the sky and its dynamics. It demands physical stamina and control and good timing but has become reasonably safe as such things go. Over the years new parachute designs have emerged, and the presently popular sky-diving chutes more closely resemble modified parawings than the original Irvin design. The new design makes them somewhat safer upon landing, less susceptible to dragging their rider with surface wind gusts. Sky diving clearly is not for everyone. But as an intimate experience with the sky, one which emphasizes the limits of our physical adaptation to the midsky while also featuring our intellectual and spiritual abilities to adapt to the sky, it is hard to beat.

Perhaps no one has expressed better how we have used our minds to cope with the sky than World War II aviation cadet John Gillespie Magee, Jr., who penned this eloquent poem.

169

HIGH FLIGHT

Oh! I have slipped the surly bonds of earth
And danced the skies on laughter-silvered wings;
Sunward I've climbed, and joined the tumbling mirth
of sun-split clouds—and done a hundred things
You have not dreamed of—wheeled and soared and swung
High in the sunlit silence. Hov'ring there,
I've chased the shouting wind along, and flung
My eager craft through footless halls of air.
Up, up, the long delirious burning blue
I've topped the wind-swept heights with easy grace
Where never lark or even eagle flew—
And, while with silent lifting mind I've trod
The high untrespassed sanctity of space,
Put out my hand and touched the face of God.

SKY-OBSERVER ACTIVITIES

• Take a sky-alert walk almost anywhere. Notice how the sky wraps itself intimately around every surface; then look at how the living things interface with it. With a 10X or better magnifying glass look at the stomates on the undersides of leaves that let the sky inside the leaf and let moisture pass out into the sky. Similarly, look at your own skin and the pores it has that likewise give two-way access to the sky. Wave your arms about and feel the pressure of the sky and the coolness as the water steals heat from your body in order to gain sufficient energy to vaporize and invisibly enter the sky.

• Drive up one of our high mountain highways, particularly in some of our national parks, and experience the change in air pressure and the thinning of the air density, particularly of oxygen.

• While swimming, open your eyes underwater. Compare your perceptions with what you see and feel while walking in the sky. Such a simple act helps us understand how much we take for granted of our basic coping adaptations for life in the sky. Follow up by hitting two stones together underwater and above water. Dive down as deep as you can, and concentrate on how your body feels. Compare it with how you feel out of the water. Only by such contrasts with other environments can we truly appreciate how regularly and finely tuned our bodies are for daily life in the sky.

• Go fly a kite! Better still, make your own. Figure 7.8 shows some common types you can build, and there are references in Further Reading that give more details. Remember that flat kites generally need some tail to stabilize them in flight. Start with a longer tail than you think you will need, and gradually trim some off until you achieve the desired stability of flight. Bowed kites are more aerodynamically stable and shouldn't need a tail. Box kites hardly appear suitable for flight, but try them; you will be surprised at their behavior. Serious kite fliers may be interested in the International Kitefliers Association, 321 E 48th St., New York, NY 10019.

170

• Check your phone book's yellow pages for organizations and businesses that can teach you one of the sport-flying skills, from hang gliding to sky diving. If you can't find any that way, contact one of the following for suggestions:

Hang Glider Association
Box 1860
Santa Monica, CA 90406
   Publication: *Hang Glider Magazine*

Soaring Society of America
Box 66071
Los Angeles, CA 90066

United States Parachute Association
806 15th Street NW, Suite 44
Washington, D.C. 20005
   Publication: *Parachutist* (monthly)

Canadian Sport Parachuting Association
333 River Road
Ottawa, ON Canada K1L 8B9
   Publication: *Canadian Parachutist* (8 times/year)

Balloon Federation of America
821 15th Street NW, Suite 430
Washington, D.C. 20005
   Publication: *Ballooning* (bimonthly)

Experimental Aircraft Association
P.O. Box 229
Hales Corners, WI 53130

FURTHER READING

AMERICAN HERITAGE EDITORIAL STAFF. *The American Heritage History of Flight.* New York: American Heritage Publishing Company, Inc., 1962.

BACH, RICHARD. *A Gift of Wings.* New York: Delacorte Press, 1974.

BENSON, ROLF. *Skydiving.* Minneapolis, MN: Lerner Publications Co., 1979.

BERNHEIM, MOLLY. *A Sky Of My Own.* New York: Macmillan, Inc., 1974.

BRUMMITT, WYATT. *Kites.* New York: Golden Press, 1971.

CARRIER, RICK. *Fly: The Complete Book of Sky Sailing.* New York Mc-Graw-Hill, 1974.

COOMBS, CHARLES. *Hot-Air Ballooning.* New York: William Morrow and Company, 1981.

———. *Ultralights—The Flying Featherweights.* New York: William Morrow and Company, 1984.

FARNHAM, MOULTON. H. *Sailing For Beginners,* rev. ed. New York: Macmillan, Inc., 1981.

FENSCH, THOMAS. *Skydiving Book.* Mountain View, CA: Anderson World, Inc., 1980.

FLAVIN, CHRISTOPHER. *Wind Power: A Turning Point.* New York: Unipub (Worldwatch Institute), 1981.

HACKLEMAN, MICHAEL A. *Wind and Windspinners.* Culver City, CA: Peace Press, Inc., 1975.

LAMBIER, JACK. *Ultra-light Aircraft.* Hummelstown, PA: Ultralight Publications, 1982.

LINCOLN, JOSEPH COLVILLE. *Soaring On The Wind.* Flagstaff, AZ: Northland Press, 1973.

LLOYD, AMBROSE. *Kites: How To Fly Them, How To Build Them.* New York: Holt, Rinehart & Winston, 1976.

LOWRY, WILLIAM P. *Weather and Life: An Introduction To Biometeorology.* New York: Academic Press, Inc., 1969.

MARIER, DONALD, and DAN WALLACE. *Windpower For The Homeowner.* Emmaus, PA: Rodale Press, Inc., 1981.

MARKOWSKI, MICHAEL A. *Hang Glider's Bible.* Blue Ridge Summit, PA: Tab Books, Inc., 1977.

MUHLHAUSEN, JOHN. *Wind and Sail: A Primer for Beginning Sailors.* New York: Times Books, 1971.

NEWMAN, LEE S., and JAY H. NEWMAN. *Kite Craft.* New York: Crown Publishers, Inc., 1974.

PERSINGER, MICHAEL A. *Weather Matrix and Human Behavior.* New York: Praeger Pubs. 1980.

POYNTER, DAN. *Hang Gliding: The Basic Handbook of Sky Surfing.* Santa Barbara, CA: Para Publishing, 1981.

ROSEN, STEPHEN. *Weathering: How The Atmosphere Conditions Your Body, Your Mind, Your Moods, and Your Health.* New York: Evans, M. and Company, Inc. 1979.

TAYLOR, GLENN. *Windsurfing: The Complete Guide.* New York: McGraw-Hill, 1980.

TORREY, VOLTA. *Windcatchers: American Windmills of Yesterday and Tomorrow.* Brattleboro, VT: Stephen Green Press, 1976.

WINNER, KEN, and ROGER JONES. *Windsurfing With Ken Winner: A Complete Illustrated Guide to a Fast Growing Sport.* New York: Harper and Row, 1981.

PART III

THE SKY AND CULTURE

CHAPTER 8

INSPIRATION FROM THE SKY

From the very earliest times the sky has had an impact on the culture of human beings. Among other things, it is the source of weather from which people took shelter; the nature of that weather had a practical impact on the form of the shelters chosen or constructed. At first, such shelters were only caves that protected the people from sun, wind, and driving rain, but suitable caves were a relatively scarce resource, and they limited mobility. Other peoples developed various temporary shelters of hides, woven mats of vegetation, or other materials which permitted them to roam farther afield. And of course, in the far north, people even learned to fashion shelters from that product of the sky—snow. In time people learned to fashion cavelike shelters from a variety of indigenous materials such as stone, man-made bricks, and wood. Today, a host of fabricated materials is used to do the same—concrete, steel, glass, fiberboard, plastic, and the like. Thus the sky is actually the father of architecture, for it is our coping with some of the more unpleasant realities of the sky that stimulated our capacity to build.

The sky contributed to the development of architecture in other ways as well. The awesome power of storms, the availability of life-giving rains, the heat and light of the sun all contributed to people's sense of vulnerability and limited control over their lives. This in turn stimulated human spirituality and the need to seek some explanations for the great mysteries. It is not surprising that people so often turned to the sky, with its great beauty and awesome forces, as a source of their most powerful deities and as a dwelling place for these gods.

The gods gave meaning and order to a people's universe, and humans, with their capacity for symbolizing, developed their buildings and even

174

whole cities with cosmological symbolism. The people of primitive and traditional cultures lived in a world that they perceived as circular, with a strong vertical dimension, and richly symbolic. To these people the circle represented the outer bounds of the sky, the horizon, and was considered a perfect form. The dome represented the whole vault of the sky, a three-dimensional symbol of heaven or its equivalent. These abstract forms appear in their art and architecture and even the layout of communities.

Spires and obelisks symbolically led the viewer into the heavens, as did ziggurats and pyramids. The pyramids were even oriented carefully to the sky so that the slope of the entrance tunnel projected upward directly toward the pole star, for the region of the pole star was thought to be the home of the dead. Such cosmologically inspired symbolic forms were prevalent in much architecture of the past and remain today, although our society and its architects tend to perceive the world in more profane, aesthetic ways, with a lower ceiling, more linear orientation, and more human scale.

You can find the symbolic image of the heavenly vault in many structures of differing cultures: the felt yurts of the Asiatic nomads, the striking Temple of Heaven in Beijing with its blue-tiled roof, and many great cathedrals such as Santa Sophia in Istanbul or St. Paul's in London. The dome was not alone in representing the arching sky; the vaulted arch served a similar purpose and was a component of many churches and cathedrals. Even in Egyptian days we find that the flat ceilings of the tombs were painted blue and had stars to represent the sky.

The earliest major buildings were primarily ceremonial in nature and devoted to the deities or to priest-kings who were the center of the perceived universe of these peoples. These buildings often became the focus of early cities, which themselves were constructed to symbolize the people's cosmology. These early ideal cities were often bounded by a circular wall or moat regardless of the natural topography, with the temples and dwellings of priests and rulers within. Serfs generally lived outside the walls. Some cities were conceived in terms of concentric circles, with social rank determining which circle one lived in. Since those with higher rank were "closer to the deities," they lived in the inner circles, which were increasingly elevated and thus closer to the sky homes of the gods. This pattern was symbolically emphasized in the architectural forms of terraces, towers, pillars, and ziggurats, with the temples and/or palaces located at greatest elevation and adorned with structures that reached even further into the sky.

Many basically circular cities enclosed rectangular walls that were oriented with their corners at the cardinal points of the compass. These points were very important in people's perception of the sky and symbolically represented the four quarters of the heaven and the four seasons generated by the sky-dwelling sun. For many cultures the circle represented the heavens and nature while the square stood for the earth and/or the artificial world of mankind. You can find such settlement patterns in pre-

175

THE SUN

SOURCE OF SYMBOLISM AND INSPIRATION

The sun has been an inspiration to people. Egyptians believed the sky was a falcon. One eye was the sun; the other was the moon.

The Inca Indians of ancient Peru worshipped the sun. When the sun went down at night it swam under the earth until morning when it rose again.

The Aztec Indians of ancient Mexico also believed the sun was a powerful god. They built their calendar around it.

Artists in northern Europe in the 15th and 16th centuries pictured the sun as a happy, caring face.

In Japan, some people welcome the sun each morning by clapping their hands.

And in some towns in Europe, men still follow an age-old custom. They tip their hats to the rising sun.

FIGURE 8.1. The sun—source of symbolism and inspiration. Plate courtesy National Center For Appropriate Technology.

dynastic Egypt and in Etruscan cities. Plato, the Greek philosopher, describes the circle and square format in his ideal city; this is linked to the cosmological doctrines of the Pythagoreans. This pattern persisted as an ideal into the Middle Ages, and you will find that the City of God described by St. Augustine was in a radial-concentric pattern.

Many of these early cities had 12 gates, named for the 12 signs of the

176

zodiac. Old Bagdad had such a pattern; so did many Greek cities, such as Athens. Jerusalem, sacred city of three major religions, had 12 gates also. Each was supposedly named for one of the 12 tribes of Israel, as prophesied in the concluding section of the biblical Book of Ezekiel, but most probably they harked back to earlier mideastern patterns geared to the zodiac.

The Chinese gave perhaps the most explicit and detailed expression of their cosmic symbols to their city designs. Yi-Fu Tuan writes:

> The Chinese imperial capital was a diagram of the universe. The palace and the principal north-south axis stood for the Polar star and the celestial meridian. The Emperor in the interior of his courts surveyed the southerly world of men. In Peking's Forbidden City the Wu or Meridian Gate pierced the south wall. The Emperor was borne through the Meridian Gate into the Forbidden City while civil and military officials entered by the east and west gates. The Four Quadrants in the heavenly vault became the Four Directions or Four Seasons of the terrestrial grid. Each side of the square may be identified with the daily position of the sun or with each of the four seasons. The east side, with the blue dragon as its symbol, was the locus of the rising sun and of spring. The south side corresponded to the sun at its zenith and to summer, symbolized by the red phoenix of *yang* ascendancy. At the west side the white tiger stood for autumn, twilight, weapon, and war. The cold region of the north lay behind man's back, and was symbolized by hibernating reptiles, the color black, and the *yin* element of water.

In more recent times cosmologies of East and West have changed greatly and have been influenced by the processes of verifiable science. Though arguably no less hypothetical than those of earlier cultures, these modern cosmologies have had less impact on architecture. However, scientific understanding of the sky has had its own new influences on architecture. In northern parts of colonial America many houses were of saltbox design, oriented so that the frigid winds of winter rode up and over, minimizing their chilling effect, while the south-facing walls received the maximum of winter sun. In the southwest region homes were designed with thick adobe walls and overhanging roofs to block the extreme effects of the searing sun. The early settlers almost intuitively designed and sited their structures to offset the extremes of sun and wind. Today our scientific technology has more and more architects designing buildings to take maximum advantage of the heating and cooling effects of sun and wind. Special materials admit light while blocking more undesirable radiations, and there are devices to trap solar energy when it is available and release it when it is not. We even see designers returning to visions of great domes, now of geodesic design and clear panels, that would arch over whole communities, providing visual access to the sky but "protecting" the inhabitants from the excesses of the sky. Whereas the peoples of the past adapted to the sky, the people of today seem ready to try and totally control its effects upon them. Increasingly, our designers give us transparent, enclosed walkways between structures, which shield us from wind and rain and blunt our awareness and sensibilities relative to our basic habitat—the sky. However, some buildings are

177

FIGURE 8.2. Home energy from the sky. C.E. Roth photo.

FIGURE 8.3. Clouds mirrored in building. C.E. Roth photo.

178

designed to mirror the sky and thus bring the sky more prominently to the attention of city dwellers.

PATTERN AND PROCESS

It is ironic that the mathematics and science that we tend to use to isolate us from the sky owe much of their origins to contemplation of the sky. Observant individuals of many cultures noted patterns of stars in the night sky and realized that these patterns and the sun and moon moved in the sky in fixed, recurrent ways. By noting and recording these events they established information about a series of cycles of varying duration that helped establish various concepts of time. Their notations were used in some cultures to develop calendars that not only recorded past events but permitted predictions of future events in the sky, often with remarkable accuracy. In such activity lies the roots of what today we recognize as science and mathematics.

A number of peoples throughout the world developed ways to record the movements of the sun throughout its yearly and multi-year cycles. Some of these were incorporated into their village designs, others were special sacred places. In some pueblo villages in the American Southwest the priests would mark on the wall of the ceremonial kiva the spot where the sun's rays first shone each day. The Hopi people have a horizon calendar; that is, the official sun watcher notes from his observation post each day where the rising sun first breaks and then sets on the hilly horizon. Each important day in the Hopi ceremonial cycle has a peak of hill or notch of valley named for it—the peak or notch on the horizon where the sun rises or sets on that day.

In areas where the horizon line was flat or tree-covered, other devices were developed. The Mayans, for example, built a large pyramid at Uaxac-

FIGURE 8.4. Hopi horizon calendar.

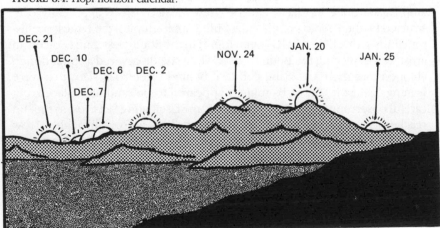

179

tun. To the east of that pyramid they constructed a platform with three small temples. They were so constructed that a priest standing on the pyramid and sighting over a stone column would spot the sun rising over the center of the roof of the appropriate temple at the solstices and equinoxes. The northern temple was for the summer solstice and the southern one for the winter solstice; the central temple marked the equinoxes. In Great Britain the remarkable structure of huge stone pillars and slabs known as Stonehenge stands on the Salisbury Plain and apparently served a similar function for early peoples of that island. It was begun sometime around 2600 B.C., built in three building phrases, and completed some twelve hundred years later around 1400 B.C. Like the Mayan temples, it was used both for religious purposes and as an observatory and calendar and was constructed with the knowledge gathered over many generations of careful observers.

Throughout Europe, North Africa, and the Near East are prehistoric stone pillars. Some stand alone; others are arranged in great circles much like Stonehenge. The pillars themselves are called *menhirs,* a Breton word meaning "long stone." When such menhirs are arranged in a circular configuration, they are called by the Breton word meaning "curved stone," *cromlech.* Dr. Alexandar Thom has been studying these stones and their alignments for many years, combining his vast knowledge of both mathematics and astronomy, and he is quite convinced that these stones were used to make long lines of sight to places where the sun, moon, and certain stars rose and set on certain dates. The longer the sightlines used (and many of these are 10 to 20 miles apart), the smaller the error. These early peoples had little or no mathematics, so such sightlines made possible an accuracy otherwise unobtainable. Not all scientists accept Dr. Thom's data and explanations for the orientation of the menhirs and cromlechs, but he has convinced many. Particularly at a site like Carnac in Brittany, where more than ten rows, including some three thousand menhirs, are laid out across the countryside over a distance of some four miles, it is fairly easy to see how they might be used to mark astronomical phenomenon.

One of the most fascinating of early sun movement records is found atop Fajada Butte in Chaco Canyon, New Mexico. It was apparently constructed by the Pueblo peoples that built Pueblo Bonito, the largest prehistoric Indian dwelling that has been found in the Southwest. Anna Sofaer, an artist, was exploring the Butte in 1977 when she discovered a spiral design chipped into the rock of the cliff face behind three rock slabs that were leaning against it. The slabs initially appeared to be randomly placed, but careful observation over time revealed some fascinating facts. Just as the sun reaches its zenith on the summer solstice, its light pierces through narrow gaps in the three slabs, and a dagger of light bisects the spiral. At the winter solstice the light emerges through the cracks so that two slivers of light bracket the spiral. There is a smaller spiral to the left of the large one, and on the vernal and autumnal equinoxes a shaft of sunlight marks its center. Because the recording device is set so that the light travels vertically across

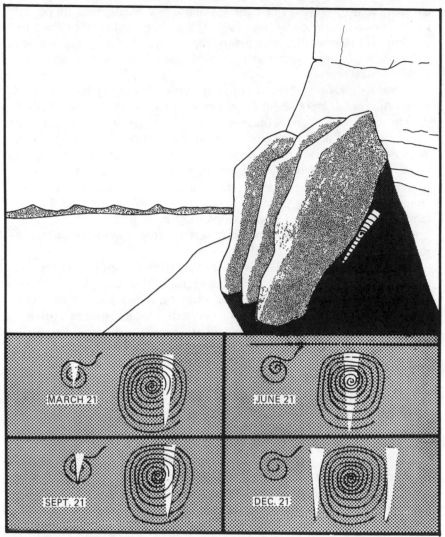

FIGURE 8.5. Fajada Butte sun dagger. Upper drawing shows arrangement of rock slabs between which light passes in certain days. Lower drawings indicate where light daggers appear around carved spirals on days of solstice and equinox.

the carving instead of horizontally, as might be expected from the sun's normal path, this remarkable astronomical marker has been called the Sun Dagger.

The spiral of the Sun Dagger has 19 grooves, and Sofaer and the researchers working with her believe that it may well record more than just solar movements. The moon, for example, has an 18.6-year cycle of movement from its highest to lowest points of declination, and they feel that the dagger may record this lunar cycle as well. They have done some simulation

181

exercises to predict what will happen, but the next major standstill period for the moon doesn't occur until 1987. At that time the hypothesis will be confirmed or rejected. The skill behind the construction of the ancient Sun Dagger is impressive, doubly so given its difficult access over rough, rattle-snake-infested terrain.

Not all early sky observations were recorded in the permanence of stone. Almost all peoples, the exceptions being some forest-dwelling peoples such as the Pygmies of Zaire, have noted the patterns of stars in the sky and invented stories and legends about them. These stories often serve as more than just campfire entertainment and explanation of the great mysteries; they are memory aids regarding what star groups are to be found in the sky at different seasons and the sequence in which they appear. In cultures without writing, only oral tradition, these stories are often impor-tant navigational aids. Polynesian peoples use them to guide them on the open ocean, and nomadic peoples of desert and steppe lands similarly turn to the stars to guide their travels.

As an example, let's take a Polynesian tale of a sailor who sets off toward an old woman's house. When he gets there, the sailor plays a trick on the woman, and she runs away. Meanwhile, he meets another man in a canoe and talks to him until he sees the old woman fall into the sea. To us it is a pretty dull story, but within that culture it has much deeper meaning, for it really indicates the stars a voyager would meet sailing eastward across the Pacific from a specific time and place. The old woman represents the constellation we call the Pleiades. The sailor moving toward her house indicates the constellation is rising. He plays his trick at the time she is at her highest point, and the woman running away represents the constellation setting toward the west. The man in the canoe represents the bright star Aldebaran, located in what we call the constallation Taurus. This is a V-shaped star cluster which the Polynesians see as the prow of a canoe. Aldebaran, rises a few hours after the Pleiades lowers to the west. Of course, the old woman falling into the sea indicates the setting of the Pleiades. This story goes on at length, with each part similarly recording the sequence and timing of the navigational stars to be encountered on the particular trip. More often than we undoubtedly recognize, folk tales of other cultures, which we may perceive as charming if a bit silly, contain similar valuable messages to those who understand that culture.

Early sky studies were primarily observational and involved the sim-ple recording of observations. This information did allow some basic pre-dicting ability once enough observations had been made and recorded over a long enough period of time. Thus, the early science was dependent upon the accumulation of records, written or oral, over many generations. Further advances depended upon the development of mathematics. The people had to develop both a system of numbers and numeration and the ability to manipulate numbers in various ways, first arithmetically and then

182

eventually in more complex ways such as algebraically, geometrically, trigonometrically, and through calculus.

Our view of the past is too foggy to say that sky observing did or did not directly foster the origin of mathematics, but it almost certainly played a strong role in its advancement. It was clearly a mutual thing, for astronomy itself was greatly advanced by mathematics. Most of what we know about the origin of mathematics indicates ancient Babylon as the cradle of the subject, with numerical, algebraic, and geometrical methods in use at least since the Hammurabic Dynasty (that is, around 1700 B.C.) Astronomy and its more illegitimate sister, astrology, were important components of Babylonian culture. In fact, it was Babylonian astronomy, which developed rapidly in the fourth and fifth centuries B.C., that acted as the main carrier of Babylonian arithmetical methods throughout the ancient civilized world! The Babylonians used a sexagesimal system rather than a decimal system such as we use today, but remnants of that system are still with us in the division of hours and minutes into 60 parts and the 360° divison of a circle (6 × 60). These current remnants of the Babylonian system, of course, are derived from time and azimuth measuring that originate in sky observation.

Major Babylonian mathematical inventions were the place-value system, in which the placing of numbers in a specific sequence affected their value, and the invention of the zero symbol to represent a place with no number while giving it a place value. This allowed expression of both very large numbers and fractions. Their system ran from 1 to 60 with 6 as the base number. So, for example, 2,30 in their notation would equal $2 + 30/60 = 2 + \frac{1}{2}$ or $2 × 60 + 30 = 150$. This allowed considerable flexibility in manipulating numbers and helped them move from simple observation of the sky to more detailed measurements of sky objects and their movements. The numbers of these measurements could then be manipulated for some basic predictions. Babylonian mathematical astronomy reached its full maturity around the third century B.C.

The mathematical methods of the Babylonians were in use by astronomers in Mesopotamia, Greece, India, and the Islamic world from about the fifth century B.C. on, and each culture began to make new contributions of its own. The fourth century B.C. found astronomer/ mathematicians struggling with the problems of spherical geometry that were suggested by the apparent motion of celestial bodies, and with the theory of the sundial. As time passed astronomical problems continued to determine the direction of further progress in theoretical mathematics, they have done so right up to the present. We see this in such ancient Greeks as Ptolemy, whose book *Almaquest* presents a theoretical astronomy using numerical and graphic methods, and Euclid, who published a spherical astronomy, through to Einstein, whose theory of relativity has some of its roots in a more modern version of theoretical astronomy.

The night sky, "painted with unnumbered sparks" in the words of

Shakespeare, has offered a great deal of inspiration across the centuries, sparking cultural components of science, math, architecture, religion, philosophy, and literature. Perhaps Mark Twain described its lure as simply and directly as anyone in the book *Huckleberry Finn* where the boy remarks: "We had the sky up there, all speckled with stars, and we used to lay on our backs and look up at them and discuss about whether they were made or just happened." From time immemorial people have looked at the stars and asked such questions, and gone on and on in their explorations of the mysteries they hold.

THE SKY IN LITERATURE

The place of the sky in oral literature has been hinted at in the story of the Polynesian sailors, but most peoples had an ample oral literature of legends about the sky. Most had their constellations and stories about the characters those star patterns represented. Many are fascinating reading. You can find a number of them from several cultures in the Olcott classic *Star Lore of All Ages*, and there are some shortened versions of primarily Western cultural star legends in Menzel and Pasachoff's *A Field Guide To The Stars and Planets*.

But the sky, both day and night, finds a place in the written literature of a number of cultures as well. It is seldom the focal point of the literature but is often drawn upon to create mood and to serve as metaphor. It is among the poets that sky phenomena get most prominent focus, and this has been equally true of Eastern as well as Western cultures. There are various periods in all cultures when nature, including the sky, gets more attention than in other periods; human affairs are the primary focus of most art and literature. In the passages from poetry and some prose that follow, it is possible to give only a small sample of how various writers have felt about or used the sky, but the *Further Reading* section will direct you to other, more extensive opportunities for exploring the sky in literature.

Poetic Expression

The Japanese have a poetic form known as *haiku* that uses only a spare three lines, each with a specific number of syllables. It is a form that often turns to the sky for subject matter. One of the ancient masters of the art is Basho, who wrote:

All day in gray rain
hollyhocks follow the sun's
invisible road

Watching the full moon,
a small hungry boy forgets
to eat his supper.

184

Some other examples of this form from other poets include:

Rain went sweeping on
in the twilight, spilling moons
on every grass blade.

SHO-U
The least of breezes
blows and the dry sky is filled
with the voice of pines . . .

ONITSURA
Out of the sky, geese
come honking in the spring's cold
early-morning light.

SOIN
In the cloudless sky
drifting white petals alone
give the wind away.

J. HACKETT
Since my house burned down,
I now own a better view
of the rising moon.

MASAHIDE

Native American peoples of a variety of tribes encompass the sky in their songs and chants. Though these are out of the oral tradition, a number have been translated and written down and can now be considered part of our available written literature. Some of these have been quoted elsewhere in this volume, more are excerpted below.

From the Pawnee people comes "The Birth of Dawn."

Breathing forth life, Earth our Mother,
Awakes, arise, and move about!
Life-renewing dawn is born.

Breathing forth life, Earth has risen.
Leaves are stirring, all things moving
Life-renewing dawn is born.

Breathing forth life, O brown eagle
Awake and rise up through the skies!
Life-renewing dawn is born.

Breathing forth life, soaring eagle
Brings the day to powers above.
Life-renewing dawn is born.

The birth of dawn from sun and darkness
Is a mystery, very sacred
Though it happens every day.

Ceremonies to bring life-giving rains were important to many tribes.

185

The following two pieces are examples of their songs, one from the Sia people, the other from the Zuni people.

SIA	ZUNI
White, floating clouds,	*Cover my earth mother four times*
Clouds like the plains,	*with many flowers.*
Come and water the earth.	*Let the heavens be covered*
Sun embrace the earth	*with piled up clouds.*
To make her more fruitful.	*Let the earth be covered with fog.*
Moon,	*Cover the earth with rains.*
Lion of the north,	*Great water, rains, cover the earth.*
Bear of the west,	*Lightning cover the earth.*
Wolf of the east,	*Let the thunder be heard over*
Shrew of the earth,	*the earth.*
Speak to the cloud people	*Let the thunder be heard.*
for us,	
So that they may water the earth.	

The sound of thunder is of import to these peoples, often in a very positive way, despite the awesome power it often implies. The Navajo people have described it as "The Voice That Beautifies the Land."

The voice that beautifies the land!
The voice above
The voice of thunder,
Among the dark clouds
Again and again it sounds,
The voice that beautifies the land.

Nancy Wood, a fine poet, has given voice to the thoughts of the Pueblo people in several fine books. The Pueblo people's sense of kinship with sky objects and others is reflected in the lines of this simple Pueblo prayer:

My brother the star, my mother the earth, my father the sun, my sister the moon, to my life give beauty, to my body give strength, to my corn give goodness, to my house give peace, to my spirit give truth, to my elders give wisdom.

Wood reflects Pueblo insight into rain:

The journey of the raindrops began in a cloud that wished to cry.
The journey of the raindrop continued on the wing of a butterfly.
The raindrop fell through the air blown by a wind from the west.
The raindrop was caught by a tree which gave it branch to branch.
The raindrop stood alone at the end of a leaf and cried to a star.
The raindrop fell to earth and went with the river that roars.
The journey of the raindrop will not end until the Great Spirit kills the sea.

186

Some of her lines reflect Pueblo attitudes toward the sky and its integration with their lives:

> *When daylight shuts her eyes*
> *And the sky is fast asleep*
> *The moon comes up with half a face*
> *And the stars put holes in the night.*
>
> *A rainbow is just*
> *The Great Spirit painting*
> *A circle around the earth.*
> *The half that belongs*
> *In my sky*
> *Is made with colors*
> *Of my life.*
> *The half that belong*
> *Below the earth*
> *Is made with colors*
> *Of my death.*

From the early Greek, Aristophanes, come this "Song of the Clouds" as translated by Oscar Wilde:

> *Cloud-maidens that float on forever,*
> *Dew-sprinkled, fleet bodies, and fair,*
> *Let us rise from our Sire's loud river,*
> *Great Ocean, and soar through the air*
> *To the peaks of the pine-covered mountains where the*
> *Pines hang as tress of hair!*
> *Let us seek the watch-towers undaunted,*
> *Where the well-watered cornfields abound.*
> *And through murmurs of rivers nymph-haunted*
> *The songs of the sea-waves resound;*
> *And the sun in the sky never wearies of spreading his*
> *Radiance around!*
> *Let us cut off the haze*
> *of the mists from our band.*
> *Till with far-seeing gaze*
> *We may look on the land!*

The German philosopher Frederick Nietzche composed some far less romantic lines that reflect a much more modern view toward an aspect of the sky. The poem is titled "Star Morals."

> *Unto a heavenly course decreed,*
> *Star of the darkness take not heed.*
>
> *Roll onward through this time and range!*
> *Its woe to thee be far and strange*
>
> *To utmost worlds thy light secure:*
> *No pity shall thy soul endure!*
> *But one command is thine: be pure.*

A prime example of the use of the sky to evoke mood comes from another German poet, Richard Dehmel. The poem, "Before the Storm," is presented here as translated by Ludwig Lewisohn.

The sky grew darker with each minute.
Outside my room, I felt within it
The clouds, disconsolate and gray.
The ash-tree yonder moved its crown
With heavy creaking up and down,
The dead leaves whirled across the way.

Then ticked, through the close room, unhurried,
As in still vaults where men are buried
The woodworm gnaws, and ticks my watch,
And through the open door close by,
Wailed the piano, thin and shy,
Beneath her touch.

Slate-like upon us weighed the heaven,
Her playing grew more sorrow-riven,
I saw her form.
Sharp gusts upon the ash-tree beat,
The air, aflame with dust and heat,
Sighed for the storm.

Pale through the walls the sounds came sobbing,
Her blind, tear-wasted hand passed throbbing
Across the keys.
Crouching she sang that song of May
That once had sung my heart away,
She panted lest the song should cease.

In the dull clouds no shadow shivered,
The aching music moaned and quivered
Like dull knives in me, stroke on stroke—
And in that song of love was blent
Two children's voices loud lament—
Then first the lightning broke.

On a brighter note, American Robert Frost brings insight into the potential joy of a different kind of sky phenomenon in his poem "To A Thawing Wind."

Come with rain, O loud Southwester!
Bring the singer, bring the nester;
Give the buried flower a dream;
Make the settled snowbank steam;
Find the brown beneath the white;
But whate'er you do tonight,
Bathe my window, make it flow,
Melt it as the ice will go;
Melt the glass and leave the sticks
Like a hermit's crucifix;
Burst into my narrow stall;
Swing the picture on the wall;

188

Run the rattling pages o'er;
Scatter poems on the floor;
Turn the poet out of door.

And finally in this sampling of poetic inspiration from the sky we turn to Longfellow and the poem whose concluding lines have become one of our off-quoted aphorisms but whose source is seldom known.

THE RAINY DAY

The day is cold, and dark, and dreary;
It rains, and wind is never weary;
The vine still clings to the mouldering wall,
But at every gust the dead leaves fall,
  And the day is dark and dreary.

My life is cold, and dark, and dreary;
It rains, and the wind is never weary;
My thoughts still cling to the mouldering Past,
But the hopes of youth fall thick in the blast,
  And the days are dark and dreary.

Be still, sad heart! and cease repining;
Behind the clouds is the sun still shining;
Thy fate is the common fate of all,
Into each life some rain must fall,
  Some days must be dark and dreary.

MUSICAL VIBRATIONS

Violinist Yehudi Menuhin has written eloquently about the very basics of music as it derives from general sound:

> Sound lies at the heart of the cycle of vibrations, beginning just where touch stops and ending just before radio waves begin. I believe profoundly that music helps keep us in touch with the entire vibrating world, and therefore centers us in our own being. . . . but these sounds are only part of a much longer continuum of vibrations found throughout the universe, some of which we can hear as distinct beats . . . and some of which we can only see, such as ocean waves, the cycle of day and night, the phases of the moon, the shift of seasons. . . . Today we realize that even noise and light have a common denominator—vibrations of different speeds.

> The cry of the newborn child is as much the intrinsic sound of music as is the staccato hammering of the woodpecker, the crash of thunder, the rustle of wind through the wheat field, the cooing of the dove, the rattle of seed pods, the clank of metal, the soft tread of feet on underbrush. Is it not in these very natural sounds that is largely found the raw material for the creation of man's music? Out of these we have built, constructed, continue building and constructing, musical languages, whether the most subtle and sophisticated monodic (melodic) and rhythmic textures such as developed thousands of years ago in India, or the most complex harmonic textures which have developed only recently in Western Europe. . . . Through the mysterious

189

vibrations of music, we are instantly able to share our own feelings and those of others. The music simply becomes part of who we are. Music has the power to combine feeling and thought without words.

The sky, as primary transmitter of sound vibrations, is basic to all our music. People use a host of devices, ranging from their vocal cords, taut strings and membranes, and enclosed air columns to generate vibrations. In the rest of nature there are similar natural sources of vibrations. Whether any of these is perceived as noise or music depends in large measure on the individual's cultural background and personal bias. Sounds that evoke pleasure to some provoke discomfort in others.

The voice was probably the earliest human device for making music, and such music may well have predated articulate speech (music being defined classically as the art of moving the feelings by combinations of sounds). Monotonous chanting probably evolved into more complex forms of melody and rhythm. The earliest music had to do with magic rituals related to the mystic realms of sun and moon, fertility, rain and wind. It focused on vital rites to protect human health and existence in the face of unknown mystical forces of good and evil; the sky-borne mysteries provoked the music and carried it away.

Sound making is one of the strongest, "magical" qualities humans can produce to generate such emotions as irritation, terror, or peace. The magical role of music has been particularly strong in the Near and Far East. The Bible relates how the walls of Jericho came tumbling down from the sound of seven ram's horns. Jewish rabbis wore bells on their garments to ward off death when they passed the threshold of the Holy of Holies. Chinese and Hindu fables are full of incidents in which singers make fire, water, or bring on a new season with their melodies. And in Greek mythology the founder of Thebes supposedly built its walls with the tones of Amphion's lyre. Among Native Americans the bone whistle or flute was blown as death approached to secure life in the hereafter. It was many centuries before music passed from its emphasis on the magical to the aesthetic. Today few of us think of music in anything but its aesthetic sense.

Much of the early magical aspect of music linked it not only to rites and religion but to cosmology and what were perceived as sky objects. For example, in ancient China:

Drums, via the skins, represent—North, winter, water
Pan pipes represent—East, spring, mountain
Zither, via silk strings represents—South, summer, fire
Bell, via metal, represents—West, autumn, dampness

The normal five notes of the Chinese scale are also symbolic:

1. North, planet Mercury, wood, black
2. East, planet Jupiter, water, violet
3. Center, planet Saturn, earth, yellow

190

4. West, planet Venus, metal, white
5. South, planet Mars, fire, red

In India the Hindu scale has seven chief tones represented as so many heavenly sisters, and various musical patterns or *ragas* are symbolically related to such things as the signs of the zodiac, the heavens, and the planets. The same is true of Arabian *magam*. But today, even in those cultures, music has passed largely from its magical stage to the aesthetic stage.

Although perception of music appears to be a human phenomenon and humans have long been makers of music, they have also found music in wild nature. The songs of birds, the calls of frog and insects are all living music carried by the sky. But the sky itself also makes music. The wind sets leaves vibrating with distinctive sounds as it caresses them in passing. There is the gentle soughing of pines, with the pitch varied by the characteristic thickness of the needles of different species. Dry oak leaves and palmetto fronds rattle in the breeze. Poplar and cottonwood leaves, with their flattened petioles, almost hum. Wind also sets wires humming, raindrops thrumming, and sleet hissing on rooftop and forest floor. At various times in musical history there have been musicians who have incorporated direct or impressionistic imitations of these sounds and rhythms from the sky into their music.

Some people used the wind directly to make music. Biblical King David, for example, is reported to have kept a lyrelike *kithara* over his bed where the midnight breezes gently plucked it and made it "sing." A more formal embodiment of this method of making random music is the aeolian harp, an instrument with 10 to 12 strings of varying thicknesses stretched over a sound box. This instrument is hung where it can be plucked by the wind, thus making serendipitous music. Its name derives from Aeolus, who in Homeric legend was the son of Hippotes, controller of the winds.

Chinese kite flyers sometimes make holes in the paper of their kites and stretch strings taut across the openings. As the kites bob and dance in the sky they make their own aerial music. Wind chimes are another instrument for producing fortuitous music with the sky. All wind chimes use a wind-blown striker of some form, but the choice of vibrators seems almost endless—varying length rods of diverse metals or glass, different-sized chunks of ceramic or natural minerals, blocks of different density woods, bones, and many others. There are also related instruments composed of hollow tubes of varying lengths sited where wind will blow over the openings, causing the air column to vibrate and emit a tone.

Most musicians demand more control over the music than such instruments provide, interesting though such random music may be in its own right. The random music exists in its own time, whereas the human musician essentially sculpts time, making it seem to come faster or slower with pulses of a weight and timbre of his or her own choosing. This imposition of will on time and vibration brings the human mind and feelings to bear on the sound. Yehudi Menuhin suggests that "the beauty of music lies in part in its placement at a point equidistant between reality and abstraction." Thus, very little of our music of the past few centuries draws its inspiration directly from sky events. However, the music may attempt to elicit emotions in their way comparable to those engendered by various sky events, such as the sense of joy and freedom of vast open skies, the foreboding of leaden overcast, the terror of tempest and thunder.

The influence of the sky is less obvious in purely instrumental music, although it can be found in places like the thunder and lightning scene of Henry Purcell's opera *Dido and Aenus* written in the late 1600s, or Claude Debussy's nocturne titled *Nuages* ("Clouds"). In that nocturne Debussy musically depicts the unchangeable appearance of the sky, with the slow and solemn march of clouds dissolving in gray agony tinted with white. In a piece like Ferde Grofe's *Grand Canyon Suite,* we hear movements that evoke sky-borne moods such as the aura of sunrise, sunset, and a cloudburst; in Rimsky-Korsakov's *Flight of the Bumblebee,* the orchestral interlude from his opera *The Tales of Tsar Saltan,* a musical picture is created of that airborne creature maneuvering through the transparent, sound-bearing medium of the sky. A few modern jazz musicians have turned to including natural sounds in their music and writing music to complement, incorporate, and decorate the natural rhythms and melodies. Foremost among these is Paul Winter and his Consort. He has focused on sky themes in pieces like *Icarus* and *Sunsinger.*

In the realm of song, that blending of words and music, the influence of the sky in musical idiom is more obvious. Here the lyrics often use sky events and objects to stimulate mood or setting for other messages. It is often difficult to separate such songs from pure poetry, and perhaps there is no real reason for doing so. A few pieces in English translation from classical music pieces through the ages may indicate something of the role of the sky in such music. As might be expected, most of it is from the Romantic era.

From the French Renaissance comes "The Return of Springtime" by Claude Le Jeune:

> *Now the sun, serenely shining*
> *Floods the land in warmth and brightness*
> *From the clouds the silent shadows*
> *Swiftly pass and change and darken.*
> *All the meadows, woods and hillsides*
> *With the aid of man, are fertile*
> *And the fields uncover flowers.*

In the Romantic period, Carl von Weber, in the music for *Der Freischutz,* wrote a song called "Und ob Die Wolke":

> *Although a cloud has covered the sky*
> *The sun shines in splendor above it,*
> *We are not governed by chance alone*
> *But by a loving father in heaven.*

192

Giuseppe Verdi wrote in Act III of *Aida:*

> *Oh my native land, never shall I see it again!*
> *Oh skies of blue, oh gentle breezes,*
> *Where the light of my life shone in tranquility.*

And finally we find in Wagner's classic opera *Die Walkure* the "Spring Song":

> *Winter storms have waned in the moon of May*
> *With tender radiance sparkles the spring;*
> *On balmy breezes, light and lovely,*
> *Weaving wonders, on it floats;*
> *O'er wood and meadow wafts its breath,*
> *Always with joy and laughter,*
> *In blithesome song of birds resounds its voice*
> *Sweetest fragrance it breathes forth:*
> *From ardent bloom joy-giving blossoms,*
> *Bud and shoot spring up by spring's might.*

In popular songs of more recent times sky themes show up from time to time. In the folk spiritual we recall that *Ezekiel Saw the Wheel* "way up in de middle ob de air." From the musical *Paint Your Wagon* comes the song "They Called the Wind Maria," and in the show *Pippin* is the tune "Corner of the Sky." And you may well be familiar with such songs as "Blue Skies," "Somewhere Over the Rainbow," "The Little White Cloud That Cried," "Moonlight Sonata," "Catch A Falling Star," "Blowin' In the Wind," "Sunny Side of the Street," or "Singing In the Rain," all of which use sky imagery. John Denver particularly uses sky images in his songs as exemplified by "Sunshine on My Shoulder" and "The Eagle and the Hawk."

Although no one claims that the sky was a major inspiration of any particular musician as it has been for some painters, the sky does crop up thematically in music and lyrics often enough to be of interest, and recognized or not, it continues to be the primary transport of all our music— good, bad, and indifferent.

THE PAINTERS

In both Eastern and Western cultures writers and musicians seem to have responded to the sky as a motif before the painters did. Early painters focused primarily on people and the expression of religious themes. Native Americans in the Southwest did fragile religious sand paintings of such sky-inspired deities as Father Sky and the Rainbow Man, but these cannot be considered paintings of the sky in any real sense. Oriental paintings of landscapes are beautiful but tend to leave the sky completely open to the viewer's imagination except for indicating some mist in mountain valleys.

FIGURE 8.6. Navajo sand painting of Father Sky. C.E. Roth photo.

One almost assumes that the paper or tapestry itself, the background for the painting, represents the sky in some undefined way.

The earliest paintings in Western tradition have a very flat, patterned quality, and the figures seldom have any background. But in time artists devised ways to represent a three-dimensionality created by the interplay of light and shadow, essentially the effects of the sky on objects. In such paintings, the sky is usually only implied and seldom included. In the religious paintings the sky may be symbolically represented by abstract, diaphanous clouds and a generally bluish color. A few show a more realistic scene with a blue sky and fluffy white clouds, a sort of painterly cliché. They seldom indicate even the moods of the sky. Sky for those early painters was simple a piece of background.

In Venice, about 1508, Giorgione created a painting he called "The Tempest," which moved the sky into a different importance. E.H. Gombrich comments in his book *The Story of Art:*

> The picture is clearly blended into a whole simply by the light and air that permeates it all. It is the wierd light of a thunderstorm and for the first time, it seems, the landscape before which the actors of the picture move is not just a background. It is there, by its own right, as the real subject of the painting. . . . Giorgione has not drawn things and persons to arrange them afterwards in space, he really thought of nature, the earth, the trees, the light, air and clouds and the human beings with their cities and bridges as one.

194

This painting was a revolutionary break with the art tradition of the times in southern Europe.

A major reason for the choice of subject matter of most paintings, portraits and religious scenes, was of course economic. Artists had to sell their work in order to eat and care for their families, and the prime patrons were the church and powerful wealthy families. There were, of course, artists in various periods who painted for themselves and chose subjects that interested them. In northern Europe there seem to have been a few more of these than in the south. Albecht Altdorfer, who painted in the early 1500s in Germany, was one of these independent northerners whose work was remarkable in that many of his watercolors and oils tell no story and contain no human beings. But then again, his skies were not particularly outstanding. There were those who would follow his lead, however, and for some of them the sky would assume greater importance as a component of their paintings. Painters had to develop a skill that strongly influenced people before patrons would buy a painting that served no other purpose than that of recording a beautiful piece of scenery.

Perhaps the first major painter to focus on landscapes was Claude Lorraine (1600–1682). He created scenes from his imagination as much as from nature, and these scenes triggered horticultural imitation in great estates and parks. His landscapes were often infused with the golden light and silvery air typical of Mediterranean regions, and the trees and skies were quite stylized. In their own way, Lorrain's landscapes were as mythical as many of the human-focused paintings of his predecessors and contemporaries. However, in many ways Claude Lorrain set the stage for wider acceptance of landscape as a legitimate subject for painters, and it was only as landscape art became important that the sky came into its own as an inspired component of the art.

It was Dutch artists of the mid-1600s who really opened the door to the sky. They had to paint their pictures first and then find a market for them, for the Protestant movement had cut off much of the patronage for religious works. These artists turned to detailed renderings of the world around them: the peasants, the sea, and other simple, profane objects. Their skill at realistic representation of surface and light was masterful. Gombrich notes that "Dutch artists could convey the atmosphere of the sea by wonderfully simple and unpretentious means. These Dutchmen were the first in the history of art to discover the beauty of the sky." Some of the men who brought realism to their skies include Simon Vlieger and Jan van Goyen. Jacob van Ruisdael came only slightly later and became, in the words of Gombrich, "a master in painting of dark and sombre clouds, of evening light when the shadows grow, of ruined castles and rushing brooks." These artists, indeed all artists who reflect nature in their art, also reflect their own feelings, enjoyments, and moods. The sky often becomes a metaphor for those moods.

The sky in landscape painting became more realistic after the publication in 1803 of Luke Howard's treatise *On the Modifications of Clouds*. In this work, Howard presented the outline of the classification of clouds that is

FIGURE 8.7. "River Scene" by Jan van Goyen. Courtesy of Museum of Fine Arts, Boston. Purchased James Fund.

FIGURE 8.8. "A Rough Sea" by Jacob Isaackszoon van Ruisdael. Courtesy Museum of Fine Arts, Boston. William Francis Warden Fund.

used with slight modifications to this day. For the first time clouds were classed as either stratus, cumulus, cirrus, or nimbus. This work brought clouds to the attention of a variety of artists and writers and stimulated closer general observation of the sky and clouds. In tune with the rising interest in science of the day, the artists, particularly landscape artists seeking to present truth in their works, became more observant and increasingly painted the appropriate cloud type for the mood they were trying to create, or painted clouds themselves for their intrinsic beauty.

Two British landscape painters are considered to be among the grand masters of landscape painting. J.M.W. Turner and John Constable were both stimulated by Luke Howard's studies and devoted considerable time and effort to painting clouds, both for their inherent beauty and as important components of their landscape paintings. Unlike the earlier master, Claude Lorrain, whose paintings so influenced the actual landscape design of England, Turner and Constable painted nature directly, recording its beauty only slightly modified by artistic conventions. One of Turner's sketchbooks done in 1814 is labeled *Skies* and contains some 79 sketches showing an enormous range of sky effects; not just clouds, but twilight and night scenes. Although many of Turner's skies were done from memory after close observation, Constable's were virtually all painted directly from nature at the time of observation. Constable's cloud studies, done in 1822, are virtually scientific notes, and each sketch is annotated with date, weather conditions, and time of day. These accurate sketches were to serve him well as references for later paintings, and his scientific realism would have impact on other groups of landscape artists. Constable believed in trying to understand nature before painting it, and his adage to students was "we see nothing truly till we understand it." More than any other painter of his time he made the portrayal of atmospheric conditions a major element of his work, commenting that the sky is "the chief organ of sentiment" in any landscape.

It was painter-writer John Ruskin, however, who probably had the most impact upon latter-day painters of skies in landscape. Born in 1819, from an early age Ruskin showed a strong interest in the budding science of meteorology, kept a weather diary during his teenage years, and joined the Meteorological Society of London in those years. At age 18 he delivered his first paper before the Society, which blended his scientific and artistic interests. It was titled "On the Formation and Colour of such Clouds as are caused by the agency of Mountains." He maintained his interest in the sky throughout his painting and writing career and devotes significant sections of his multivolume treatise *Modern Painters* to the sky. It was this material that had such influence on other landscape painters of the day. Though clearly lacking in accuracy by today's standards, it was none the less very influential. Actually, Ruskin was less interested in the dynamics of the sky than in its overall beauty and the complexity of clouds, and he opened new lines of observations for ordinary observers. Writing in *Modern Painters* he suggested that "if artists were more in the habit of sketching clouds rapidly and as accurately as possible in the outline, from nature, instead of daubing

FIGURE 8.9. "The Slave Ship" by Joseph Mallard William Turner. Courtesy Museum of Fine Arts, Boston. Henry Lillie Pierce Fund.

FIGURE 8.10. "Weymouth Bay" by John Constable. Courtesy Museum of Fine Arts, Boston. Bequest of Mr. & Mrs. William Caleb Loring, November 6, 1930.

198

down what they call 'effects' with the brush, they would soon find there is more beauty about their forms than can be arrived at by any random felicity of invention, however brilliant, and more essential character than can be violated without incurring the charge of falsehood. . . ." As an example of what he meant he wrote:

> If you watch for the next sunset when there are a considerable number of . . . cirri in the sky you will see . . . that the sky does not remain the same color for two inches together; one cloud has a dark side of cold blue, and a fringe of milky white; another, above it, has a dark side of purple and an edge of red; another, nearer the sun, has an underside of orange and an edge of gold; these you will find mingled with, and passing into the blue of the sky, which in places you will not be able to distinguish from the cool gray of the darker clouds, and which will be itself full of gradation, now pure and deep, now faint and feeble. . . .

But Ruskin was quite wary of scientific truth that was not elevated by artistic truth, and it becomes difficult to separate the symbolism he saw in cloud forms and meteorological events from the atmospheric science that he put forth. Basically Ruskin, along with most of his generation, held to a teleological view of the world and believed that the beauty of the skies was divinely inspired, as might be interpreted from the first lines of the nineteenth Psalm:

> *The heavens declare the glory of God*
> *and the firmament of his handiwork.*

According to Ruskin, all beauty "is either the record of conscience, written in things external, or it is a symbolising of Divine attributes in matter, or it is the felicity of living things, or its perfect fulfillment of their duties and function. In all cases it is something Divine, either the approving voice of God, the glorious symbol of Him, the evidence of His kind presence, or the obedience to His will by Him induced and supported." It is such recording of the divine presence, the skies being one element thereof, that became typical of much landscape work of the period both in England and in America. Most would agree with Ruskin that "the simplest forms of nature are strangely animated by the sense of the Divine presence; the trees and flowers seem all, in a sort, children of God . . . I much question whether anyone who knows optics, however religious he may be, can feel in equal degree the pleasure or reverence which an unlettered peasant may feel at the sight of a rainbow."

The sky probably reaches its greatest importance as a component of landscape art among nineteenth-century American painters of the Hudson River School. Painters in this tradition used the sky to reach the emotions of gloom, dread, and fear or to stimulate feelings of joy and gladness. Their

199

FIGURE 8.11. "Moonlight Sonata" by Ralph Albert Blakelock. Courtesy Museum of Fine Arts, Boston. Charles Henry Hayden Fund.

skies are often used symbolically, but they were nonetheless devoted to careful, almost scientific sketches and observations of the clouds and atmosphere. The notebooks of Frederick Church, Thomas Cole, Jasper Cropsey, and Albert Bierstadt, among others, are full of careful cloud studies. This was difficult work, for things in the sky change so rapidly that even the most rapid sketching, with written notes and coded abbreviations, fails to catch all of what is happening in the sky at any moment.

Perhaps Thomas Cole used the sky as symbolically as any of the Hudson River masters. For example, one of his great works is a five-painting set titled *Course of Empire.* The series explores various stages in the development of civilization. In it he uses the sky as metaphor, with the sunrise symbolic of beginnings, puffy clouds for maturity, sunset for old age, and the like. The first painting represents the savage state and thus shows wilderness with the sun rising from the sea and the clouds of night retiring over the mountains. The second painting is pastoral and has the day further advanced, with light clouds lying about the mountains. For the mature stage he chooses a noonday sky with puffy cumulus clouds. The decline is represented by a tempest of storm clouds, and the final painting features a sunset. The clouds are not stylized, but they are used symbolically.

However, it is Cole's student, Frederick Church, who was most devoted to rendering the sky. In the mid-1800s Church was America's best-known landscape painter, both at home and abroad. He painted large canvases that were faithful copies of nature and very popular. But by the last quarter of the century, with the rise of Impressionism and the advent of photography, his work was no longer fashionable. Particularly during the last 30 years of his life, when his paintings were no longer in demand, he devoted himself to vast numbers of oil sketches of the sky done with great looseness and bravura. A contemporary, Henry Tuckerman, wrote: "It has long been his daily custom to ascend a hill, near his country home, to observe the sunset; and in his landscapes 'the earth is always painted with reference to the skies' which is one reason for their truth to nature." Art writer and critic John Howat has commented that Church's "oil sky sketches alone are enough to establish [him] as one of the finest Hudson River School masters."

Other painters of this school also rendered the sky with skill and beauty. The interested viewer should seek out the works of Jasper Francis Cropsey, George Innes, Asher Durand, Edward Moran, Alfred Bierstadt, and Winslow Homer. Their styles vary considerably, but all regularly depict the sky with great force and beauty.

By the end of the nineteenth century, landscape painting was out of vogue. Painting was moving away from copying nature and toward French Impressionism and modernism; that is, toward greater and greater abstraction. Artists were looking to the paint for its own sake. They saw the painted

201

FIGURE 8.12. "The Harp of the Winds" by Frederick Edwin Church. Courtesy Museum of Fine Arts, Boston. M. & M. Karolik Collection.

surface as having a life of its own quite apart from the subject depicted, and technique as admirable, indeed as beautiful, as content. The sky again appears stylized in most of these paintings but is not entirely lost from the work of such painters as van Gogh, who used bright colors and strong brush strokes to represent the sun and clouds. By the twentieth century the sky is largely absent from paintings and remains so until the second half of the century, when public taste slowly began to swing back toward more realism and a greater appreciation for the natural world. Most avant-garde painting still tends to exclude the sky, but there is greater acceptance of other schools of art.

In the midtwentieth century, Eric Sloane focused his efforts on

FIGURE 8.13. "The Buffalo Trail" by Albert Bierstadt. Courtesy Museum of Fine Arts, Boston. M. & M. Karolik Collection.

FIGURE 8.14. "Storm over Lake Otsego" by John Steuart Curry. Courtesy Museum of Fine Arts, Boston. Gift of Mr. and Mrs. Donald C. Starr.

203

meteorology understandable to the layperson and as an illustrator of the sky was very successful. As an artist he went on to join two of his passionate interests—the sky and the barns, bridges, and other structures of Americana. Sky and buildings are often of equal importance in his compositions. One of his major compositions is the great mural in the National Museum of Space and Aeronautics in Washington, D.C. which illustrates the various cloud types over the Grand Canyon.

Wildlife art has become increasingly popular in recent years. While many of the artists focus their efforts on the wildlife per se, a number are as much interested in the total environment of the animal as in the animal itself. Outstanding among such artists is Maynard Reece, who focuses much of his work on waterfowl. While the sky is essentially background, it is rendered with loving care and appreciation. Others, like Robert Bateman, make the sky an integral part of their paintings, less by including large expanses of it than by incorporating atmospheric effects such as haze, fog, and intense sunlight that establish mood and sense of place to the overall painting.

At least one young American artist, Karen Gunderson, is currently painting pictures of clouds almost exclusively. Her work is gaining acceptance in art circles as true art, not simply illustration. Her paintings are dynamic and fully realized. They play sky and clouds against each other, creating opposites and contradictions that, as art critic Theodor Wolff states, "meet, clash, and resolve themselves into stunning icons of wholeness." Her images of light-drenched clouds and blue skies can easily be enjoyed for themselves alone, just as their inspiration can. Wolff suggests that Gunderson can easily become one of those rare artists "for whom art is not merely the flat out depiction of pictorial ideas but the dynamic embodiment of those ideas within highly charged and generative forms, symbols, or images."

PHOTOGRAPHY

Perhaps no general art form is more dependent upon the sky than photography, since it depends, in large measure, on the sun as a source of light. Yet relatively few serious photographers have turned to the sky for subject matter. Like the early painters, photographers have made the activities of people the prime target for their lenses. Scientists, of course, have used the camera to record the various phenomena of the sky, and such photos are often of great beauty as well as utility, but this is different from turning to the sky for artistic statement and expression. At the forefront of black and white

FIGURE 8.15. "Cloud, Sierra Nevada, California 1936" by Ansel Adams. Courtesy of the Ansel Adams Publishing Rights Trust. Copyright © 1985 by the Trustees of the Ansel Adams Publishing Rights Trust. All rights reserved.

photographers who used sky phenomena as key components of their compositions was Ansel Adams. He would often wait patiently long hours for the lighting and cloud structure to be just right before he would open his lens shutter. The results are often spectacular. Joseph and David Muench are also skilled photographers of the sky working in both black and white and in color. The public is indebted to the regional magazine *Arizona Highways* for regularly presenting the work of these three photographers to the public. No magazine so frequently presents outstanding photographs of the sky by so many superb photographers, or articles about sky activities and phenomena. It is a rich treasure of the beauty and wonder of the aerial realm in which we live.

AVANT-GARDE ART OF THE SKY

The painters of the mideighteenth century recorded nature and the sky as part of nature. Today, except for the realist school of painters, avant-garde artists tend to see the sky less as nature than as a vast canvas upon which to execute rather transitory expressions of the artist. Perhaps such an approach goes back to China and the invention of aerial fireworks, for this modern sky artistry is similar in putting colorful and/or spectacular objects into the sky for various periods of time. In a sense, kites and hot-air balloons are also forerunners of these art forms, which often consist of various lighter-than-air inflatables of diverse shapes and textures sent aloft either tethered or as drifters. For example, at the opening ceremony of the Olympics in Mexico City a huge series of inflated colored rings arranged in the Olympic symbol was allowed to rise into the sky. Like that example, much of this modern sky art is really a short-term event staged before large audiences and soon gone. In part this is designed to emphasize the transient nature of all things.

The night sky is a favored backdrop for light shows in which powerful colored lights are aimed skyward to reflect and refract in the atmospheric haze and the base of clouds. Behind such works is an implicit sense that the sky is just another thing to be utilized, one way or another, by people; a thing with little or no intrinsic value of its own. This is quite different from the eighteenth-century perception of the sky as a reflection of the Creator. This art reflects a much more cynical view of the world around us. Psychiatrist Quentin Regestein gets at this view when he states: "I believe that the quivering self-deprecation imbuing us moderns prevents our enjoying the sky, because the sky represents uncertainty, and we've swallowed all the uncertainty we can manage. Consider what it means to look into the 'wild blue yonder' and realize that we know nothing about what is ultimately beyond us. It becomes more painful if we also don't know what is proximately around us; awfully difficult if we lack a coherent set of values." Much of the avant-garde sky art seems to reflect this confusion of values. It tends to be very personal, very transient statements of the "ooh-aah" variety that call very little attention to the sky per se and its inherent beauty, but instead stress technological wizardry and the variety of human attempts to control the sky.

Among such attempts are the plans of an artist, working in cooperation with NASA, to artificially stimulate aurora borealis in the upper atmosphere. Joe Davis has persuaded NASA to take aboard the the space shuttle a device that will shoot a beam of electrons some 37 miles out into the ionosphere, exciting the gases there and inducing the floating, ethereal beauty of an aurora in latitudes where they do not normally appear. This artistic endeavor Davis calls New Wave Ruby Falls; NASA calls it Getaway Special 266A. NASA is less interested in the art of this project than in the scientific information it may reveal about the ionosphere. In a similar artistic-cum-scientific endeavor called his Lightning Project, Davis is creating a tri-masted sculpture 106 feet high that is supposed to change the color of any lightning bolt that strikes it. The age-old conflict between those who would live with and appreciate nature and those who feel compelled to dominate nature is alive and well in the world of art.

On the other hand, there are those among the avant-garde sky artists who see their efforts more as a union of art and science, craft and nature. Their perception is that they are a much more mature embodiment of the ideas simplistically set forth by Ruskin a century ago that stimulated the efforts of some of the realist landscape artists. To them, their technological sky manipulation is truly in tune with the changing dynamics of the sky, a truer expression of the reality of the sky than the fossilized images of a moment in time recorded by the painters and photographers. They are often stunned by the accusations of sky pollution leveled at them by some critics.

The importance of the sky as a source of artistic inspiration ultimately seems tied to a culture's changing views of the basic relationship between people and nature, their oneness or separateness from nature. During those periods when, because of either religious or scientific beliefs, humans have a perception of a closer relationship, the sky plays a dynamic and often vital role; in those periods when mankind views itself as above and apart from nature, with nature only as a handservant to provide for human needs, the sky seems to shift into deep background if it is perceived at all.

SKY-OBSERVER ACTIVITIES

• Look for announcements of art shows featuring works of the Hudson River School or such British landscape masters as Turner and Constable Visit the exhibits, and pay particular attention to the sky vistas in the paintings. There are, of course, art books featuring the works of these artists (see *Further Reading*) which you can peruse, but the reproductions, seldom have the full impact of the originals, many of which are very large canvases.

• Spend an inclement day or two perusing back issues of *Arizona Highways,* with their array of spectacular photos by many of the outstanding photographers of the sky.

• If visiting New York State in summer, you might wish to visit the homes of Frederick Church and Thomas Cole in the town of Catskill. Church's Olana is an ornate, Persian-style villa, of interest in its own right, constructed and landscaped by the artist. It has walls laden with his sketches and paintings. Walking the trails, you can always view the skies that he spent so much time sketching. Not far away is Cedar Grove, the home of Church's mentor Cole. Less flamboyant than Olana, Cedar Grove has been restored for summer visitation and houses exhibitions of Cole's work and that of his followers.

• When traveling to any of the world's older cities, take time to note the orientation of major streets, plazas, and monuments. Compare them with your observations of the daily pathway of the sun. If the older part of the city is walled, note the orientation of the corners of the walls and the location and number of gates. See if there is any correlation with some of the cosmological orientations indicated in this chapter. (Note: Don't forget to carry a compass with you on such excursions.)

• If possible, make a horizon calendar from a viewpoint near or at your home. Make a careful, detailed, scalled drawing of your eastern and western horizon lines. For each day, or at least for special days in your annual schedule, note the point on hill, tree, rooftop, or other horizon feature where the sun rises and sets.

• Plot a "solar window" for the plot where your home stands. This involves determining the elevation of the sun above the horizon at both the summer and winter solstices and the number of hours per day that the sun's rays clear horizon obstructions, such as trees and hills, to fall on your property. This solar window indicates the feasibility of using passive or active solar-heating systems for your home. Of course, you are more apt to be able to use the data when siting a new building, but you may find that your present building is well enough sited to make some solar mechanisms feasible for your use.

• Explore what Murray Shafer, in his book *The Timing of The World,* has called "soundscapes." All about you, wherever you may be, is a whole world of sound vibrations, most of which we tend to tune out of our minds. Close your eyes and listen hard. Make a mental, or physical, list of the sounds you hear in that situation. How do you feel about the different sounds? Even when you are not consciously aware of these various sounds, your always-on-duty ears are taking them in and your mind is subconsciously screening them. Some of their emotional meaning seeps through and contributes subliminally to your overall mood. As you familiarize yourself with various sky-borne soundscapes, you will have heightened your consciousness and perhaps discovered some delightful rhythms, tones, melodies, and other aspects of natural music among the general noise.

● Choose some of the books in the Further Reading section for some inspirational prose and poetry focused on the sky.

FURTHER READING

BAIGELL, MATTHEW. *Albert Bierstadt*. New York: Watson-Guptill Publications, 1981.

BASKETT, JOHN. *Constable Oil Sketches*. New York: Watson-Guptill Publications, 1966.

BENEDIKT, MICHAEL. *Sky*. New York: Wesleyan University Press, 1970.

BUTLIN, MARTIN. *Turner Watercolors*. New York: Watson-Guptil Publications, 1965.

CLAUSE, ROGER, and LEOPOLD FACY. *The Clouds*. New York: Grove Press, 1961. (Of special interest is the final chapter, "Clouds and Men.")

COGNIAT, R. *The Century of the Impressionists*. New York: Crown Publishers, Inc., 1968.

DE COCK, LILLANE, ED. *Ansel Adams*. Boston: New York Graphic Society, 1972. (Includes many of Adams's most famous sky-oriented photos, along with many others.)

DOVER, K.J. *Clouds* (abbrev. ed. of work by Aristophanes). New York: Oxford University Press, 1970.

DUNWOOD, H.H., and others. *Weather Proverbs* New York: Gordon and Science Publishers, Inc., 1977.

EXUPERY, ANTOINE DE SAINT. *Wind, Sand and Stars*. Translated by Lewis Galantiere. New York: Harcourt, Brace & World, 1940.

HIRSH, DIANA, and TIME-LIFE BOOKS EDITORIAL STAFF. *The World of Turner 1775−1851*. New York: Time-Life Books, 1969. (This volume also contains a number of works by John Constable.)

HOWAT, JOHN K. *The Hudson River and Its Painters*. New York: Viking Press, 1972.

HUDSON, TRAVIS, and ERNEST UNDERHAY. *Crystals In The Sky: An Intellectual Odyssey Involving Chumush Astronomy, Cosmology and Rock Art*. Socorro, NM: Ballena Press, 1978.

HULSKER, JAN. *The Complete Van Gogh*. New York: Harry N. Abrams, Inc., 1980.

KOMAROFF, KATHERINE. *Sky Gods: The Sun and Moon in Art and Myth*. New York: Universe Books, Inc., 1976.

LEWIS, CECIL. *Sagittarius Rising*. (This record of a World War I pilot's experiences has many interesting sky passages. Among the best is one published under the title "The Birth of A Cloud" in the Winter 1984 issue of *Orion Nature Quarterly*.)

LINDBERGH, ANNE MORROW. *Listen, The Wind*. New York: Harcourt, Brace & World, 1938.

MENUHIN, YEHUDI, and CURTIS W. DAVIS. *The Music of Man.* New York: Methuen, 1979.

MURCHIE, GUY. *Song of the Sky.* Boston: Houghton Mifflin, 1954.

MYKEL, A.W. *Wind Chime Legacy.* New York: Bantam Books, Inc., 1981.

NOVAK, BARBARA. *Nature and Culture: American Landscape and Painting 1825—1875.* New York: Oxford University Press, Inc., 1980.

OLCOTT, WILLIAM TYLER. *Star Lore Of All Ages.* New York: G.P. Putnam's Sons, 1911.

SHAFER, MURRAY R. *Turning of the World.* New York: Alfred A. Knopf, Inc., 1977.

SLOANE, ERIC. *For Spacious Skies.* New York: Thomas Y. Crowell, 1978.

————. *Look at the Sky.* New York: Duell, Sloan & Pierce, 1961.

STUART, G.E. *Storm.* New York: Random House, 1941.

TUAN, YI-FU. *Topophilia: A study of Environmental Perception, Attitudes, and Values.* Englewood Cliffs, NJ: Prentice-Hall, Inc., 1974.

WAINRIGHT, GERALD A. *Sky-Religion in Egypt: Its Antiquity and Effects.* Westport, CT: Greenwood Press, 1971.

WILLIAMSON, RAY A. *Living in the Sky—The Cosmos of the American Indian.* Boston: Houghton-Mifflin, Co. 1984.

WISSLER, CLARK. *Star Legends Among the American Indians* (Science Guide No. 91). New York: America Museum of Natural History, 1956.

INDEX

211

213

214